Almost Everything You Need to Know About

Goldendoodles

Diane Klumb

Almost Everything You Need to Know About Goldendoodles

Copyright 2012

Diane Klumb

Table Of Contents

Acknowledgements   page 5

CHAPTER ONE: Goldendoodle Basics   page 7

CHAPTER TWO: Coats and Colors   page 27

CHAPTER THREE: Finding that Perfect Puppy   page 41

CHAPTER FOUR: Being Prepared   page 65

CHAPTER FIVE: Off to a Good Start   page 93

CHAPTER SIX: Feeding Your Dood   page 111

CHAPTER SEVEN: The Holistic Dood   page 133

CHAPTER EIGHT: Goldendoodle Grooming   page 179

CHAPTER NINE: Beyond the Basics   page 213

Index   page 226

D1364751

Acknowledgements

This book would not have been possible without the help and generosity of the many wonderful Goldendoodles owners and breeders I had the pleasure to meet over the last year while I was researching and writing it.

Being a longtime writer for the Purebred Fancy, I found, does not really prepare one for writing a book about hybrids! A lot of new material needed to be covered, both about the breed itself (and an extra thanks to everyone who cheerfully allowed me to "go over" their dogs their dogs on beaches, in parks and on city streets) and about the science and genetics of hybrids in general. For the latter I owe a debt of gratitude to the clinical vets and geneticists who patiently answered my many questions, as well as the groomers, both professional and amateur...hopefully this book will make their job a little easier!

And last but certainly not least, I'd like to thank the many wonderful Goldendoodles in all their wonderful sizes and colors I met along the way, who were equally gracious and never failed to charm.

CHAPTER ONE:

GOLDENDOODLE BASICS

(or...what am I really getting myself into here?)

With his casually tousled locks and sunny personality, the Goldendoodle has risen with astonishing speed from the ranks of just another "designer dog" to one of the most popular breeds among the pet-loving American public. And if the hallmarks of a great companion dog are robust health, a great temperament and attractive looks, this breed is certainly well-deserving of its popularity, because he excels in all three areas.

A (very!) Brief History of Goldendoodles

Unlike many breeds, the history of the Goldendoodle is mercifully brief and hardly warrants an entire chapter. The first litters started appearing in the early 1990s as the result of deliberate pairings of Golden Retrievers with Standard Poodles. Since the recipe for the Goldendoodle is right there in his name, there is little dispute about his origins, and they are not likely to become "obscured by the mists of time", as has happened with so many older breeds.

The first Goldendoodles appeared shortly on the heels of the Labradoodle, a breed deliberately developed in Australia in an effort to produce a hypoallergenic guide dog. Goldendoodle breeders adopted a similar portmanteau name largely because the "doodle" suffix had already gained recognition among the public. And like his Labradoodle cousin, many Goldendoodles excel as service dogs and therapy dogs.

Now, because it was never registered anywhere, the matter of who actually produced the first litter of Goldendoodles is unfortunately impossible to ascertain, with many breeders in both the US and Australia claiming the honor. In the long run, of course, it doesn't really *matter* – regardless of who first came up with it, the idea itself turned out to be a world-beater.

From Total Obscurity to Soaring Popularity ...

What are the reasons behind the Goldendoodle's popularity? Without a doubt, a large part of it is his looks.

Back in the fifties, when a man wore a suit and tie to rob a bank and a woman sported an elaborate beehive hairdo and pearls to make dinner, elaborately groomed pets were all the rage. (Not surprisingly, this was the heyday of the Poodle.)

The Goldendoodle's characteristically tousled appearance is much more reflective of today's world, where a guy worth billions of dollars can sport a two-day beard and a tee shirt under a sports jacket, and casual chic is the general order of the day. Likewise, an illustrious pedigree tied to the landed aristocracy of England or Europe just doesn't open as many doors as it used to, especially if brains and a winning personality are not part of the package. Short on the former but long on the latter, the Goldendoodle is in many ways the quintessential Modern American Dog, and simply mirrors our current cultural ethos.

A decidedly upscale fellow, the Goldendoodle counts among his fans many Very Rich and Famous Personages, and is now found in growing numbers in affluent neighborhoods across America.

Positively ubiquitous in dog parks everywhere, the Goldendoodle is equally likely to be spotted in marinas from Maine to southern California, where there it would seem there's an unwritten ordinance requiring a percentage of sailboats to have one of these water-loving canines on deck.

A surprising number are also showing up in duck blinds and cornfields throughout the Midwest, where they serve a dual purpose as weekend hunting dogs/ full-time family dogs. Many more are found working as service and therapy dogs, tasks for which they are equally well-suited. A few are even certified Search and Rescue Dogs. The Goldendoodle, it appears, is adaptable to a fault.

And because for no particular reason he also happens to be one of the most absolutely *photogenic* fellows to come along in the world of dogs, he's rapidly become a darling of the advertising world as well – ads featuring Goldendoodles are now appearing regularly in national magazines, a sure sign that a breed has *arrived*.

In short, the Goldendoodle has become a Phenomenon, no less than America's newest canine sweetheart. If there are three people left in this country who haven't heard of the Goldendoodle, it appears one would be hard-pressed to find them.

But... Is the Goldendoodle Actually a *Breed*?

Simply *assuming* that based only upon its burgeoning popularity really begs the question, and as this is technically a "breed book", the issue probably needs to be addressed right out the gate, because it is certainly a matter of some dispute. While Goldendoodle owners and breeders view them as a breed that's simply not recognized by AKC, the traditionalists in the purebred dog fancy dismiss them as "overpriced mutts" and insist with no small measure of vehemence that the public is being fleeced by money-hungry opportunists out to make a quick buck. *Who is right?*

Let's start with a definition of the word "breed". **To begin with, the term is simply not part of scientific taxonomy.** All domestic dogs, purebred and mongrel alike, are classified by taxonomists as members of *Canis Lupus Familiaris,* a subspecies of the species *Canis Lupus,* which is a member of the genus *Canis,* of the much larger family *Canidae,* which is of course a member of the order *Carnivore.* Subspecies are commonly divided into landraces, races, strains, or breeds by breeders and livestock geneticists, but not by taxonomists. The reason for this is pretty simple – without human intervention, most would happily revert back to the single larger subspecies (in the case of dogs that would be mutts of "primitive type, with short coats, long legs and ears that stick up) with no problems whatsoever. A "breed" is an entirely manmade phenomenon, and does not occur in nature, so there is no definitive scientific definition for the term.

However, it *is* found in any dictionary, and both Merriam Webster and the venerable American Kennel Club define "breed" similarly.

Breed: A race of animals, selected and maintained by humans, with a characterized appearance and a common gene pool.

Adhering strictly to this definition, the Goldendoodle, like several other (but certainly not all) hybrids, is most decidedly a breed.

To begin with, the Goldendoodle is, in the vernacular of the purebred dog enthusiast, simply "dripping in breed type". In fact, the sheer consistency in breed type exceeds that of many far older purebreds, including one of its own "parent" breeds, which is actually pretty funny if you think about it.

Unlike the Goldendoodle, there have always been two very distinct types (or "characterized appearances") within the Golden Retriever breed, and as European and American show breeders have selected for different styles of dogs over the years there are now actually *three*, each physically and genetically differing enough from the others to qualify as separate breeds.

One often reads about "American Goldens" and "English Cream Goldens" but that's only part of the story. Within the Golden Retriever gene pool worldwide, there also exists a longstanding split between the performance/field-bred dogs and the show-bred dogs of both American and English type. Yet when any of these three very different strains are crossed with a poodle *of any of the three size varieties*, the resulting offspring are immediately and easily recognizable as Goldendoodles.

There is really no other breed for which the average Goldendoodle can be mistaken, which is the basic definition of breed type.

And as it is produced solely by the deliberate crossing of the purebred Poodle and the purebred Golden Retriever with no other admixtures, all Goldendoodles by definition share "a common gene pool".

And just as "old money" was once "new money", the vast majority of purebred dogs are in fact themselves the descendents of various crosses of older breeds, although the purebred dog fancy seems inclined to conveniently forget that.

Golden Beginnings

In fact, the Golden Retriever itself is what livestock geneticists call a "composite breed", and began as a hybrid. It was first developed in Scotland around 1867 *by the deliberate crossing of a Yellow Retriever with a Tweed Water Spaniel.*

This pairing produced four yellow puppies – Crocus, Cowslip, Primrose and Ada. These pups represent what geneticists refer to as F1 hybrids. Cowslip was then bred back to a Tweed Water Spaniel in what any breeder would recognize as an F1b backcross. A bitch puppy from *that* litter was subsequently bred back to a descendent of Ada in one of the earliest documented programs of deliberate inbreeding, and the Golden Retriever was on its way.

Highly popular in England right out the gate, the first Golden (a bitch named Mary) was registered with the American Kennel Club in 1889, *a mere 22 years after the first deliberate cross.*

And What About the Poodle?

The origins and subsequent recognition of the three varieties of Poodles as a single breed are somewhat more obscure. Although the AKC recognizes all three size varieties as a single breed, recent DNA research reveals that they are in fact three genetically distinct entities, with the Miniature and Toy varieties more closely related to each other than to the Standard variety. The traditional written history of the Poodle breed actually supports these genetic differences. The Standard Poodle appears to have developed from a landrace (the term used to describe a loose grouping of dogs developed in a geographic area for a specific purpose long before the deliberate "gentrification" of breeds into smaller groups) of hunting dogs developed for water retrieving around Germany as early as the 16th century, while the smaller ones appear to have their origins in an unrelated landrace—a diminutive dog of similar build and coat apparently developed in the Caribbean that made its way to England and France around 1700.

So it appears, with no small amount of irony, that neither the Golden Retriever nor the Poodle, both long-recognized and registered as "breeds", really technically fits the AKC's own definition of one (failing to display a single common phenotype in the case of the Golden or a common gene pool in the case of the Poodle), while the Goldendoodle, universally dismissed by the Dog Fancy as an overpriced mutt, actually does.

In light of this uncomfortable collision between twenty-first century molecular science and long-held tradition, perhaps the most accurate definition of a breed is that of one O. Lloyd-Jones, in a paper in the venerable Journal of Heredity entitled "What is a Breed?" published way back in 1915.

With as useful a definition as any, Mr. Lloyd-Jones suggested that, in the final analysis, "a breed is a group of domestic animals, termed such by common consent of the breeders."

In the face of what is surely a period of exuberant new-breed development unseen since the end of the nineteenth century, this might well prove in the long run to be the best definition of all.

While it may indeed be a breed, the Goldendoodle is not a *purebred dog*, and this distinction is very probably the source of much of the confusion.

The American Kennel Club (for better or worse the authority on all things related to purebred dogs in America) defines "purebred dog" as "*a dog whose sire and dam belong to the same breed and are themselves of unmixed descent since recognition of the breed*". This insistence upon unmixed descent (or "genetic purity") in fact represents the heart and soul of the American Kennel Club for the last one hundred and thirty years.

By definition, *genetic purity* requires a closed stud book. This means that the breed has a registry for which only the descendents of the designated original cross or crosses that went into making the breed are eligible. After multiple generations of breeding without the introduction of any new foundation breeding stock from either parent breed, the breed is "recognized" by some governing body like AKC .

So in order to become a "purebred" dog, many generations of Goldendoodles would have to be bred only to each other, with no backcrosses to either parent breed—in other words, they would need *a closed stud book*.

The Goldendoodle breed does not *have* a closed stud book, nor has there been an effort to develop one. Most are still deliberately produced by F1 and F1b crosses of the parent breeds, and are what geneticists refer to as crossbreeds, or *hybrids*.

A *hybrid*, just for the record, is defined by geneticists as the result of the deliberate crossing of two separate inbred strains, or homogeneous populations.

It does not require, as is often erroneously stated (mostly by a wealth internet "dog experts" with an agenda) two separate *species* or even two *breeds* to qualify, but simply two *strains*, which is an important distinction. One can have hybrid cattle like the Brangus, hybrid dogs like the Goldendoodle, or hybrid tomatoes like the famous Big Boy– hybridization is not limited to animals.

And by definition, hybrids display what geneticists recognize as *heterosis,* often called *hybrid vigor.* This is the chief advantage to creating a new hybrid, right after getting to pick out a cool new name for it. And what exactly *is* heterosis?

Here's how it's defined by geneticists:

Heterosis: The average increase in performance traits (i.e. size, hardiness and disease-resistance) displayed by the offspring of a deliberate cross of two different strains when compared to the averages of the original parent strains.

And that's a Good Thing. As the science of population genetics gains purchase, it has become all too apparent that it is the closed studbook required to maintain genetic purity and achieve recognition by all-breed registries that is actually responsible in large part for the appalling number of genetic disorders and immune dysfunction plaguing purebred dogs. First-hand experience with these health issues accounts in no small part for the recent popularity of hybrids among the pet-owning American public.

So, through possession of a single characterized appearance, a common gene pool and the common consent of its breeders, it appears that the Goldendoodle is indeed a breed, albeit not a purebred one. This still leaves the larger, and really far more important, question to be answered.....................

Is It the Right Breed For You?

Thanks to the miracles of hybrid vigor, the average Goldendoodle will often live for 13- 15 years, which represents a long-term commitment to dog ownership. And with the Standards topping out at a possible 80—100 pounds it's physically *a lot of dog*. That's why it's really, *really* important to decide if it is indeed the right breed for your household before falling in love with an adorable Goldendoodle puppy.

There is no perfect breed, and there is no perfect dog. Some breeds are absolutely perfect for some people, while for others….well… not so much. And that's where both breed type and breed character come in.

The term *breed type* generally refers to the physical characteristics that define a breed – a combination of what old breeders referred to as "shape and make" and "fancy points" back in simpler times. *Breed character* generally refers to a commonality of character and personality traits that for reasons of genetics, most well-bred and well-socialized members of any given breed will share.

In both areas, what is right for one family may well be wrong for another. This is the strongest argument for buying a particular breed in the first place, rather than adopting a mixed breed of unknown heritage from a shelter. With the latter, it's pretty hard to predict adult size, weight, build, coat or temperament.

As with most breeds, in both breed type and breed character the Goldendoodle is a genetic blend of the breeds from which it was developed. However, because some traits are controlled by dominant genes and others by recessive ones, these characteristics are not evenly inherited….in some ways the Goldendoodle more closely resembles the Golden Retriever, and in some ways his Poodle ancestry shines through. So let's look at breed type and breed character separately, because both ideally need to be a good fit

Author's Note: In spite of a new and alarming trend toward replacing the term "dog owner" with "dog guardian", and "dog ownership with the term "dog guardianship" and God only knows what other linguistic idiocy brought to us courtesy of PETA, dogs are still legally considered property and people still own them. This, of course, may change once they have evolved past rolling in dead fish, eating their own poop and drinking out of toilets, but for now it's still probably a good idea and really does not constitute enslavement by our species over theirs.

So, if for no other reason than to avoid ridiculous literary awkwardness, the term "owner" will be used throughout this book rather than "guardian" or "humom" or any such silliness. ("Manhole covers" will likewise not be referred to as "personhole covers" and mangrove trees will not be referred to as "persongrove trees" purely out of respect for the late George Carlin.)

And unless specifically referring to a bitch (or other female) the pronoun "he" will be used as the default.

Breed Type..........a Product of Genetics

Breed type is defined as a particular set of physical characteristics which set one breed apart from all others. Traditionally laid out in a breed's standard, it often provides the best initial clues to whether or not a breed is a good physical fit for one's lifestyle. Although the Goldendoodle does not have an official written standard, their physical appearance is astonishingly consistent from an anatomical standpoint – in other words, regardless of size, the relative lengths of their various bones and the angles of articulation between them vary little from dog to dog, resulting in a very uniform outline. So what does the typical Goldendoodle look like?

Although size can vary greatly, most Goldendoodles end up larger than expected– they can easily reach 100 pounds or more. Minis can weigh up to 60 pounds.

No matter what his size, the average Goldendoodle is a squarely-built dog and relatively high on leg.

His neck is typically rather long, clean and very strong, and blends well into his shoulders.

He typically displays a classic "Poodle front", with a sloping shoulder blade and a long, rather upright upper arm, simply because that front assembly tends to be dominant over that of the Golden, where the legs are set well under the body.

He typically displays a well-angulated rear, long from stifle to hock and short from hock to heel.

This body type makes him both fast and very agile, with tremendous endurance. This is not a breed that will tire easily.

His tail is set on level with the back, long and typically carried in a gentle sickle; its carriage usually reflects his worldview at any given point.

The classic Goldendoodle head is certainly a defining characteristic and his alone. (In other words, this is a "head breed", as much of essential breed type is to be found here.)

The ears are typically of medium length and dropped. The muzzle is long, well-chiseled beneath the eyes, rectangular and clean-lipped. The stop is slight, and the planes of the muzzle and skull are divergent rather than parallel, making him slightly down-faced. With large almond-shaped eyes set widely and rather obliquely, these elements combine to produce the typically winsome and totally melting expression that make him immediately identifiable as a Goldendoodle.

It is worth noting that the Goldendoodle displays none of the manmade anatomical exaggeration that define many modern breeds, and all his parts fit together pretty seamlessly into a pretty balanced whole. In fact, students of anatomy may notice with some amusement that the skeleton of a typical Goldendoodle is remarkably similar to Mother Nature's own *Canis lupus,* a pretty well-designed fellow by anyone's standards. (This explains a lot about his endurance levels.)

Breed Character..... Another Product of Genetics

In order for any dog to live up to his full genetic potential and develop into a well-adjusted and essentially happy fellow, he has *three very different sets of needs* which must be met. These needs, common to all pack animals, are hard-wired into his DNA and have been carried down for millennia from his wolf ancestors. (It's amazing how many people do not know this.)

These three needs are: physical, social, and intellectual. (There is no particular order, here- all of them are equally critical to the dog's well-being, and all of them must be adequately met.)

Virtually all behavioral problems in dogs are, without exception, a result of one or more of its essential needs not being met by unwitting but well-meaning owners.

(Write that down somewhere, as it is an immutable tenet of dog ownership.)

Because most breeds were developed for very different and very specific tasks, the requirements for meeting these needs vary greatly from breed to breed (and to a lesser extent from individual to individual) based upon *breed character*.

Breed character, like breed type, is nearly always related to a breed's original function; in temperament as in physical appearance, the rule that "form follows function" invariably applies.

Although most people never give it a moment's thought, simple logic should tell us that the specific physical, social and intellectual needs of a herding dog like the Border Collie are going to be very different than the needs of a scenthound like a Basset Hound, as the work they were originally bred to do is very different and requires very different thought processes, relationships with their handlers and "ways of going". The chief advantage of choosing a particular breed in the first place is that one can have a fair idea in advance of how these needs are manifested in a particular breed and what will be required to sufficiently meet them, and understanding that failure to do so will result in an ill-behaved (and often neurotic) dog.

In other words, *breed character* provides a lot of information about what is needed to meet the basic needs of a dog of that breed, and whether or not it is the right breed for you. Let's go through these needs one by one, as they apply specifically to the character of the Goldendoodle:

Meeting the Breed's Physical Needs

The most obvious physical need of any dog after food and water is *exercise*, and its importance cannot be understated.

Although the term "laid-back" is often used when describing the Goldendoodle, it really refers to the dog's overall easygoing and non-quarrelsome *temperament* rather than a need for little or no exercise. Laid-back is *not* a synonym for lazy in man or beast, and failure to understand the definition of a term on the owner's part does not constitute dishonesty on the breeder's part.

Many breeders' websites describe the exercise requirements of a Goldendoodle as "moderate", and that is probably accurate. What you really need to understand is what it is being compared to, and there's a wide spectrum in the world of dogs. A Goldendoodle's exercise needs are moderate when compared to those of a Border Collie or a Brittany, but not so much when compared to those of a Basset Hound or a Pekingese. Essentially, this is an active breed rather than a lazy one. In fact, the most common reason given for a Goldendoodle needing to be rehomed (or even worse, ending up in a shelter) is that the dog is too "hyper".

Almost without exception,

a dog is labeled "hyper" when his basic exercise needs are not being met.

As has often been pointed out, "a tired dog is a well-behaved dog". The thing is, it just takes a lot more to tire some dogs out!

And make no mistake about it, because of their build and size (and this includes the smaller ones) it takes a fair amount of directed exercise to tire out a Goldendoodle, especially in the first two years of his life.

Directed exercise means just that, by the way – another common misconception of dog ownership is that turning the dog out into a fenced yard a couple times a day will somehow take care of his exercise requirements. It won't. Unless he has another dog to chase and play with (and a lot of Goldendoodles live in multiple dog families for just this reason) the average Goldendoodle will not self-exercise – the exercise needs to be actually *directed* by a human. This is because he is descended from retrieving breeds, which are by definition bred to work *with* a handler, rather than independently (as is the case with most hound breeds).

You might as well know right now that a few walks on a leash will not do it either – in fact, that's another major misconception of dog ownership, and the source of a lot of behavioral problems in dogs of all breeds.

Most dogs of reasonable size can walk a lot farther than most people can without getting tired – unlike us, they're actually built for it. (*Because, like their common ancestor the wolf, most domestic dogs are built to cover long distances, dogs can walk almost indefinitely and trot for miles and miles without tiring.*) So odds are, by the time you are back in the house and ready to plop your butt in front of the tube, your Dood is just getting warmed up. To burn off excess energy, dogs actually need to *run*.

However, this does not need to be accomplished by actually running with them for miles every day – in fact, that's probably not a good idea at all in the first 18 months or so, especially on concrete sidewalks.

A puppy's exercise should be more like nature intended, in frequent short bursts of all-out energy, and on soft outdoor surfaces like grass or sand. And through a stroke of pure luck, the same "sporting dog DNA" that causes them to *require* a fair amount of exercise to stay both physically and mentally fit also provides a reasonably painless method of *delivering* it.

Since the Goldendoodle is descended from retrievers on both sides of his family tree,

teaching a puppy to retrieve early on is hands-down the best way to exercise him.

In addition to a couple daily walks, even fifteen minutes chasing a tennis ball or Frisbee in the back yard or your local dog park at full speed a couple times a day will go a long way toward burning off a dog's excess energy, while requiring very *little* actual energy expenditure on the owner's part. (For most dogs, once they've mastered it, retrieving is a self-rewarding exercise — as long as you keep throwing, the dog really doesn't care if you're sitting on a bench reading a book or talking on your cell phone while you're doing it, and he certainly does not need a treat every time he returns a Frisbee or a tennis ball.)

If you honestly cannot manage that, you really need to seriously consider whether this is the right breed for you, as you are surely going to have behavior problems, and it won't be the dog's fault.

Meeting the Breed's Social Needs

Just as there are clues to a dog's physical needs written into each breed's standard, there are clues to a dog's social and intellectual needs in there as well, and the differences between the Goldendoodle's parent breeds in this area are pretty clear.

The standard for the Golden, for instance, uses words like "friendly", while the Poodle standard uses words like "dignity". (The word "dignity" is actually used twice!)

Big difference there. Although the Goldendoodle physically favors the Poodle, socially he's a lot more like the Golden Retriever.

In fact, I've yet to meet a *single person* who's used the word "dignity" when describing a Goldendoodle. Intelligent, friendly, patient with children and small animals — the Goldendoodle displays all these qualities in spades. Dignity? Not so much. If dignity and "an air of distinction" are important character traits for you in a dog, get a Poodle. Or a Chow.

On the other hand, if "friendly" is more important to you, the Goldendoodle is a real contender, as this appears to be a universal character trait.

"Friendly" is really another way of saying "has strong social needs", and the Goldendoodle, like the Golden Retriever, has *very* strong social needs. He's a pack animal through and through, although he rarely wants to be the pack *leader*, which makes him a good choice for the novice owner and families with kids.

What does this mean to the owner? With a well-socialized Goldendoodle, this means he pretty much views every stranger on the planet as a friend he just hasn't met yet, and for the most part he'd rather endure neutering without anesthesia than the agony of being left alone.

Although this may not sit well with some breeders, the truth is that the Goldendoodle's strong social needs mean it is really not a good breed for the household where no one is home all day. (In fact, professional trainers report that one of the most common behavioral issues in Goldendoodles is "separation anxiety", which is basically a doggy panic attack triggered by being left alone.)

These dogs really do need to interact socially to at least some degree more or less nonstop during their waking hours and they are not happy left on their own for extended periods of time, especially when young. (If they were people, they'd be on their cell phones 24/7. In fact, as soon as someone develops cell phones for dogs – which someone no doubt will – Goldendoodles will be the first to use them.)

The good news is that the Goldendoodle is also extremely *socially adaptable* – they are rarely if ever "one-person" dogs, loyalty is *not* their strongest suit, and "social interaction" does not even necessarily require *human* company. They enjoy doggy daycare, with its nearly endless opportunities to make new human friends, and they adore spending time in the company of other dogs. They have no problem with a stranger coming into their home in the middle of the day to play with them and take them for a walk. (In truth, they have no problem with a stranger coming into their home in the middle of the day to steal the family silver and the flat-screen TV, either, but that's not really an upside….) They have no problem sharing their home with another animal – in fact, they *love* it. They have no problem with other breeds of dogs at all, large or small.

A Brief Goldendoodle Worldview:

Burglars? *Hey, come on in guys, I'm lonely in here all by myself!*

Another big dog with his hackles raised? *Hey, dude, wanna play tag?*

Kids? *Oh look – I see KIDS!!!! I LOVE kids!!!!!*

Cats? *Whoa, the dude was waggin' his tail...how's I supposed to know he was ticked off?*

Being alone? *Nooooooooooooooooo!!! Not alooooooooooooooooone!!!*

Personal space? *Ummmm...what's personal space?*

When it comes to cats, Goldendoodles tend to be innately fonder of cats than cats are of Goldendoodles, mostly due to that "lack of personal space" thing, but they invariably work it out.

So if one wants to keep a Goldendoodle from turning into a neurotic mess in a home where no one is home most of the day, arrangements will have to be made to avoid leaving him alone for extended periods.

Because they adore everyone indiscriminately

and are universally lacking in defensive aggression,

as personal protection dogs Goldendoodles are total non-starters.

Because they're also pretty deficient in territorial aggression, most owners report they're not even much good as watchdogs, although they may bark in delight when a stranger shows up at the door. (And even the largest of them are unlikely to inspire fear in anyone except the most dogophobic – they just don't have the face for it somehow.)

On the other hand, because of the lack of aggression, if he's intelligently raised, you really don't need to worry about your Goldendoodle biting anybody. ("Intelligently raised" is the key phrase here. Any dog inadvertently forced to assume a position of pack dominance is going to have some issues, especially if they are not temperamentally cut out for the job. In addition, because they are descended from retrievers this is a seriously "mouthy" breed, and as puppies they really need to be trained not to grab humans by the arm or leg in play, which they are inclined to do. Although not an aggressive act, it can easily be mistaken for such, especially in a large dog, and jerking one's arm or leg away in fear can result in an unintended bite, which will be traumatic for both the biter and the bitee.)

Because he rarely outgrows his playful nature with adulthood and is not easily threatened, the Goldendoodle is a natural lover of children and an ideal family dog. Like most sporting dogs (and remember, this is a breed created from two "repurposed" sporting breeds) they are tolerant of small children and extremely patient with toddlers, which many smaller breeds rightly consider a threat to their safety and well-being. Puppies raised with children need to be trained early on to control their mouthy instincts, though, or they will be inclined to haul them around, which will invariably get them into trouble.

Another consideration is how you feel about personal space, because Goldendoodles as a group have little or no sense of it.

This again is a gift from the Golden ancestry rather than the Poodle's contribution – the Poodle, bless his heart, generally has an exquisite sense of personal space, especially with strangers, which is probably what that "dignity" thing is about.) Like the Golden, this is an "in-your-face" breed, and if you find that frankly annoying, you might want to think long and hard about owning one, because you are unlikely to change it. According to some breeders and trainers, the F1b Goldendoodles (who are likely carrying more Poodle DNA) are as a whole better in this department than the F1s, but I wouldn't bank on it if you really want a dog who understands the concept. (For the record, many breeders with experience in both breeds claim the Labradoodle has a better sense of personal space than the Goldendoodle.)

The upside of this personal space thing is that in spite of his size, the Goldendoodle does not require a particularly large house. Owners report that ninety-pound Goldendoodles can get by just fine in a house that's only 1,500 square feet. In fact, according to one Manhattan-based trainer who works with a lot of them, as long as the dog gets adequate daily exercise, the average Goldendoodle will do just fine in an efficiency apartment, since they always want to be in whatever room you're in, anyway.

Intellectual Needs

High intelligence is a trait that the Goldendoodle has inherited from both parent breeds. Out of 110 breeds, over 200 professional obedience trainers rated the Poodle #2 and the Golden #4 in intelligence. High intelligence in a dog, however, is not always a good thing.

Intelligence in dogs is generally measured by their ability to solve problems without a lot of direction, while trainability is a different character trait entirely.

What this means to the owner is that when bored and finding themselves without human direction, intelligent dogs (who get bored a whole lot easier than dumb ones) will often engage their problem-solving abilities to the owner's peril. For example, most Goldendoodle owners report that their dogs could not be reliably left alone in the house without being crated until they were at least two years old. This has nothing to do with housebreaking (Goldendoodles are typically reliable in that department at an early age) and everything to do with "creative destruction".

In general, the more intelligent the dog,

the greater his powers of creative destruction when young..

In all fairness, however, dogs do not view this as destruction, and rarely does a dog destroy its owner's property out of spite —that's a common misconception based entirely upon anthropomorphism. Odds are the dog wasn't angry that you left him alone, he was just bored. Bear in mind that dogs have no innate sense of the value of your property (they're a lot like teenagers in this regard) and they tend to view your most valued heirlooms as toys they simply haven't had the opportunity to play with yet. Too often this involves solving the age-old problem of what's inside of it, because curiosity is also tied to intelligence and Goldendoodles are innately curious.

The high intelligence of this breed also means they absolutely require formal training

or they will train themselves,

and the results are not likely to be what the owner had in mind.

This formal training should ideally start at around 7 or 8 weeks of age, when the puppy first arrives in his new home.

Trainability, which any trainer will tell you is pretty unrelated to intelligence, does correlate heavily with an innate desire to please, and thanks to his Golden ancestry, the Goldendoodle ranks high on this scale as well. Because training involves interaction with people and Goldendoodles love people, Goldendoodle puppies uniformly love training and take to it like so many little ducklings to water.

With short, positive daily training sessions, the average pup can pretty well master the puppy basics — "come", "sit", "stay", "no biting!", walking on lead and ringing a bell to go outside — by 12 weeks of age. This basic repertoire, it should be noted, probably exceeds that of the average American adult dog by some bit, but for the Goldendoodle, that is just the beginning.

Because they are so innately social, Goldendoodles benefit more from training classes (where they learn to reliably follow commands even when there are serious Doodle-y distractions like new people to greet and other puppies to play with) than from individual in-house training sessions. Once they are old enough, training classes are highly recommended, even if your pup has learned the basics at home. Many owners report that their Goldendoodle graduated at the top of his class, which is a real confidence-builder for the novice owner.

Once the basics are mastered, advanced training depends on the individual desires of the owner – depending on the owner, this can take the form of "stupid pet tricks", competitive Agility, Therapy or even life-saving Search and Rescue work. The important thing to remember is this:

The Goldendoodle is a breed that both enjoys a fair amount of training

and actually requires it in order to thrive.

Because of this, no matter what their other attributes (and they are many) the breed is not really well-suited to those who find training a dog boring.

Typical F1 coat development
from 7 week old puppy
to trimmed adult

CHAPTER TWO:

Coats and Colors

(or...unraveling the Myths and Mysteries)

When asked what originally attracted them to the breed in the first place, a majority of Goldendoodle owners say it was a combination of the breed's temperament, lack of serious health issues and always.... the famous hypoallergenic, low-shedding and attractive Goldendoodle *coat*. In fact, for many owners, the coat was the *first* consideration.

Given that, it is unfortunate that there is so much conflicting information, as well as flat-out *misinformation*, floating around the internet about the Goldendoodle coat.

There is no doubt the Goldendoodle's casually tousled locks contribute greatly to his overall charm, but do his widely touted hypoallergenic and low-shedding qualities represent any sort of reality... or, as many suggest, just sales hype?

Is there any way to predict what sort of coat a Goldendoodle will have as an adult, or is it, as many suggest, a total crapshoot?

And exactly how much work is *really* involved in taking care of a Goldendoodle coat?

Let's look at the "hypoallergenic" part first:

Over the past couple of years the term "allergy-friendly" has largely replaced the term "hypoallergenic" on virtually all breeders' websites, as it is now generally accepted that there is "really no such thing as a hypoallergenic dog".

This is an unfortunate mistake. The *only* reason it is now generally accepted that there is really no such thing as a hypoallergenic dog is because that particular bit of misinformation been *widely disseminated on the internet*, apparently by persons one can only charitably assume have no access to a dictionary.

From the American Heritage Dictionary:

Hypoallergenic adj. :

Having a decreased tendency to provoke an allergic reaction.

In other words, a "hypoallergenic dog" simply has a decreased (i.e. lower) tendency to produce an allergic reaction in people with allergies when compared to a dog that is not hypoallergenic. That's pretty cut-and-dried. So why the confusion?

What's actually happened here is that way too many self-styled "internet dog experts" have unfortunately confused the word "hypoallergenic" with "nonallergenic", which is an entirely different word with an entirely different meaning.

Nonallergenic adj.:

Not producing an allergic reaction.

There are in fact *many* hypoallergenic breeds, and the Goldendoodle is definitely one of them.

On the other hand, there are no nonallergenic breeds at all, even those which are entirely devoid of hair, because all dogs are covered from nose to tail in SKIN, which is where the allergens are actually produced.

The Science of Dog Hair

Most dog allergies in humans are produced by reactions to the rather awkwardly named *Can f 1* and *Can f 2* proteins. These proteins are produced in canine epithelial tissue, and end up in the dog's dander (which consists of shed skin cells) some of which sticks to the hair before becoming airborne. (These proteins are also found in canine saliva, which is why dogs that drool heavily are a poor choice for people with allergies.)

Some breeds have been shown to carry measurably greater amounts of these proteins on their hair, and the differences are actually connected to *seborrhoeac levels* rather than hair length. (*Seborrhoeac* in this context simply refers to dogs that naturally produce a lot of *sebum*, as opposed to dogs with a pathological skin condition.)

Sebum is the oily substance produced by the sebaceous gland, a small gland connected to the hair follicle which lubricates the hair shaft. Not surprisingly, the oilier "waterproof" breeds like Labs were found to have the highest levels of Can f proteins on their hair, because instead of the normal 21-day cycle, the epidermal turnover time of seborrhoeac dogs is only 3-4 days. In other words, oily-coated dogs simply produce more dander, and the Can f proteins are in the dander, which sticks to the hair. Less oily breeds like the Poodle produce considerably less. The Golden Retriever probably falls somewhere in the middle.

Although hair length does not significantly affect the amount of Can f proteins produced, the more hairs that are shed, the more these allergens are dispersed throughout the house, both on surfaces and in the air. This is where the "non-shedding/low-shedding" part comes in, and hair length (largely determined by variations on the canine RSPO2 and FGF5 genes) is a definite factor in shedding, another area where misinformation abounds. So let's look at that next.

Shedding and Genetic Coat Variations

To begin with, except for a very few totally hairless breeds, *all dogs shed*. There is simply no such thing as a non-shedding coated dog, or a non-shedding coated mammal of *any kind,* for that matter. Even *elephants* shed, for Heaven's sake. Some dogs simply contribute less hair to the environment than others, for a couple of different reasons.

Each mammalian hair goes through a basic three-phase cycle — *anagen, catagen* and *telogen* — although not all hairs are on the same cycle. (If that were the case, shorthaired dogs would be totally bald for a couple of weeks several times a year, which they clearly are not.)

Although it can be affected by temperature, daylight, endocrine function and the animal's individual health, most shedding is genetically determined.

Anagen is the "growth" phase, and the length of this cycle varies greatly based on the dog's genes. Longhaired dogs logically spend a lot more time in the anagen phase than short-haired ones do.

Catagen is the "transitional" phase, which lasts 1-2 weeks.

Telogen is the "resting" phase, which lasts 5-6 weeks, during which time the hair doesn't grow. At the end of this cycle, the hair detaches from the follicle and is pushed out, or shed, as a new hair develops beneath it.

So what's happening is basically this: a shorthaired dog is genetically programmed to whip through the anagen or "growth" phase a lot faster than a longhaired one – the anagen phase in a dog like the Lab, whose hair grows to about an inch or two at best, may only last a couple of months, whereas the anagen phase in a Poodle, whose hair can reach 10 inches before shedding out, may last a couple of years. (Contrary to popular belief, a Poodle's hair will *not* continue to grow indefinitely!)

In other words, a shorthaired dog sheds out each individual hair a lot more often.

This results in more dog hair lying around, which carries more dander

and, depending on the seborrhoeac levels, more Can f proteins.

There are several more factors which affect shedding that are a lot less straightforward.

The first involves the amount of curl in the dog's hair, which is largely controlled by variations on the KRT71 gene. Although we can't see them, each hair shaft is covered with scales, sort of like a fish. In straighter-coated breeds, these scales lie flat against the hair shaft, whereas on curly or wavy hair, which consists of a series of s-curves, the scales are forced open at each outside curve, sort of like what you'd see if you bend a fish.

When curly or wavy haired breeds shed, the hair that's just been shed

tends to catch in open scales of the surrounding hairs and get stuck there,

rather than falling clean off the dog and landing on the couch.

These breeds are said to "shed into their coats", and if not brushed regularly to remove the shed hairs they will rapidly turn into a matted mess. The tradeoff for this higher grooming requirement is less dog hair floating around the house.

The second factor in shedding is the *pattern* of coat growth, which is largely controlled by two different genes. A typically longhaired breed like the Golden retriever carries two copies of a variation on the *FGF5* gene, which causes the hair on the bottom half of the dog to be long while the hair on the face, front of the legs and feet is short, with the hair on the back of intermediate length.

Longhaired breeds shed less than shorthaired breeds

because a large percentage of their hair spends more time in the anagen phase.

They are generally considered to be "moderate" shedders. Many people are surprised to learn that longhaired breeds shed less than shorthaired ones, but it is a fact nonetheless. As anyone who's owned one can attest, in the shedding department the otherwise adorable Pug is the hands-down winner. The Pug's coat is both short *and* dense, which translates to a *lot* of hair pretty much everywhere.

To further complicate things, dogs with facial furnishings and furry feet all carry at least one copy of a dominant variant on the *RSPO2* gene which causes the hair all over the dog to stay in a longer anagen cycle.

Breeds that carry two copies of the recessive "longhaired" (FGF5) variant and at least one copy of the dominant "furnishings" (RSPO2) variant have long hair from nose to tail and will logically shed less than a longhaired breed without the RSPO2 mutation. Breeds carrying this genetic combination are referred to as "drop-coated", and include the Bearded Collie, the Tibetan Terrier, the Lhasa Apso and the Maltese.

When the gene variants that produce a drop coat are combined with the variants that produce a curly coat you end up with the breeds likely to be lowest-shedding and most hypoallergenic.

The Poodle, the Portuguese Water Dog, the Bedlington Terrier and the Bichon Frise all fall into this category. (For reasons not yet fully understood, these breeds also tend not to produce a lot of sebum, which is why they rarely have a "doggy" odor.)

This brings us to the third factor affecting shedding – coat *density*, which is defined as the number of hairs per square inch. The denser the coat, the more hairs are logically shed on a daily basis.

Depending upon the amount of curl, this extra hair will either end up on the furniture or being shed into the coat, where it will rapidly form mats.

Coat density is inherited independently of all the other coat genes. Poodles carry a uniformly dense coat, while coat density in Goldens varies quite a bit. (It's probably worth noting that as well as typically carrying more wave, the "English" Golden carries a softer, denser coat than American Goldens, and groomers generally agree that the coats on English Cream Goldendoodles are the most difficult to maintain.)

The final factor is the difference between guard hair and undercoat. These are produced by two different types of hair follicles, which cycle differently—as everyone who's ever owned a double-coated dog has already noticed, undercoat cycles faster than guard hair.

As juveniles, all mammals produce only softer undercoat, which is insulating. Around six months, some of the undercoat follicles are replaced by those which will produce guard hair, which is coarser and more waterproof.

This is the period called "blowing puppy coat", and it generally lasts for several months, during which time tangles form almost overnight as undercoat is literally pushed out and if the puppy is not brushed almost daily he will rapidly become a matted mess.

In adults, the ratio of guard hair to undercoat varies from breed to breed and in the case of the Goldendoodle from dog to dog. Because undercoat cycles faster, in general, the greater the proportion of undercoat, the greater the coat maintenance requirements. (Again, the "English" style Golden Retrievers carry proportionally more undercoat than the American dogs.)

It's also worth knowing that research has shown that no matter what its genetics, the single most effective tool in reducing the amount of Can f proteins on the dog and by extension in the house is frequent bathing. When a dog is bathed, a lot of dander (and Can f protein) is washed down the drain.

The amount of Can f allergens dispersed throughout the house can be reduced by up to 84% by simply bathing the dog twice a week.

Which, let's face it, no one is really going to do. But it is a strong argument for considering a dog on the smaller end of the Goldendoodle size scale when allergies are a factor. It's simply a lot less work to bathe a smaller dog than a great big one, and for that reason alone a smaller dog is likely to get bathed more often, especially in the winter, when dry indoor air causes a dog's skin to be flakier.

So… what do all these combinations of gene variations in canine coats (which frankly few people on the planet even had a clue about prior to 2009) have to do with the Goldendoodle? A lot.

. These genes explain why the F1 Goldendoodle puppy often looks more like a Golden Retriever puppy at 8 weeks, while some (but not all) of the F1b puppies have fluffier faces and coats at the same age, and look more like untrimmed Poodle puppies.

They also explain the greater variations seen in the adult coats of F2 and F3 Goldendoodles (the result of breeding Goldendoodle to Goldendoodle), where a pup or two invariably ends up with a "Golden Retriever" coat. (The appearance of these so-called "retriever coats" is the main reason cited by breeders who don't breed F1 Goldendoodles together. Although they still maintain a high level of hybrid vigor, these coats are less hypoallergenic and shed more than the "typical" Goldendoodle coat.)

Goldendoodle Coat Genetics

Assuming the coat genotypes of both the Golden Retriever and the Poodle are relatively "fixed", all the F1 puppies will come out with exactly the same coat genotype, which they inherit in basic Mendelian fashion. And although it is different than either parent, it is the same in all the puppies, and it is this specific genotype that produces the typical "Goldendoodle" coat.

The Golden Retriever is genetically ll, CC, ff. This means he carries two copies of the recessive longhaired variant at FGF5, two copies of the wavy variant at KRT71, and two copies of the recessive "clean-faced" variant at RSPO2.

The Poodle is ll, cc, FF. This means he also carries two copies of the ll variant, as well as two copies of the curly variant and two copies of the dominant "head furnishings" RSPO2 variant.

(Although not desirable, a small percentage of Poodles are heterozygous for the curly gene allele – in other words, they also carry one copy of the wavy variant. This genotype is more likely to occur in the rarer colors because selective pressure for a coat that can be easily sculpted into the more extreme show trims has not been as great. This explains why occasionally some F1b Goldendoodles are not as curly or even wavy as might be expected.)

Coat Variations in the F1 Goldendoodle

F1 breeding	**Sire** cc ll FF long, curly, with furnishings	
Dam ll CC ff long, wavy, no furnishings	**ll Cc Ff** long, wavy, with furnishings	**ll Cc Ff** long, wavy, with furnishings
	ll Cc Ff long, wavy, with furnishings	**ll Cc Ff** **long, wavy,** **with furnishings**

In any breed with variance in RSPO2, the heterozygous puppies develop facial furnishings later than the pups that received two copies. And although they each carry at least one copy of the curly gene, the *amount* of curl displayed on F1 puppies can vary, because there is yet another gene involved that determines whether a coat is straight or wavy/curly. When present, a single copy of this gene can "mask" both wave and curl. As the Golden Retriever standard allows for both straight and wavy coats, this trait is not "fixed" in the breed. (It is entirely missing in the Poodle.) So pups with a straight-coated Golden parent will often display less wave than will Doods with a wavy-coated Golden parent.

Coat Variations in the F1B Backcross

F1b breeding	**Sire** **ll cc FF** long, curly, with furnishings	
Dam **ll Cc Ff** long, wavy, with furnishings	**ll Cc FF** long, wavy, with furnishings	**ll cc Ff** long, curly, with furnishings
	ll cc FF long, curly, with furnishings	**ll Cc Ff** long, wavy, with furnishings

When an F1 Goldendoodle is bred to another Poodle in an F1b backcross, the variation in puppies becomes greater, because the Goldendoodle is not genetically "fixed" (i.e. *homozygous*) for either curl or head furnishings. As a result, some of the F1b pups may inherit a copy of the curly gene from each parent and be curly (cc) like a Poodle, while others may inherit one of each variant and end up Cc, with a wavy coat. But because each pup will have inherited one copy of the dominant F variant from the poodle parent, none will end up with a "retriever coat". The pups with the Poodle coat phenotype are likely to be the most hypoallergenic. Pups can be gene-tested at 2-3 weeks of age with a cheek swab, at a cost of only $75 per pup.

Coat Variations in the F2 Goldendoodle

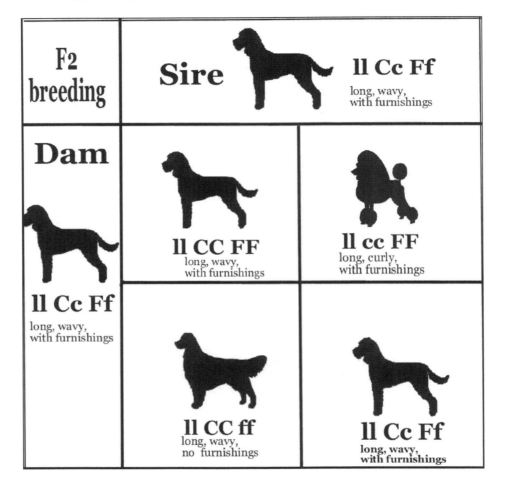

F2 breeding	**Sire** ll Cc Ff long, wavy, with furnishings	
Dam ll Cc Ff long, wavy, with furnishings	ll CC FF long, wavy, with furnishings	ll cc FF long, curly, with furnishings
	ll CC ff long, wavy, no furnishings	ll Cc Ff long, wavy, with furnishings

In addition to the variation in curl, the fact that both parents are Ff means that some pups in these litters will be FF, some will be Ff, and some (statistically 25%) will be ff. The pups with the last combination will display the "retriever coat" pattern and will not develop head furnishings at all.

These pups are least likely to be hypoallergenic and will be moderate shedders like the Golden, so are probably a poor choice for families where allergies are a problem. However, for those families who really prefer the "clean-faced" looks of the Golden Retriever and are less concerned with shedding and more concerned with the health advantages provided by hybrid vigor (F2 animals generally display only slightly less hybrid vigor than F1s and certainly more than either of the parent breeds) they may be perfect. These pups can also be identified within a few weeks of birth by gene testing.

Although most Goldendoodle breeders are unaware of its existence, the widespread use of coat gene testing would be a Really Good Idea for this breed, as it takes out a lot of the "guesswork" in predicting adult coats and ultimately allows breeders to do a better job matching puppies with the needs and desires of the new owners.

In addition to that, if it were used in conjunction with the newly available gene testing for DLA haplotypes, coat gene testing would also allow serious breeders to produce consistent F3 puppies maintaining both critical genetic diversity and the desired wavy Goldendoodle coats, rather than essentially turning the breed back into Poodles through repeated backcrosses that reduce hybrid vigor.

How would this work? Obviously, given his coat genes, the F2 pup in the upper left, who is homozygous (or pure) for both the wavy coat and the "furnishings" gene, could be bred to any unrelated F1, or even an unrelated and similarly tested F2, or F1b, without fear of producing any "retriever coats", because a puppy needs to inherit a copy of the RSPO2 "wild type" allele from each parent to display it, and this dog has none to pass on.

Genetics of Coat Color

It has long been noted that "a good dog cannot come in a bad color", and color in the Goldendoodle is largely a matter of personal preference.

Goldendoodles can display virtually any color or pattern, and they may change color as they mature. However, there are more variations in the multigenerational Doods than in the F1s.

This is because the Golden Retriever is genetically "fixed" for color, and has been since the early development of the breed.

The color genotype for the typical Golden Retriever is BB, ee, SS.

For the two or three people on the planet who may actually be interested in this stuff, this is the recipe for a solid-colored homozygous dominant black dog also homozygous for a recessive variant on the E locus that prevents the extension of *eumelanin* on the hair shaft, leaving only *phaeomelanin*, resulting in every hair ending up some shade of cream, gold or red while the pigment on the nose, lips and pads stays black. Although a percentage of Goldens may be heterozygous on the A and K loci (thus allowing for tan patterning) the pattern is masked by the ee genotype common to the breed.

The Poodle breed, on the other hand, does not have a common color genotype.

Every canine color variant identified to date has been found in the Poodle.

Although solid white, black, brown, silver and apricot are the most common colors (and the only ones actually listed in the AKC Poodle Standard) red, black and tan, phantom, brindle, merle and sable are also found in the breed, as well as piebalds (commonly referred to as parti-colored), in which any of the above colors and color patterns appear as patches on a white dog.

The reason for this difference is easily explained. The Golden Retriever literally began as a "designer breed" with a limited gene pool originally selected for a single color (gold), while the Poodle more or less evolved from at least two separate landraces with a much larger gene pool over a much longer period of time. This allowed for the introduction of a lot of recessive color gene variants from his various early ancestors. However, in order for a recessive gene variant to be expressed, *both* parents must be carrying a copy.

Because the genes of the Golden are fixed,

the possible colors in F1 Goldendoodle puppies are limited.

F1 puppies are most commonly some shade of gold, running the gamut from almost-white to fairly deep red, or black, and they will be primarily solid-colored, sometimes with white markings on the toes, chest, and possibly the muzzle, often referred to as "abstract" markings for no logical reason. (This happens when the Poodle parent is carrying the piebald gene.)

Depending upon whether or not the Poodle parent is carrying the dominant gene variant for silvering (where only one parent needs to be carrying the gene), black puppies may lighten to silver at adulthood, and reds and creams may lighten as well.

Occasionally black and tan puppies can appear in F1 crosses, because both Goldens and Poodles can carry the gene alleles for the black and tan pattern. These puppies, marked like Dobermans, are sometimes referred to as "phantoms", but black and tan and phantom are not really the same thing genetically. "Phantom" refers to incomplete expression of the classic tan pattern on a black or chocolate dog due to heterozygosity on the K locus. Very common in cockers, this can also occur in

Goldendoodles and Poodles, but it is not genetically the same as a true tan-patterned dog.)

And F1 Goldendoodles will have black noses. The gene variant that produces brown (or chocolate) in both the skin and the hair (bb) is not found in the purebred Golden retriever, so neither chocolate puppies nor the color combination called "caramel" by some breeders (i.e. a gold puppy with a brown nose) is likely to occur.

In multigenerational Goldendoodles, including F1 bs,

virtually any color and/or combination of colors is possible.

While the earliest Goldendoodles were usually the result of crosses between Golden Retrievers and white Standard Poodles, recent years have brought a surge of new colors and a lot of size variation to the breed, through the introduction of the less-common colored (and smaller-sized) Poodles. From the standpoint of genetic diversity, this is a Very Good Thing.

Why is that?

Geneticists often point out that in any domestic species, breeds predicated upon a single color or pattern or even size are invariably the most vulnerable to genetic disorders and problems linked to inbreeding depression, because their gene pools have been artificially (and often drastically) reduced in size in order to "cement" the desired traits. So besides simply giving puppy buyers more options, the dizzying array of colors and sizes now emerging in the Goldendoodle will actually help to preserve the robust health and longevity that is a result of hybrid vigor and which is in no small measure responsible for its popularity.

CHAPTER THREE:

Finding that Perfect Puppy

(or...where's match.com when you really need it?)

Once you've decided that the Goldendoodle is the right breed for your family, the next step is sorting out all the "flavors" suddenly available. F1s, F2s, F1bs, F2bs, Multi-gens, English Goldendoodles, Teddybear Goldendoodles, English Teddybears, Moyens, Minidoodles, Lapdoodles – the sheer number of options out there are enough to make one's head spin.

Let's start out with some definitions.

When geneticists use the letter F with a number and or extra letter, what they are describing is the genetic "recipe" used in creating the specific animal. (The F stands for "filial", just for the record.)

F1 Goldendoodles

These are the product of a first-generation cross between a purebred Poodle and a purebred Golden Retriever. Genetically, they all inherit 50% of their genes from the Golden Retriever parent and the other 50% from the Poodle parent. Most Goldendoodles are in fact F1s, and display the highest level of heterosis, or hybrid vigor.

F1b Goldendoodles

These are the product of a breeding between an F1 Goldendoodle and a second (usually unrelated) purebred Poodle. (The b in this case stands for "backcross", because the breeder has backcrossed to the Poodle.) Although it is common to say that these F1b dogs are "75% Poodle and 25% Golden Retriever", from a genetic standpoint *this is actually highly unlikely*. Here's why:

In an F1 backcross, the Goldendoodle parent has inherited one gene variant at each locus from the Poodle parent and one gene variant from the Golden Retriever parent, *but they will be passed to each puppy randomly*. When thousands of genes split individually, the possibility of a straight 50/50 split is to say the least statistically improbable. It is entirely possible (although also unlikely) that the F1 parent passed all his Poodle genes to one puppy and all his Golden Retriever genes to another. In reality, it's most likely to be a crapshoot.

So it would really be more accurate to say that an F1b Goldendoodle is likely to carry a greater percentage of Poodle DNA than an F1 would be, and so is more likely to display a greater percentage of Poodle characteristics, including the poodle coat qualities. The downside of the "backcross" dogs is that for the reasons explained above, the pups randomly receiving the greatest number of Poodle genes from their F1 parent will lack the highbred vigor of the F1s, and are more susceptible to development of the health issues that plague purebred Poodles.

F2 Goldendoodles

These are the result of crossing an F1 Goldendoodle with another F1 Goldendoodle. For the reasons explained previously, these dogs are far less consistent in looks, size and temperament than the F1 or even the F1b, and for this reason are hard to make any generalizations about. Some look like F1s, some like F1bs (with more Poodle characteristics) and some look almost exactly like Golden Retrievers.

These last pups still retain a high level of heterozygosity, however, and are less likely to suffer from the genetic disorders that plague Golden Retrievers and Poodles. For those who really love Goldens but are put off by the health issues in the breed, the "retriever-coated" pups in an F2 litter may be a great option.

"Multi-gen" or Multi-generational Goldendoodles

This is a term that can refer to any dog whose parents are Goldendoodles rather than Poodles or Golden Retrievers. It is also commonly used to refer to F2b Goldendoodles (produced by breeding F1b females back once more to a Poodle sire) although some dispute this use of the term, as that really represents what is called "top-crossing" in livestock genetics. They can also refer to F2 and F3 Goldendoodles. These multi-generational crosses are typically more common in the Labradoodle. Multi-generational Doods produced by backcrossing typically do not display the highbred vigor of F1s although gene testing for DLA haplotypes could mitigate that greatly.

Teddybear Goldendoodles, English Cream Goldendoodles, English Goldendoodles, English Teddybear Goldendoodles

These are all terms the buyer will run into when looking for a pup, and there's a LOT of confusion here. Often these pups are considerably more expensive, leading to the claim by many breeders (especially those who use American Goldens) that they simply represent a "marketing gimmick", and that there actually is no difference. So what's the real story?

To begin with, all these names refer to pups out of Golden Retrievers imported from England or Eastern Europe rather than out of American-bred dogs. These Goldens are usually a light cream color, mostly because that shade is simply more popular in the show ring there. (There is really no disqualification for any shade of red/gold/cream in Goldens anywhere.) At present, show breeders on this side of the pond currently prefer a brighter gold dog than those on the other, although that has not always been the case and it will no doubt change again in the future.

In terms of conformation the English-type dogs tend to be significantly more substantial (i.e. broader throughout and heavier in bone) and display significantly less angulation, with a broader muzzle and back skull when compared to the field-type "American" Golden. (American show-type Goldens, for the record, are more substantial than the field-bred dogs but more elegant than the English type, with silkier coats and better angulation both fore and aft. They are rarely used to produce Goldendoodle pups because American show breeders keep pretty tight control on intact animals and are frankly unwilling to put them in the hands of Goldendoodle breeders, whom they universally view with fear and loathing.)

Aside from personal preference, the downside of crossing the English-style Golden with the Poodle is that they tend to be "unlike-to-unlike" breedings. As every show breeder knows, the genes that determine substance, angulation and bone length in both the front and rear are inherited independently. (This is Mendel's Law of Independent Assortment, the bane of breeders everywhere.)

When dogs who are radically different in these areas are crossed (even within a breed) the potential for "unbalanced" puppies, where the parts simply do not fit together well, is much higher. Dogs that lack balance are at higher risk for structural problems because more stress will be brought to bear on the straighter angles as the dog moves. Vets and owners are already starting to see these problems in Goldendoodles, which is more than a little alarming. No matter what country the parents hail from, dogs with similar structure and angulation are more likely to produce sound puppies.

And although they tend to produce puppies with blockier heads and really cute "teddy bear" faces, because of the extra substance these English-type dogs will tend to weigh quite a bit more for their height as adults, which is also a factor worth considering.

In addition, English and European Goldens tend to display a denser, softer and often wavier coat than their American counterparts of either bench or field type. Often fluffier as puppies, the English Cream Goldendoodles consequently tend to carry denser, wavier coats as adults than the offspring of American dogs. When freshly bathed and groomed, their coats have a lovely plush "whipped cream" look rather than a "shaggy dog" look, reminiscent of a Soft Coated Wheaten Terrier puppy more than anything else. Although lovely, this is a much higher-maintenance coat, which is also a factor to consider.

Many breeders claim that the "English Cream Goldens" are more laid-back and mellow than their American counterparts – true or false?

Mostly true, although the temperament of the individual parents is still most important. American Goldens from working lines (the ones most often used in producing Goldendoodles) were selected more for "performance traits" like intelligence, trainability and drive (which translates into a desire to work) than their bench-bred counterparts on either side of the pond, where winning really is a beauty contest, and performance traits rarely factor into breeding decisions.

Trainers who work with Detection, Service and Search and Rescue dogs tend to prefer dogs with more drive, while the pet owner may well prefer a dog with less, because unless directed with adequate training and exercise, this "drive" will translate into a hyper dog.

That said, whether from English or American Goldens, a Goldendoodle with laid-back parents is much more likely to be a laid-back dog than one whose parents are on the high-energy end of the scale, which is why it's good to meet the parents if at all possible no matter *what* country they're from.

It is also often claimed that the "English Cream Goldens" are healthier than the American dogs, and will by definition produce healthier puppies – true or false?

Without a large health database for Goldendoodles, which does not exist, this claim is honestly pretty hard to prove one way or the other. Statistics for Eastern European countries like Hungary (where a lot of so-called "English" Goldens actually hail from) are simply not available, and screening for hip dysplasia and single-gene disorders in those countries is frankly not as commonly performed.

Cancer rates in Goldens in England appear to be somewhat lower than in the US (close to 40% of Goldens in England will ultimately die of cancer compared to 60% in the US) but both are higher than most other breeds and frankly appalling.

On the other hand, one form of PRA (GR_PRA1) has been primarily found in the European Goldens, with around 1 in 20 found to be carrying the causative gene mutation in England, compared to 1 in 200 in the US. And a recently-available gene test for ICTA (which causes chronic skin problems) has revealed that 70% of the Goldens in France are carrying either one or two copies of the causative mutation. Clearly, health issues in Goldens (and Poodles, for that matter) are not limited to the American dogs, and "better health" should NOT ethically be used as a selling point.

So the bottom line is basically this...the robust health and improved immune function of F1 Goldendoodles is primarily a function of *heterosis*, and as such is not particularly influenced by the country of origin of either parent breed. (This is covered in more detail in the Health Chapter.) More important than which country a Golden hails from is really whether or not health information on the parents and ideally the grandparents is available, and it's a little dicey to breed a dog without health-screening for the genetic diseases in its breed no matter *where* it's from.

What puppy buyers really need to understand is that there really is no breed called the "English Golden Retriever" –for better or worse, all Goldens worldwide are registered simply as Golden Retrievers no matter what country they come from and may be interbred so long as the registry of one country recognizes the stud book of the other. And because none of these terms are trademarked, anyone can call their Goldendoodle puppies pretty much anything they want and no one can stop them.

If you prefer a Goldendoodle pup out of an "English-type" Golden Retriever because of its face, or body type, or temperament, or coat type, it's probably wise to ask to see the pedigrees and/or registration certificates on the parents to make sure the parent is actually from England or Europe, and to look at either the parent itself or photos to assure yourself it's the style of dog you prefer, because unfortunately all breeders are not entirely honest in this regard.

Now, in terms of finding a dog that's going to fit your lifestyle, size really can matter, so let's look at that next.

Moyens, Mini Goldendoodles, Miniature Goldendoodles, Petite Goldendoodles

These are all terms used to identify Goldendoodles produced by crossing Golden Retriever bitches with smaller Poodles in an effort to bring down size.

In addition to the above, **Microminidoodles** and **Lapdoodles** are terms some breeders are now using to describe F1 crosses between Golden Retriever females and very tiny Toy Poodle males weighing 4-6 pounds. (These breedings are invariably the result of artificial insemination.)

Poodles in the US come in three sizes- Standards are over 15 inches at the shoulder, Miniatures are less than 15 inches but not more than 10, and Toys are 10 inches or less. (Although the historical term Moyen is often used to describe small Standards, technically they do not exist as a Variety in the US.)

The Golden Retriever standards call for a dog between 21 ½ and 24 inches at the shoulder the world around, with weights between 55 and 75 pounds.

Many websites explain that crossing two breeds of different sizes will generally result in puppies halfway in between. Although this sounds logical at first blush, it rarely proves to be the case in real life, because hybrid vigor tends to increase size as well as increasing longevity and immune function in the progeny, generally to the tune of 20% or more.

F1 Goldendoodles with a Standard Poodle parent will usually weigh somewhere between 50 and 80 pounds as adults, and can (and do) end up weighing closer to 100 pounds. It is not uncommon for them to stand 28 inches at the shoulder or more.

Miniature Goldendoodles (alternatively referred to as any or all of the names listed above) are generally smaller than Standard Goldendoodles, thanks to their Miniature or Toy Poodle parent and/or grandparent. But in spite of the breeders' best efforts, even those with a 6-pound Toy parent rarely end up much less than 15-20 pounds, and some are likely to end up closer to 45 pounds.

The reason for this is simple genetics. Because Goldens uniformly lack the variation in FGF1 gene expression that is a fixed genetic trait in all breeds under 20 lbs including Miniature and Toy Poodles, all the resulting offspring are heterozygotes by definition. Without a gene test, which is commercially unavailable at this time, reaching homozygosis would take several generations of backcrosses, by which time you'd functionally end up with a small Poodle rather than a Goldendoodle and all gains in genetic diversity (hybrid vigor) would be lost. Consistently reducing size takes many years and lots of generations, and larger "throwbacks" can show up at any time, just like "retriever coats" and for the same reason.

However, there is a *big* difference between a dog that may end up weighing 45 pounds and a dog that may end up weighing 100 pounds, so if size is a factor, you're definitely better off looking for a breeder who specializes in Minis. But beyond that, any breeder who absolutely guarantees adult size should be viewed with caution. And if you truly need a dog that will finish out under 20 pounds because of zoning or Homeowners Association rules, no Goldendoodle is really a safe bet unless it's already an adult, and you'd be better off with an Island Minidoodle or a Maltipoo puppy.

The amazing thing about all these different "varieties" is that with the exception of size variation, most Goldendoodles actually look remarkably similar and have remarkably similar temperaments and activity levels. If properly socialized, all are great with kids and other animals, and tend to share the same greater overall robust health and longevity than their purebred cousins.

Even the much-discussed coat differences between the F1 and F2 dogs are probably a little overrated – a survey of nearly a thousand Goldendoodle owners revealed that over 70% of the F1 dogs were rated as "light-to-non-shedding". And even more surprising….

Over 85% of the owners of F1 Goldendoodles reported

friends and family members with allergies had "no problems" with the dog.

A whopping 96% of the F2 dogs were rated as light-to-non-shedding by their owners, and 91% of them produced no problems in friends and family members with allergies.

If allergies are a serious consideration, the F2s are still probably a better bet; otherwise you can probably own an F1 Goldendoodle (which will display the greatest amount of hybrid vigor) without having to worry about tons of dog hair floating around your house.

So…………… now that we've sorted out all that confusing name stuff, it's time to actually start looking for a breeder.

Locating a Good Breeder

It is an unfortunate truth that puppy buyers as a whole put a lot more time (and a whole lot more research!) into choosing the right breed than they put into choosing the right breeder or the right puppy. Once they've done their research and decided that a breed is perfect for their family, way too many otherwise intelligent people immediately go out and buy the first available puppy of that breed that they find on the internet.

This is a *really* big mistake.

As is true in any other breed, all Goldendoodle puppies are NOT created equal, nor are all the breeders producing them. Your odds of getting the right puppy – ideally a healthy, happy, east-to-train fellow that's going to end up with the looks, coat and temperament you want – are really pretty dependent upon choosing *the right breeder*. And since a Goldendoodle can live 13-15 years, it's well-worth the extra time it takes to do that.

Unfortunately, given the current market situation, where you can hardly (virtually) swing a cat without (virtually of course!) whacking someone selling Goldendoodle puppies, finding the right breeder can be daunting. *But not impossible* As is true in any breed, all Goldendoodle puppies are NOT created equal, nor are all breeders– especially if you know what to look for. What's amazing is how many otherwise savvy consumers *don't*. So let's look first at what you definitely want to avoid:

Pet Shops

Buying a dog from a pet shop is a poor choice on many levels. It does not allow you to either meet the parents or to get any sort of idea how the puppy was raised in the critical early weeks of his life, both of which are important factors that affect things like temperament and trainability. It also keeps substandard breeders in business, because no matter what the nice kids in the pet shop tell you, responsible breeders do *not* sell their puppies through pet shops. Only the bottom-feeders of the dog-breeding world sell puppies wholesale. Because of that, you'll also want to avoid:

Virtual Pet Shops (aka Online Dog Brokers).

Buyers who want to avoid pet shops usually end up looking on the internet, where the odds are the first puppies they will find will be offered for sale in *virtual pet shops*, otherwise known as dog brokers.

The main difference between traditional brick-and-mortar pet shops and their virtual counterparts is that in the latter case, most people don't realize that they are buying from one.

And because these guys usually have cleverly-designed websites and pay top-dollar for website optimization, they pop up at the top of the results on an internet search for *almost any breed*. How to avoid them? Here are a couple of clues that should tip you off that you're really visiting an online pet store:

The first clue is that they have a *lot* of breeds available, while responsible breeders rarely have more than a few at most, and more often only one.

The second clue is that they only display "staged" photos of adorable puppies...there are never any parents in evidence. In fact, if you visit their sites repeatedly, you may notice that the same puppy photos often appear over and over, with different names attached – this month's "Freddy" may well be next month's "Phoebe". And some of these pictures are actually swiped from other websites, honest to God, which means you're actually getting a totally different puppy than the cutie you fell in love with.

Just like the brick-and-mortar pet shops, these guys are buying puppies wholesale from commercial breeders and selling them retail – they're just less honest about it. But *unlike* a neighborhood pet shop, they don't have any ties to the community – in fact, since the puppies are often drop-shipped from the breeder, it's often pretty hard to figure out just where on the planet they are located. (Some are based in Indonesia; the largest one in the US is based in FL but their puppies are dropped-shipped from all over the country.)

This means they needn't worry about customer satisfaction or maintaining any sort of long-term relationship with their customers, who are hardly going to stop in to buy food and supplies for their dog over the years.

And because they sell over the internet, they are not even regulated by the USDA, so there are no USDA inspections or bare-minimum standards for the care and condition of their dogs, as there are with breeders who sell to pet shops. They are the worst of the worst, and they practically own the internet when it comes to online puppy sales. *Steer clear of them.*

Sorting Out Breeders

What you want to find is a *breeder*, which in simple legal terms means the person selling you the puppy is the same person who owns the parents and bred and raised the litter. But because they come in all stripes, and all advertise in pretty much the same places, even after you actually locate a couple you're still not home free, because along with respon*sible breeders,* a lot of breeders who advertise puppies on the internet or in newspapers are what we might euphemistically call *substandard breeders.* They may be actual puppy mills, or they may be smaller home-based breeders, but either way they represent the worst of dog-breeding.

Buying a puppy directly from a substandard breeding operation either in person or over the internet because you feel sorry for him (which some kindhearted people actually admit to doing) may *seem* like a kindness but in the long run it's entirely counterproductive – every puppy purchased for this reason ensures that another one will produced right behind him.

Buying a puppy from a substandard breeder because you *didn't realize you were dealing with one* is really no better because the end result is the same, but unfortunately this happens a lot more often. And thanks to the internet, it's getting more frequent every year.

The scary truth is this: ANY dog breeder can make himself look good on the internet.

No matter how irresponsible or downright awful they may be, absolutely *no one* advertises themselves as an irresponsible breeder.

Absolutely no *one runs* an internet ad for puppies explaining that they're just cranking out puppies to make a quick buck, even if they really *are* just cranking out puppies to make a quick buck.

And absolutely *no one* runs an internet ad for puppies explaining that their puppies are whelped and raised in an unused chicken coop out back, even if they *are* whelped and raised in an unused chicken coop out back. Nope, what substandard breeders invariably tell the buying public is this:

"We raise dogs as a family hobby."

"Our pups are raised underfoot with lots of love."

"Our pups get lots of socialization playing with our kids/grandkids."

"Our dogs and puppies are health-checked by our vet."

"Our puppies are dewormed and are current on all vaccinations."

And my personal favorite: "Our puppies come pre-spoiled", which is about as intelligent as selling pre-spoiled groceries.

The problem with all this, of course, is that a whole lot of perfectly *responsible* breeders say a lot of the same things. (Of course, the big difference is they're probably telling the truth.) But by itself, this list does not guarantee or even indicate you're dealing with a responsible breeder, and *if that's all they got*, it's a big red flag and you'd do better to look elsewhere.

Buying From a Local Breeder

The absolutely best way to determine if a breeder's advertising is an honest representation of their breeding practices or a total load of horse manure is to simply *visit* them, meet the parent dogs and see where and how their puppies are raised. This gets a whole lot easier if the breeder lives within an hour or two of you.

And there are many other advantages to buying from a breeder close to home. You can see firsthand if the parents have the size and temperament you are looking for *before* you put down a deposit. You can easily just drive over and pick your puppy up when he's ready to go home without having to worry about the time and costs involved in getting a puppy from one end of the country to another. You can see if you and the breeder "click", which is important if you consider your puppy's breeder to be your first resource when it comes to advice in the first year or so, which you should. And, even best of all, if several or all the puppies in a litter end up in the same area, they can get together for play days and "Doodle Romps" (wonderful for social dogs like Goldendoodles) and their owners can take turns pet sitting for each other when needed.

Unfortunately, finding breeders in your own area is a lot harder than it used to be back when people regularly advertised puppies for sale in the newspaper. A few still do, and it seems to be increasing, especially as the "buy local" idea catches on, but it's probably wise to extend your search a little beyond that, which really only leaves the internet.

Now, before you begin your internet search for a local breeder, you need to be VERY careful. And here's why:

If you Google "*your state here* Goldendoodle puppies for sale", or anything even remotely like that, I will guarantee you that most of the websites that pop up will actually be the above-mentioned dog brokers *masquerading as local breeders*. These bandits have collectively purchased *thousands* of those domain names, in every breed and including every state and major metro area in the domain name itself. (According to an investigation launched by HSUS, one Florida-based broker alone *owns over 800 of these "local" domain names* and ships a reported 20,000 puppies a year.) In a masterful marketing move, these commercial brokers for substandard breeding operations swarmed in like a plague of locusts early on with a lot of capital and now practically own the internet when it comes to puppy searches. *Caveat Emptor.*

Where to Look

Two good places to find real local breeders on the internet are EBay Classifieds and Puppysites.com, both of which list breeders within a couple of hours driving time based on your zip code. Some of these breeders will be good and some will probably be awful, but at least you can drive over and check them out your veryownself, because they'll all be within driving distance.

Puppysites.com allows you to choose the breed first and then lists breeders by distance from you, while EBay Classifieds sorts entirely by city instead of breed, which means you'll have to plow through all the Bulldogs and Schnauzers and rescue Greyhounds and shelter dogs also listed in your area to find the Goldendoodles.

If you can't find a local Goldendoodle breeder you're comfortable with, you'll have to widen your search, and you'll probably end up buying a puppy sight-unseen from a breeder over the internet. And in spite of the perils, the internet can be a useful tool for finding a good breeder you are confident buying a puppy sight-unseen from, as long as you know what to look for. So what *should* you look for?

Redefining "Responsible Breeder"

There's a lot of information on the internet defining what constitutes responsible dog breeding, but most of the time what you're really getting is someone's personal opinion, and usually that person is a longtime purebred dog show enthusiast. In other words, a "show breeder".

Serious show breeders (*who may or may not also be responsible breeders*) generally "breed for themselves", and to give them their due, very few are in it to make a profit—in fact, breeding good show dogs is right up there with compulsive gambling as far as a money-loser goes. *Showing dogs* is really their hobby and the show breeder generally only breeds in order to produce another show dog – a dog which will do a lot of winning in the ring, finish to its championship and then be added to their breeding program.

A lot of them honestly believe that producing a litter of puppies for *any other reason* is irresponsible if not downright unethical, and are not shy about saying so. Although many of them are also concerned with health and temperament, show breeders are primarily breeding for *conformation to the standard of their breed* – in other words, their breeding decisions are largely based on looks, which is what the sport of breeding show dogs is all about. The ultimate goal in this sport (above and beyond winning) is to produce a dog that perfectly conforms to its written standard.

Of course, since breeding dogs is an inexact science at best, all puppies in a litter are statistically unlikely to be "show quality". Those puppies which do not closely match the written standard of their breed (which can include such minutia as the actual number of teeth in its mouth, a spot of white on its chest or the desired shade of brown in the iris of the eye) or do not have the "look at me" personality required of a successful show dog are sold as pets.

If the show breeder is responsible, these pups will be well-socialized and come from health-screened parents with sound temperaments and will be sold on spay/neuter contracts, where minor conformation flaws will probably not even be noticed. (The loss of a big chunk of this pet market to hybrids produced entirely as pets is the major reason show breeders loathe the new "designer breeds", by the way. Without a ready pet market for their non-show quality pups, show breeders cannot breed.)

It should be pretty obvious by now that if you're looking for a Goldendoodle a lot of the information provided by dog show enthusiasts on what constitutes responsible breeding just doesn't apply – hybrids do not have dog shows, or written standards to adhere to or argue over, or even National

Parent Clubs with a written Code of Ethics for the breeder to belong to.

Unlike show dogs, hybrids are produced exclusively as companions and service animals, and conformation to a physical standard is less important than a good temperament, trainability, soundness, health and longevity, all of which also are (or at least should be) important to show breeders but are frankly not that upon which they ultimately base their breeding decisions.

And a lot of the criteria for responsible breeding laid forth with such certainty by show breeders is frankly out of date even if you *are* looking for a purebred, because the sport is graying rapidly and so most of them are, well….*OLD*…and haven't exactly kept up with the technological advances of the modern world.

A spectacular example of this is found on one of the many "How to Identify a Responsible Breeder" websites out there, which states unequivocally (*and I swear I am not making this up*) that "only puppy mills accept Paypal", and so acceptance of Paypal should be considered a red flag.

Excuse me???? With the exception of Amazon, pretty much the whole *world* takes Paypal, and how accepting only handwritten checks sent via snail mail could somehow make one a more responsible breeder simply defies the imagination. (Actually, when it comes to payment, the only *real* red flag is the breeder who accepts "cash only", because odds are pretty good they've got some issues with the IRS and you've got little recourse if things go south… *don't go there.*)

So, with all that in mind and without further ado, here's what you need to look for to find a responsible breeder of Goldendoodles on the internet:

Look for reviews…and get recommendations

One of the greatest advances of the twenty-first century surely came from Amazon. In fact, it's completely revolutionized the way America makes its collective purchasing decisions. You guessed it….it's the consumer review. And it's the best thing that's ever happened to puppy buyers.

Many breeders' websites now have testimonial letters from previous puppy buyers, with accompanying photos of said puppies all grown up in their new homes, which is pretty cool. But don't assume that's enough by itself, because the brokers also now have "testimonials" from buyers on their websites as well. Are they real? Hard to tell. A responsible breeder will also provide you with names and contact information for people who own their puppies if you ask.

Some breeders also have forums for their puppy owners set up either on their own websites or on one of the big Doodle sites that anyone can read. Since logic tells us these would be pretty hard to fake unless one had a ridiculous amount of time on their hands, they're probably worth checking out.

Bottom line is this: *No matter what breeders say about themselves or their dogs, it's not going to be nearly as useful as what people who actually own the puppies they've bred have to say.*

Now it goes without saying that breeders who've been at it the longest, and those who've produced a lot of puppies, are going to have more puppy owners out there than those who breed less frequently, so don't assume tons of references are automatically better than a few– this is one of those "quality-over-quantity" issues. Even breeders who do not produce enough puppies to maintain a forum for their puppy buyers should be able to give you recommendations.

Responsible breeders have information on the parents.

The laws of genetics being what they are, the parents of any particular puppy, even a hybrid, offer the best clues about how it's likely to turn out. (This is why you're not buying from a pet shop, remember?) Ideally, photos of the parents and information about them should be on the breeder's website.

This information should include health screening results. Responsible breeders health-screen their breeding dogs for genetic problems known to exist in their breed (or breeds) before they produce puppies. In Goldendoodles, this screening should ideally include:

Hip dysplasia screening

Out of tens of thousands of dogs in around 200 breeds, OFA currently ranks hybrids 29th in incidence of canine hip dysplasia (CHD), so even though 28 breeds have a higher incidence, it's pretty clear hybrid vigor is not a total panacea here. (Both Goldens and Poodles are susceptible to hip dysplasia, although the incidence is far higher in Standard Poodles than in Miniatures and Toys.)

Although after 40 years of continuous research and untold millions spent trying, there are still few definitive answers about the genetics of hip dysplasia, which appears to be between 25% to 48% heritable and is clearly not a single gene disorder.

Studies *have* shown, however, that breedings between two dogs affected with CHD produce an average of 75% affected offspring, which compares pretty unfavorably with the 25% affected offspring produced on average by dogs certified clear of it. Currently, the only way to screen for CHD is with a hip x-ray. The results of x-rays may be registered with PennHip, OFA, or a foreign registry.

.CERF exam.

Performed by a Board-certified canine ophthalmologist, this will exclude any genetic ocular diseases (primarily cataracts, pra/prcd, lens luxation and glaucoma, all of which can be heritable) present at the time of exam.

OFA Cardiac exam.

Performed after a year of age, this will rule out congenital heart defects like SAS (subvalvular aortic stenosis) which is unfortunately far too common in Golden Retrievers. Although less common, SAS also occurs in Poodles (primarily Standards) and is believed to be genetic in origin. Virtually all congenital heart defects can be ruled out by *auscultation,* which means a vet simply checks the heart with a stethoscope and signs an OFA form certifying the heart is normal. It's the cheapest and least invasive of all health screenings one can perform prior to breeding.

Although health-screening breeding dogs does not guarantee a pup will not end up with any of these problems, it does significantly lower the odds. Most screenings only need to be performed once in a dog's life. And since the cost of totally health-screening a breeding dog is far less than the price of a single puppy, there's really no reason for a breeder *not* to do it.

In addition to those listed above, some breeders also screen their breeding dogs for elbow dysplasia and gene-test for PRA/PRCD, which causes irreversible blindness. Although relatively rare, the causative single-gene defects for PRA occur in both Golden Retrievers and Poodles, as does the gene defect for VonWillebrand's disease, which causes a form of hemophilia. Dogs who have been gene-tested clear of these disorders cannot pass the genes on to the next generation.

Temperament:

Since temperament is every bit as heritable as health, breeders should also be able to provide information about the parents' individual temperaments and personalities. And any owner should be able to come up with something a little more informative than "Sadie is a real sweetheart and loves belly-rubs". Does Sadie love to retrieve? Does she like kids? Is she quiet or exuberant? Outgoing or cautious with strangers? Quick to learn? Willing to please? High-energy or low energy? To a large degree, these are all heritable traits.

Responsible breeders have a sales contract.

Every breeder should provide one, and usually they are posted on their website. If it's not, ask for a copy prior to putting down a deposit. Sales contracts assure that both the breeder and the buyer understand and agree on what will be done in any contingency that may arise both prior to and after sale of the puppy. Read through these carefully before committing yourself to a puppy, because they are NOT all the same, and the devil is in the details

Deposits:

Most breeders accept deposits to hold a puppy, and some to hold a place in line on an upcoming litter. Some are refundable if they cannot provide a puppy meeting your requirements within a specified time, and some are flat-out non-refundable for any reason whatsoever. (You probably want to avoid these, especially if they only accept cash.)

Few if any breeders will refund a deposit if you've simply changed your mind, nor should they be expected to. Putting down deposits with several breeders and then expecting to have all but one refunded once you've made up your mind is a *really bad idea* – don't do it. Many breeders plan their breedings based on the number of deposits in hand, and even if they don't return the deposits they've probably turned away puppy buyers if they assume a litter is all spoken for.

Payment:

More and more breeders are now requiring that you pay in full prior to picking up your puppy, sometimes weeks in advance. (The *reason* they are now doing this is explained in the preceding paragraph.) If you choose to go this route, make sure the contract allows for a "back-out" clause in case things don't work out as planned. (What things? Illness or other family emergencies, illness or death of the puppy prior to pickup…lots can happen in the space of a few weeks and it's best to know what your options are in those circumstances.)

More and more breeders now accept Paypal, which is safe and convenient for both buyer and seller; usually the seller is asked to pay the points for this convenience. Some breeders accept personal checks and others do not – it is best to find out ahead of time. But do beware the breeder who only accepts cash….that really IS the mark of a sleazy breeder.

Responsible breeders provide a health warranty.

Some breeders will guarantee against all "life-threatening" genetic defects, which sounds good, but should be considered a red flag. For example, hip dysplasia, which is frankly the most *likely* genetic defect, can be crippling and may require expensive surgery to alleviate pain, but no vet will declare it to be life-threatening because it's not. A contract that covers only life-threatening defects is in reality not much of a warranty at all.

Some contracts require that you return the puppy prior to replacement or reimbursement for medical costs associated with a genetic defect. The breeder is really counting on the fact that you won't do this, and in fact most states' Puppy Lemon Laws do not require it. (In any state, consumer laws supersede individual contracts.) Currently, 19 states have enacted specific Puppy Lemon Laws; in other states, puppy purchasers may be protected under the state's consumer protection laws, but there may be a filing fee required.

Many Goldendoodle breeders state that they will not guarantee the dog against hip dysplasia if he is overweight – there's a good reason for this. The heritability of hip dysplasia is estimated to be as low as 25%, which means 75% is environmental, and overweight is one of the environmental factors with strong science behind it.

Contingencies:

Some health warranties are contingent upon the new owner following specific instructions, which may be reasonable or downright weird. For example, specific vaccination protocols make sense, because over-vaccination can actually result in chronic health problems, especially in vaccine-sensitive animals. Requiring that the owner feed a *specific brand* of vitamins or supplement in order for the warranty to be valid, on the other hand, may simply reflect the breeder's involvement in a multi-level marketing plan. Some dog food companies are now engaging in this practice as well, so it's always good to check that out when the breeder requires a specific food be fed in order for the health warranty to be valid. There's a big difference between recommending and requiring.

Responsible breeders take dogs back.

All responsible breeders are concerned with the welfare of puppies they've bred even after they have been sold, and will take them back and/or assist in rehoming them if the owner cannot keep them for any reason at any time in the dog's life. Some will reimburse the owner for part of the purchase price while others do not. (The breeder's policies in this regard should be clearly stated in writing.)

But beware *anyone* who is unwilling to offer a place in their home to any dog whose existence they've called into being, because *they are the people responsible for dogs ending up in shelters*. In fact, don't buy a puppy from them.

Responsible breeders only own as many dogs as they can take care of.

There is really no correct number here – it depends entirely upon the breeder's resources. But a responsible breeder keeps only as many dogs as they can appropriately house, socialize, exercise, groom and provide professional routine veterinary care for.

With dogs the size of Goldendoodles, this very likely means that if they have more than a couple dogs they'll have some kind of "kennel" setup, although no one except maybe Purina Farms ever has photos of their kennel on their website, which is really too bad. Contrary to popular belief, kennels are not a bad thing — they allow dogs to get adequate fresh air and exercise, both of which are critical to their health and well-being, and they get to interact with other dogs, which is very important to a social breed like the Goldendoodle. Kenneled dogs should be clean, well-groomed, well-socialized and friendly, however, and the kennel runs themselves should be safe, clean, well-shaded with plantings and surfaced with something like pea rock or pavers so they may be easily cleaned.

Many Goldendoodle breeders use "guardian homes" for some of their breeding dogs, which is generally a win/win situation. These dogs (usually the best pups in their litters) are placed as puppies in nearby pet homes. When they are old enough and have passed their health-screening they come back to the breeder's home to be bred and (in the case of females) whelp a litter or two, after which time they are spayed and spend the rest of their lives as pets in the same home they started out in. This system allows the breeder to maintain more genetic diversity in their line than they would under the traditional breeding system (where genetic diversity is often limited by the number of dogs a breeder can practically keep) and it's a terrific deal for the dogs themselves, who get more individual attention than they would at the breeder's home. In fact, in a society where most people are restricted by law or practicality in the number of dogs they are allowed to own, the "guardian home system" probably represents the future of dog breeding.

Responsible breeders ask YOU questions.

Responsible breeders will either ask you to fill out an application and will conduct a phone interview prior to accepting a deposit. They'll ask lots of questions about your living situation, the hours you work, and your family. Because they want their puppies to be successful, they want to find out in advance if one of their puppies is likely to be a good fit for your family situation, and will tell you flat-out if they don't think it is. An irresponsible breeder will ask no questions and take anyone's money.

Responsible breeders provide ongoing support.

Responsible breeders are there 24/7 to answer questions, no matter how dumb they may be, for the life of the dog. They provide written instructions for things like vaccination, worming, housebreaking, early training, grooming and all the other things you need to know to get off to a good start. And they are available for advice at any hour by phone in an emergency. Do not, under any circumstances, buy a puppy from a breeder who will not provide you with his/her personal phone number—odds are, there's a good reason why.

Responsible breeders want you to come and pick up your puppy.

This one is probably the most important of all, and a lot of people get it wrong. Because of the possibility of infectious diseases like distemper and parvo, most breeders cannot allow their home or kennel to be used as a petting zoo by everyone considering the possible purchase of a puppy. In fact, some breeders only allow those puppy buyers who actually have a deposit on a puppy to visit after the puppies have received their first vaccinations for this reason. But you should never buy a dog from a breeder who will not allow you on the premises to pick up your puppy. NEVER.

Before you plunk down a single red cent (and even if the breeder is half a continent away), *always* ask if you can come and pick up the puppy. If the breeder demurs and immediately offers to ship or meet you *anywhere* other than their home, they have not just raised a red flag… *they've hoisted the JOLLY ROGER,* and odds are pretty good you're dealing with a pirate. No sane breeder is THAT paranoid about parvo! They may ask you to remove your shoes, or wash your hands, but they will *not* keep you from entering their homes, or seeing the whole litter, or the mother, or the area where the dogs are kept.

Responsible breeders do not hand puppies over to their new owners

and collect payment for them in the Wal-Mart parking lot.

They just *don't.*

Choosing the Right Puppy

Choosing a good breeder makes choosing the right puppy in a litter a whole lot easier, because you will have what amounts to professional help, but there's a lot you can do to help the breeder in this regard.

Dispelling the "pick of the litter" myth.

If one phrase should disappear from the world of dogs, that phrase should be "pick of the litter." Unless one is looking for a show dog, *there is simply no such thing.* (Even then it's pretty dicey – many a Westminster Winner over the years was "third-pick puppy" in his litter!)

Since puppies are in essence fraternal rather than identical twins, every puppy in a given litter is going to be a little different, in both looks and personality. As with human siblings, one is invariably going to be the liveliest, one the smartest, one the most assertive, and one the most easy-going.

A good breeder will spend time interviewing each new owner

either in person or by phone

and will try to match each puppy with the family into which he best fits.

For example, the most assertive puppy is probably not the best choice for a family with very young children. The "genius puppy" in a litter is probably not the best choice for an owner who is not all that interested in doing a lot of training – remember, in general, the higher the puppy's IQ, the more challenging training him will be. The liveliest puppy is not the best choice for the more sedentary owner.

A good breeder has spent a lot of time with the puppies by the time they are 7 weeks old, which is really when neurological development is pretty much complete in the canine and its innate personality is revealed. What the owner sees in an hour's visit may not be reality at all – for example, the "live-wire" puppy may simply be tired at that point from running around all morning and give a pretty good impression of Mr. Mellow, which will change once he gets home and has a chance to recharge his little batteries.

Choosing a puppy based on photographs is not a great idea either.

The most *photogenic* puppy in a litter—the guy who literally mugs for the camera and is so cute you could just scoop him up right off your computer screen – is almost guaranteed to be the most challenging, while the one who looks a little like he's facing a firing squad and really just wants someone to take this silly bow off his neck is likely to be the easiest to live with. (No one *ever* believes me on this, but 40 years of taking puppy pictures has convinced me that I'm right. So if you want to live with the Mick Jagger of Goldendoodles, go for it.)

Color and gender are two other areas where people put more emphasis than they should when choosing a puppy.

If you end up with a higher-energy puppy than you intended, the particular shade of gold he displayed at 7 weeks is not going to matter much, especially since it may lighten or darken anyway. A good dog just never comes in a bad color.

The same is true of gender. In the Goldendoodle, where the genes for either defensive or dominance aggression are unlikely to exist, there just isn't enough difference between males and females to figure into the equation. This is *not* a high-testosterone breed, and neutering removes a lot of what may exist naturally.

It's really best to explain your family situation, previous dog-owning (or child-rearing) experience and what sort of dog appeals to you and then let the breeder, who interacts with the puppies 24/7, choose the right puppy for you. For reasons no one has really ever figured out, most good breeders have an intuitive gift for choosing the right puppies for each family. (Puppy owners will often attest to this, which is why it's good to read the reviews.) Maybe it's just part of being a good breeder. But whatever the reason, when choosing which puppy is right for your family, it's really in the new owner's best interest to trust a good breeder's judgment.

A note of caution: The breeder who expects puppy buyers to choose their puppy at birth or shortly thereafter based entirely on photographs of what look essentially like little slugs on a baby blanket is either lacking in experience or is primarily producing puppies for profit. In either case you may want to proceed carefully or better yet "just slip out the back, Jack".

A Word About Price...

Currently, the price of a Goldendoodle puppy ranges anywhere from around $400 to $3,000.

Although there are certainly exceptions, by and large the differences in price reflect the differences in experience levels, breeding expertise, customer support provided and marketing skills that exist among breeders.

In general, puppies on the lowest end of the scale are mostly produced by substandard breeders, who are unlikely to do a lot of health-screening on the parents or critical early socialization of the puppies, both of which are critical. (The exception to this rule are the slick online brokers, who are essentially selling $400 puppies produced by substandard breeders for thousands of dollars because of their deceptive advertising practices.)

In the middle range are usually small home-based breeders who probably don't do a lot of health-screening and may not be particularly knowledgeable about canine genetics. On the plus side, as a general rule the puppies are raised in a clean environment (usually the kitchen rather than a kennel) and get a fair amount of casually administered early socialization, which is another way of saying they get picked up, cuddled, and played with quite a lot by the family, which is great.

At the highest end are the breeders who put the most time, money and energy into their breeding program, and offer the greatest amount of support both prior to and after purchase. Their breeding dogs are health-screened and their puppies are put through the early neurological stimulation program in addition to extensive socialization and early training.

When it comes to deciding how much you are willing to spend on the initial price of a puppy, it's always good to remember that the cost of the puppy is a mere drop in the bucket compared to the lifetime cost of feeding, grooming and providing veterinary care for a dog. If you simply want a low-cost pet for the kids, get a guinea pig.

CHAPTER FOUR

Being Prepared

(or...how to spend lots of money waiting for your puppy)

Odds are, if you've done your research and chosen a puppy from a responsible breeder, there will be some lag time between when you plunk down your deposit and when you actually pick up your puppy.

This time can best be used for collecting the astonishing amount of equipment, supplies and assorted paraphernalia required for successful puppy management, getting your home ready for the new family addition, and learning what you need to know to make the transition as smooth as possible for everyone concerned.

Raising a Puppy the way Nature Intended

At 8 weeks, a puppy of any breed is still pretty immature. It is important to understand that removing him from his mother and littermates at that age is *not* the natural course of events for a canine. In the wild, most wolf pups commonly stay with their parents for up to a year and if resources permit, often for life. The same is true of foxes and coyotes – in most wild canids, packs are really extended families, and domestic dogs are still psychologically hard-wired for that lifestyle.

What we are doing when we "adopt" a puppy is taking an incredibly immature pack animal out of his natal pack and incorporating him into another *very different* pack – one that's probably comprised of members of another species altogether, and where no one speaks his language nor shares the same social rules of the pack into which he was born. It's really a credit to the inherent adaptability of the dog that so many of them manage to do so well…just try to imagine for a moment how well the process would work in reverse!

Raising a puppy successfully is a lot easier

if we work *with* his psychological hard-wiring instead of *against* it.

In order to do that, we need to understand what Mother Nature intended, and the best way to do that is to look at how wolf cubs develop and are raised in the wild, and try to adapt that to our own situation, because that's also how our puppies are hard-wired.

Wolf cubs are born in a den, and stay there for the first few weeks of life with their mother. She rarely leaves them during this time, and her food is provided by the litter's sire (usually the alpha male) who delivers it to her door, bless his heart. At 4 weeks or so, the cubs first toddle outside the den into the spring sunshine, where they are greeted enthusiastically by the entire pack. At this point, the litter is beginning to be weaned, and the other pack members provide regurgitated solid food for them.

When the cubs are around 8 weeks old (not coincidentally when neurological development in the canine is completed), the pack moves them from the den to a carefully chosen *rendezvous site* within the pack's territory where they will stay until they are 7-8 months old, at which time they are nearly full-grown and are ready to become full-fledged members of the pack.

During this time, they are usually left in the care of a babysitter (most often a young wolf from the pack of either gender) during the day, and alone when necessary. Their days are spent playing with "toys" and learning the skills they'll need to become useful functioning pack members. Food is still delivered to them, and they sleep with the pack at night. These rendezvous sites are chosen carefully by the pack, with the physical needs (like access to shallow water) and safety of the cubs given highest priority. They are taken on short outings as they grow, but are still largely confined to the rendezvous area until they are mature.

Because this method has worked so well for untold millennia, it simply makes sense to stick to it when raising our own puppies, who share over 99% of their DNA with their wolf ancestors, including those that determine neurological and psychological development.

Setting up the Rendezvous Area

When we bring an 8-10 week old pup home, what we need to do is transition from the "den with mom" to the next naturally-occurring phase, which is moving him to a *rendezvous area*. We are also moving him into a new pack, which is going to be fairly stressful for the first week or two.

The territory of this new pack comprises your entire house and yard, and at his age, your pup should not have the run of it any more than a wolf cub would in the wild, and for exactly the same reason — safety. It is absolutely astonishing how much trouble a puppy can get himself into if he is granted full territorial privileges before he's ready for them.

So what the new owner needs to do before the puppy arrives is decide which area of the house is going to be the *rendezvous site*, and plan on confining him to that area, (usually with baby gates) when he is unattended.

As with a wild pack, this area should be the place where the older pack members congregate to relax when they are not working. This will vary from family to family and depends upon the layout of the house, but it is usually the kitchen/family room area. In some homes, if it is directly off the kitchen and not isolated but can be blocked off with a gate, a laundry area can work. It should also include a corner for the puppy's crate, which is where he will sleep during the day, and a door that leads directly to the area (whether that is the back yard, a terrace or the sidewalk) where he will eliminate, so he can learn to go directly to the door to signal when he needs to go outside.

Never, ever use a bathroom or laundry room with the door shut- for a young pack animal, that constitutes psychological torture, plain and simple.

Pet Gates...An Absolute Necessity!

Since it is entirely counterproductive to give a young puppy free access to the entire "pack territory", this rendezvous area will need to be cordoned off with baby gates—how many you will need depends entirely upon layout. It should also have flooring other than carpeting for purely practical reasons.

With smaller breeds and very young Dood puppies, an exercise pen can serve as a rendezvous area (and in fact is what your puppy was probably raised in at the breeder's), but a standard-sized Goldendoodle will outgrow one within a couple of months, so that should be taken into consideration prior to purchase. Consider borrowing one or check out yard sales.

Pet gates now come in a dizzying array of sizes and designs, from doorway-sized to eight or more feet wide, and one of which will certainly work no matter what the layout of one's home. The best place to start looking is Amazon, which has the inarguably largest selection anywhere, and many of which qualify for Amazon Prime's free shipping.

There are really only two caveats when selecting pet gates. The first (and most critical) caveat is to only select from those made with vertical bars, with no horizontal crossbars between the top and the bottom. These are the only gates that are climb-proof and *nothing* is more discouraging than installing a new gate only to watch your puppy immediately scamper over it like an oversized squirrel. The second caveat concerns height – there's not much purpose in a gate under 30 inches, and for most Doods, 36-40 inches is even better.

That said, the choice of materials (plastic, wood or metal) and color is really up to the homeowner, and you might as well get something that isn't going to look downright ugly. Wood gates should be sprayed with Bitter Apple right off though, or they'll soon look like they've been attacked by beavers. Some gates have walk-through doors, which make sense, and some have little "dog doors" built right in, which make considerably less sense, although I'm certain there is some purpose there that escapes obvious notice. Exactly where to put the gates is a matter of traffic flow- it's a good idea to figure this out and live with it for a while before the puppy arrives, because you may well decide to move it. Better to figure that out before the puppy arrives than confuse him by rearranging it later.

Puppy-proofing

Once you've decided where the gates are going to go, everything inside that becomes the rendezvous area and needs to be *puppy-proofed*. The best way to do this is to remove everything that can potentially be dangerous or disassembled that's within three feet of the floor – electrical cords (there is an unknown magnetic force that attracts puppies to outlets with electrical cords plugged into them), houseplants, knickknacks, books, magazines, antiques, sporting equipment, electronics and basically anything else of value that you do not wish to have damaged or turned into confetti or woodchips by industrious puppy teeth.

Anything that cannot be removed (like the woodwork!) should be sprayed with Bitter Apple *before* the puppy sinks his teeth into it rather than after. So you'll want to put a spray bottle of Grannick's Bitter Apple on your growing list of Things You Absolutely Need. It's under ten bucks on Amazon.

Although it sounds weird, the best way to puppy-proof is to get down on your knees, lay your forearms flat on the floor, and look around. You now have the puppy's view of his new world, and it's amazing what you'll see that you may have missed standing up.

Food and Water

The rendezvous site should also contain the puppy's water and food dishes because this is where he is going to eat. As with pretty much everything else, there's a wide variety from which to choose, ranging from the most utilitarian to the most decorative. (As you've probably figured out by now, the days when dog ownership required a dog house, a feed pan, a water bowl and a nice butcher's bone are long gone....of course, those were also the days when a kid owned one pair of shoes, used a bicycle to get everywhere he needed to go and got an orange in his Christmas stocking. Right.)

Choosing the Right Bowls and Dishes

The main considerations in choosing dog dishes are that they be durable, easy to clean (ideally you should be able to pop them in the dishwasher) and not easily tipped over. The kind with sloped sides and a non-slip base are a good choice, and stainless steel is far and away the easiest to keep clean, the least toxic, and the most durable. Some owners prefer the "double diner" dishes because they tend to keep the dishes tidily in one place- if you go this route, make sure the dishes are removable from the platform for cleaning.

One of the newest additions to the world of dog dishes are those designed to slow down the rate at which the dog inhales his food and water. (In the wild this is not a problem, because the wild canine has to work quite a bit harder for both his food and water.) The food dishes have raised areas that the dog has to work around in order to scarf up his kibble, which slows him down a bit and lessens the chances of post-prandial barfing and general indigestion. The water bowls have a sort of "float" inside that keeps the dog from submerging his entire muzzle and filling both his mouth and facial furnishings with water, much of which invariable ends up dripping onto the floor.

In addition to making less of a mess, both these dishes are a good choice for breeds (like Goldendoodles) that are susceptible to bloat. Unfortunately, most of them seem to be made of plastic instead of stainless steel, which means if they are left with an unattended puppy they'll end up as chew toys.

Dog Food Storage

Unless you plan to prepare fresh home-cooked meals for your Goldendoodle every day (which really is the healthiest option even though you probably won't do it), you will need something in which to store his dry dog food (AKA kibble) to avoid creating a fast-food drive-thru for the local rodentia, which is what will happen if you leave it in the bag.

The best choice here is probably a tall plastic dog food storage bin with a tight flip-top lid and little castors so you can roll it out to fill it. It is *not* a good idea to keep this in the rendezvous area, however, because even a toy-breed puppy with motivation and a set of industrial little teeth can turn a plastic storage bin into a self-feeder in no time flat by gnawing a hole in the bottom corner – the laundry room or pantry is a better choice. If you absolutely need a chewproof one, you can also get stainless steel model, but it will cost you about a hundred dollars more.

A "step-on" stainless kitchen garbage can will *not* work, just for the record— any Doodle worth his salt will quickly figure out that stepping on the lever turns it into an all-you-can-eat buffet, whether it's used for kibble or actual garbage. The "touchless" ones with infrared sensors? Pure magic for the hungry puppy! (You may want to keep this in mind when puppy-proofing your kitchen...)

Yes, you DO need a crate!

No matter what PETA says, a crate is not a cage, it's a den. And when properly introduced, a crate is an invaluable asset to training. It will help speed the housetraining process considerably, as well as preventing property destruction when a young dog needs to be left unattended.

Some Doods will outgrow the need for a crate when they reach maturity (rarely before a year and often closer to two), while others consider the crate to be their personal "den" and prefer to sleep in it their whole lives; the difference is largely temperamental. Either way, you're going to end up needing a crate large enough to hold a full-sized dog.

Crates come in a dizzying array of sizes, shapes and materials, and once again, the best place to start looking is Amazon, which pretty much carries every dog crate known to man. For Goldendoodles, the wire crate is usually better than the plastic "airline crate", because these are social dogs and they like to see what's going on around them.

You can also buy really nice-looking wooden crates that look like furniture, but these are really only appropriate for dogs with no teeth or no imagination, because any other dog will turn them into a big pile of toothpicks in short order. (Been there, done that.)

However, for every problem it seems like someone comes up with a solution and one of the *coolest* additions to the world of crates is the new specially-designed wooden end table that slips right *over* the crate.

This allows you to incorporate the crate right into the furnishings of the family room where you can even put a lamp on it, which beats having what unfortunately looks a lot like a circus tiger cage plunked unceremoniously in the corner of the room.

These are also available on Amazon; just make sure you buy the right sized-crate to fit it, because they are *not* adjustable. (Note: these tables are designed for the Midwest "i-crate" line of crates, not their Life Stages crate.)

Midwest crates, by the way, are an overall good value – many show breeders have been hauling the same Midwest crates around to dog shows for thirty years or more, which subjects them to a lot more abuse than anything the average pet owner can come up with.

The basic Midwest wire crate sizes are as follows:

Extra-Large: 48" x 33" wide x 33" high- good for the largest Doods and "sprawlers"

Large: 42" x 30" wide x 33" high- good for most standard-sized Goldendoodles and large minis

Medium: 36" x 24" wide x 27" high- good for most minis

Other manufacturers' crates may vary by an inch or two either way. In general, it's best to err on the side of too big rather than too small, because a dog who feels cramped is going to put up more of a fuss in his crate, and Goldendoodles tend to sleep sprawled out like Goldens rather than tidily curled up like Poodles.

It's also a good idea to buy a crate with 2 doors, one on the end and one on the side, which gives you a lot more flexibility when figuring out where to put it, especially if you're going to make it into an end table. (A puppy is likely to learn the "kennel up" command more quickly if he doesn't have to execute a maze to get in there.) Now, the major problem with these crates is that during the first few months most baby Doods are going to do better sleeping in a crate in the bedroom with their new senior pack members, and all of them need to be crated in the car until they're old enough for a seat-belt harness.

These adult-sized wire crates are a real pain to carry around, especially if they've got a table wrapped around them. They are also too big to use successfully for housetraining – any puppy with more than three brain cells will soon figure out he can use half the crate for a bathroom and still have a comfy dry spot left to sleep in. Some crate models come with a removable divider panel to solve that problem, but that still won't make them any easier to schlep it into the bedroom every night, nor will it make it any easier to hoist into the backseat of a car. Wire dog crates were originally invented to go in the folded-down-flat backseats of station wagons and they still only really fit well in vans, since the backseats of many SUVs now no longer fold down totally flat for no apparent reason besides stupidity on the part of non-dog owning SUV designers.

The best way to get around this whole problem is to simply add a second, smaller plastic crate to your ever-growing list of supplies.

If your puppy was shipped via airline, you can use the crate he came in until he outgrows it, at which time he can probably move to his permanent crate at night and he'll be old enough to use a seat-belt harness in the car. If you're driving to pick up the puppy from the breeder, you'll have to purchase or borrow one, because you'll definitely need it for the ride home. Try yard sales first, where they are usually cheap and usually almost brand-new. Or ask around—it's amazing how many people have a puppy crate stashed in their garage. Just make sure you wash it out with a bleach/water solution before using it- bleach kills every virus that can infect a dog.

If you can't find one to borrow or buy used, there are a lot of models available from Amazon; look for something in the 26-28" range, and don't bother with a top-of-line-model, because you'll only need it for a couple of months. The KennelCab Large is a good, inexpensive Doodle puppy crate. Just make sure you get the Large and not the Intermediate, which is too small for most Dood puppies much over 8 weeks of age.

Crate Pads and Dog Beds

Now that we've got the crate issues sorted out, it's time to look at dogs beds, and there are lots of options here as well. In fact, the world of dog beds has expanded to the point where it's almost impossible to figure out where to start!

The major factors to consider in choosing dog beds are washability, durability and good looks, since it's going to be part of your home décor for years to come unless it gets chewed up. Many gorgeous and very pricey dog beds score well in the good-looks area, but fall down badly in the first two.

Because dog beds can be expensive (Orvis carries a nice one that costs $350) this is one place where you really want to read the reviews.

When he's still a baby, it's pretty simple – the best choice in bedding for his "little" crate is a fluffy bath towel. You'll actually need two, so they can be laundered as needed. In spite of everyone's best efforts, puppies and accidents go hand in hand, and there's no sense in getting upset about it.

Some "experts" claim that if a puppy pees in his bed you'll never be able to

reliably housetrain him, but this is sheer idiocy

and causes a lot of undue worry on the new owner's part.

I mean, *think* about it…little kids wet the bed with appalling regularity, yet most outgrow it and enjoy many years of a dry bed…at least until very old age sets in and we end up back where we started in the bladder-control department. It's much the same scenario with dogs. Where people come up with this stuff is a mystery.

When taking him for a ride in the car in his little crate, it's a good idea to take the extra towel along for the ride, because puppies also upchuck, although 99.99% of them outgrow that, too. (Put the extra towel in a small plastic bag – that way, if he barfs on the first one you can just switch them around and tie the bag closed, which will keep the car smelling fresher for the duration of the trip than it would if you didn't have the bag…many a perfectly good towel has ended up in a rest-stop trash can for this very reason.)

When it comes to choosing a bed for his "real" crate, the most popular one among dog owners is probably **Midwest's Quiet Time Bolster Pet Bed,** which is available pretty much everywhere. (It currently ranks #26 in Amazon's Pet Products with 486 reviews at the time of writing.) Get two, so you can launder them frequently…they wash easily and dry fast, and can be laundered probably 100 times without falling apart. These beds are specifically sized for Midwest crates, which makes choosing the right size a whole lot easier.

Floor beds

Most dog owners also have a dog bed or two on the floor…in fact, some have one in every room, honest to God. Essentially "dog furniture", they will help keep the family Dood off yours. These beds are usually big squashy things and dogs universally love them.

The main thing to look for here is a bed with a *removable machine-washable cover,*

because most comfy plump Goldendoodle-sized floor beds

simply won't fit in a washing machine.

And because they're pretty expensive, you want one that has a record of durability and a cover that won't fall apart after a couple launderings.

One of the best places to check here is **L.L. Bean.** They've been making tough dog beds for tough sporting dogs for many years, and as far as durability and quality for the price goes, they're hard to beat. (If your Dood is inclined to "de-stuff" the bolster on his crate bed, Bean also makes one of the most indestructible crate pads on the market—resistant to chewing and digging, they can literally be hosed off if need be.) Bean also sells replacement covers for many of its beds, which is brilliant. The denim covers are the most durable and least attractive to dog hair – you can choose a color that best blends with your décor and doesn't show dirt.

Grooming Stuff

Unless you are planning to have your dog groomed professionally on a weekly basis (which at $50-$100 per session is prohibitively expensive for most owners), you will need some basic grooming tools and supplies to keep him clean and mat-free between scheduled appointments.

In fact, having the *right* grooming supplies (and a basic knowledge on how to use them) will save you a lot of money in the long run in a couple of ways. You'll be able to stretch the time between grooming appointments without ending up with a matted dog that has to be shaved from nose to tail, which is frankly unattractive and which most Dood owners hate.

And you can end up with a smaller grooming bill when you do take him in, because most groomers base their fees on the amount of time it takes to actually groom a dog, and that is often based on the condition of his coat and how well he is "trained to the table" as much as size.

A survey of professional groomers unfortunately reveals that the poor Goldendoodle is often deficient on both counts, which is why groomers often charge more for them than other breeds of the same size. Besides a lack of training, groomers most often cite the fact that Goldendoodle owners are using the wrong grooming tools at home, resulting in a dog that looks good on the outside, but is often matted at the skin, which is why they end up shaved down.

Trying to figure out which tools you need, however, can be a little daunting, because there are literally hundreds of dog brushes and combs on the market, all designed for different coat types.

To make this a whole lot easier, what follows is a list of what you really need to have on hand when your Goldendoodle puppy arrives, so you can get off to a positive start, as well as supplies and equipment you'll want to add later on. (Proper grooming techniques are covered farther along in the Grooming Chapter.)

Grooming table and grooming post

The single most important purchase after a pet gate and a crate is a *grooming table with a grooming post*, and it's astonishing how many Goldendoodle breeders never even mention this critical item to the new puppy owner. There's simply no way around it – the Goldendoodle is a high-maintenance breed, and yours will require a fair amount of grooming over his lifetime. (Because of the textural difference, most professional groomers agree that the typical Goldendoodle coat is actually higher-maintenance than that of the Poodle.)

This will be a whole lot cheaper and easier for everyone concerned if the dog is trained to enjoy being groomed on a table *from early puppyhood*, which is why you want to have it on hand right from the get-go. In fact, it's probably close to impossible to keep your Dood free of mats without one.

If you buy your grooming table before your puppy arrives, and you put him on it every single time you run a comb or brush through him from his first day at home, you will have a dog that is a piece of cake to groom. If you don't, you won't, and it will get worse and worse as he grows. It's that simple.

Unless you are a professional, a grooming table that can be folded flat and easily carried to whatever location you prefer is by far the best choice. (In nice weather, you may want to groom outside on a patio or deck, and move into the laundry room or basement in inclement weather.) The grooming post attaches easily to the table with a screw-on clamp and comes off for storage. The best place to check out the available options is once again Amazon, where you have the advantage of being able to read the reviews.

Virtually all Goldendoodles will fit on a 36" grooming table. If yours is a mini, you can get by with one of the less expensive tables, which generally come with a 34" grooming post. (These start at under $70 including the post, which is a great price.) On the other hand, if you have a standard, you'll probably want to buy Midwest's 36" model, which is both sturdy and comes with a 44" grooming post. It costs around $130 on Amazon with the post included, and will probably outlast your dog.

The 36" grooming table is generally about 33" high, which puts the dog at just the right height for most people to groom without a lot of back strain. Those who are a lot taller or shorter than average, or who own a *really* big Dood, may want to consider a table with adjustable legs – the legs adjust from 24' to 36", so the owner can easily find a height that is comfortable. An adjustable table and post can be purchased for around $200, and may be well worth the extra cost if 33" is just not the right height for you..

Comb and Small Scissors

A comb (the kind with rotating teeth that literally slide through the coat without pulling are best for puppies) and a 5-6 inch straight grooming scissors with rounded tips (for trimming hair around his eyes, pads, and under his tail, as well as cutting out things like gum that may get stuck in his coat and are impossible to brush out) are the other two grooming tools you really need to have on hand when the puppy arrives. The rest of the grooming supplies you'll need are listed in Chapter Eight.

Toys and Chew Bones

This may well be the longest treatise ever written on dog toys and dog chews, but reading through it *before you buy a single toy* can save you literally thousands of dollars and several trips to the vet's office, so it's probably well-worth the effort.

In order to satisfy his needs for both intellectual stimulation and chewing, Goldendoodle puppies require lots of toys. In order to keep yours safe, these need to be broken down into two categories – the kind he can play with under supervision, and the kind that can go into his crate with him when he's left alone. (The latter category is frankly pretty limited.)

Besides the more immediate and often life-threatening dangers of choking, every year hundreds of dogs end up having whole plastic, rubber and nylon "chew toys" as well as various parts of said chew toys surgically removed from their digestive tracts via extremely expensive gastric surgery because of intestinal blockage. (In the last few years, the number of dogs – primarily those of the sporting breeds – who've had to have entire cell phones surgically removed from their guts has been on the increase as well…consider yourself warned.)

Along with hard chew toys, soft stuffed plush toys are immensely popular – virtually all Goldendoodle puppies love to play with them, and will retrieve them endlessly. They also love to snuggle with them. On the other hand, the average Dood puppy is entirely capable of totally eviscerating his favorite beloved stuffed toy (and ingesting both its stuffing and its squeaker) in ten minutes flat when no one is looking for no apparent reason and with apparently very little forethought. This puzzles owners no end – they simply cannot understand why a dog would systematically destroy (and very probably ingest) what was obviously a favorite toy.

The short answer is…..*they do it because they're dogs.*

Before buying a single dog toy, you need understand the hard-wired instincts driving a puppy's behavior, because once again you will be more successful working *with* a dog's DNA than *against* it.

In the wild, when a litter of wolf cubs is moved to its rendezvous area, the adults deliver whole small animals and birds as well as "leftovers" (like legs and antlers) from large kills as soon as the cubs have graduated beyond the regurgitated-food stage.

These items provide training, entertainment *and* nutrition all in the same package – Mother Nature is nothing if not efficient. The bony leftovers satisfy the need to chew during teething while providing needed calcium and trace minerals for the growing cubs.

Small whole animals are dual-purpose as well – they are "hunted", captured and played with, tossed, used for games of tug-o-war, and then ultimately *eviscerated*, because in addition to protein, the internal organs provide vital nutrients like Vitamin A, various amino acids and cholesterol, all critical for optimum physical and brain development in the cubs. (Ironically, these highly nutritious organs are all classified by law as "byproducts" by the FDA and no one wants them in their dog food.)

Once the insides are eaten, the cubs will then ultimately consume around 85% of the rest, including hide, fur and feathers, all of which provide protein and fiber.

So what happens is when we, as senior pack members, present our own cub with toys (often modeled after human baby toys), his ancient canine DNA takes over. Consequently, he will gnaw industriously on his brightly-colored hard plastic teething toys shaped like car keys or baby pacifiers until he can break them into pieces he can ingest, even though they have zero nutritional value, and he will play with his latest plush "gingerbread man" or soccer ball until he gets bored, at which points his eviscerating instincts take over and he guts it, eats the polyester stuffing and the plastic squeaker, and then shreds the rest of it.

This happens because he is a baby *canid*, not a baby *human*. As with humans, "playing" for immature canids is how they practice the skills they will need as an adult, and their "toys" often reflect that. (If this makes you wonder why anyone would design toys for an animal lacking opposable thumbs in the shape of *keys* you're not alone...chalk it up to a bad case of anthropomorphism.)

Unfortunately for his digestive system, however, a puppy's DNA does not allow him to distinguish between plastic and natural bone, real fur and acrylic, or even entrails and polyester fiberfill – it is the *behaviors themselves* that are hard-wired in.

This is the same reason that a dog will "bury" a bowl of food on a tile floor with imaginary dirt and leaves in an elaborate ritual and then smugly walk away, satisfied that it is well-hidden even though it's clearly still in plain sight.

Once we understand what Mother Nature had in mind and work with it, choosing both the right chew toys and soft toys gets a whole lot easier. Amazon reviews also help a lot, since virtually every bone and dog toy they sell has multiple reviews—one has an astonishing 670 reviews as of today. (That's not a typo, that's actually *670 reviews for a nine-dollar toy*...and I swear I am not making this up.) Although the ultimate decisions are yours, the following rundown of the most popular will at least give you a place to start, so you don't have to spend the rest of your natural life reading dog toy reviews.

Chew Toys.

All puppies need something acceptable to chew on, especially when they are teething. With only one possible exception, none of them are totally without risk, but then, neither is driving a car – the key is to find a risk level you are personally comfortable with.

Chew toys can be divided into two basic categories- inedible (usually made of plastic and rubber) and edible (usually substances that used to be working parts of animals). Which you prefer is largely a matter of individual temperament and personal philosophy, because puppies will chew up and swallow pretty much anything. Those who don't like the idea of their dog constantly gnawing on and ultimately ingesting artificially-colored rubber and various plastic polymers will probably want to go the more "natural" route, while those who are not comfortable having parts of dead animals lying around their house will probably prefer the "artificial" options, which is what we'll start with.

Fake Stuff for Dogs to Chew On

In the artificial category, **Nylabone** products are probably among the best-known and the safest, if your puppy will chew on them – some will while others just ignore them completely. The larger bone-shaped and wishbone-shaped nylon Nylabones are good choices as long as someone's in the house. (The manufacturer specifically warns against leaving their products with an unattended dog.)

One thing worth knowing about classic Nylabones however is if swallowed in whole or in part *they do not show up on an x-ray*, which can be problematic. Nylabone's puppy keys and teething rings are certainly cute and fun for small puppies, but probably only for the first month or two for a full-sized Dood from a safety standpoint. (The good news is that at least the bright colors mean they'll show up on an x-ray if ingested.) *Most Nylabone products average 3-4 star ratings from Amazon customers.*

The ubiquitous **Kong** is another popular chew toy, and being made of rubber

it also bounces, which makes it fun. Filled with peanut butter, it will usually keep a puppy entertained for quite a while, but again, should not be left with an unattended dog. You might as well start right off with a big one so you never have to worry about it being accidentally swallowed. **Kong's Stuff-a-Ball** is one of the more durable and popular "treat toys" (as well as the hands-down quietest) and the **Kong Extreme Ball** rates a solid 5 stars, although it's not really a chew toy. *Kong products average 3.5 to 4.5 stars across the board.*

Real Stuff for Dogs to Chew On

In the "natural" department, let's start with what you *don't* want to give your puppy, and those are chopped and compressed "bone-shaped things" of any sort. Although most big dogs can crunch them up, swallow the pieces and manage to get them all the way through their digestive tracts, they represent a real hazard for puppies and small breed dogs, who can pretty easily break off a chunk just large enough to choke on or to cause an intestinal obstruction. For the record, the ubiquitous Greenie falls in this category—although the manufacturer clearly states they are only for *adult dogs* weighing over 15 pounds, it seems like everyone knows someone who's lost a small dog or a puppy to a Greenie. *Stay away from anything that uses the word "compressed" or looks like it's made from chopped-up stuff.*

Real Bones

When it comes to bones, **Marrow and knuckle bones** are the time-honored natural chew toys for dogs, who've been happily gnawing on them for untold millennia, but they are not without inherent risk either; leaving a dog alone with even a huge one when no one is around is not recommended. Cooked bones can splinter, presenting a risk of both choking and intestinal perforation, even though untold thousands of them are consumed by dogs around the world every single day without incident.

Raw bones, as their proponents are quick to point out, do not splinter as easily, but they do come with the inherent risk of food-borne pathogens like e-coli, campylobacter, and salmonella, to name just a few. Although dogs are indeed less susceptible to them than are people, most dogs *live* with people and can spread these pathogens via their saliva to their human pack members.

"Smoked bones" with bits of meat attached are a favorite of nearly all dogs, but they *are* strong-smelling and fairly messy, and many owners limit them to outdoors or crates for that reason. Both raw and cooked bones can cause stomach upset in some dogs, while others have no problem with them at all. Always monitor bone-chewing carefully and replace bones when they start to get small or chunks start to get chewed off. *Overall, most natural bones get an average rating of 3.5-4.5 stars from Amazon's dog-owning customers.*

Assorted Animal Parts

An alternative to actual bones are various other "natural parts", all of which puppies and indeed dogs of all ages adore, all of which are pretty nutritious and some of which you may find palatable enough to actually have around. The downside of all these "natural" chews, however, is that they're all pretty expensive.

This is really pretty hilarious if you consider that when they used to be included in dog food as a cheap protein source, FDA required them to be labeled as "byproducts".

When dog owner decided they didn't want to feed their dogs food that contained "byproducts", those parts ended up dried, smoked, shrink-wrapped in plastic and sold individually at exorbitant prices to those same dog owners as "natural treats" for those same dogs. Go figure.

Anyhow, it's been a real windfall for the slaughterhouse industry, which just goes to prove once again that it's an ill wind that blows nobody good.

Pig's ears and the even less-appealing **pig snouts,** both of which big dogs merrily crunch up like large overpriced potato chips, *will* last awhile for puppies, and puppies adore them. On the other hand, they are, not surprisingly, greasy and "piggy-smelling" and have a tendency to stain everything they come in contact with.

Lamb's ears, which are dry, white, and odorless, are a cleaner choice and being less fatty are less likely to cause stomach upset. *In the customer review department, pig's ears and snouts probably average 3.5 stars while lamb's ears average 4-5 stars, with the 5 star ratings mostly from owners of puppies and small dogs.*

Rawhide. Although most dogs really like it a lot, giving dogs rawhide in any shape is pretty controversial— although independent research has shown ingestion of rawhide is safe, large chunks of rawhide can be bitten off and swallowed, presenting the same choking hazard found in chopped compressed bones, so a lot of vets advise against it. (Of course, if you ask a vet, they'll tell you *nothing* is really safe for a dog to chew on, because the only time vets see a lot of this stuff is when they're surgically removing it from a dog's digestive tract.)

In spite of that, America's dog population probably consumes untold tons of rawhide chips, rolls and knotted bones on an annual basis. The key to rawhide chews for puppies if you choose to give it is to stick to big knotted rawhide bones and toss them as soon as the puppy starts to untie the ends into slimy strips he could ultimately swallow. Depending on the puppy, this can take anywhere from days to weeks, by which time it's probably pretty disgusting anyway. *Rawhide products rate 3.5-.4.5 stars on average.*

Cow's hooves are another chew toy option for puppies. Once again, they all like them and will chew away merrily for hours without the hooves themselves getting slimy. Although they're not greasy like pig parts, they do have an odor and some people find them unappealing to have lying around the house, since they look a lot like, well…hooves. Totally unprocessed and pretty safe for young puppies, older dogs who are strong chewers can break chunks off if they work at it for awhile. *Cow's hooves have an Amazon customer rating of 3.5-4.5 stars.*

Bully sticks, also sold as "pizzle sticks" and "beef tendons", are universally loved by dogs, and are about as natural as you can get, since they are in reality simply raw bull or steer penises which are hung and dried without any cooking, processing or chemicals. (The name "beef tendon" was recently adopted because it turns out some dog owners are just not comfortable with the idea of their dog chewing on a penis, but they're really all the same thing.) They do have a fair amount of nutritional value, and because they are low in fat, they are unlikely to cause stomach upset.

Many owners feel bully sticks have a "calming" effect on their dogs, most likely related to the fact that they're high in taurine, an amino acid known to be protective against glutamate excitotoxicity in the brain – in fact, taurine is used to treat both seizures and head tremors in dogs. They're considered safer than rawhide from a choking standpoint, especially if you buy the thickest ones. In fact, if it weren't for the "yuck" factor, and the fact that they all smell pretty awful (even the so-called "odorless" ones), bully sticks would probably rate 5 stars based on safety, palatability and nutritional value. But what can you say about a product where one of the 5 star reviews actually starts out with "Gross, but worth it"? *Overall, 4 stars.*

OK, assuming you haven't fallen off your chair in a coma by now, you've probably figured out that a "5 star chew toy" would be 100% natural, nontoxic, nutritious *and* incapable of splintering or breaking off into chunks so you could leave it in his crate with him when no one's around, as well as odorless, not greasy, messy, or disgusting to look at or pick up, and hopefully not something you'll have a hard time explaining to Aunt Eleanor when she comes over at Christmas and asks what the dog is chewing on. "Sustainably harvested" seems like too much too ask, but what the heck, let's throw it in there anyway. Oh yeah, and dogs should actually *like* it.

Well, Mick, it might not happen often, but if you try sometimes, you just might find you get what you want *and* what you need....

The absolute BEST puppy chew toy at any price

is a good-sized chunk of antler.

Elk, whitetail, mulie or moose, doesn't matter, good quality antler meets all of the above criteria, *and is probably the only thing on God's green earth that's safe enough to leave with an unattended puppy.*

And unlike bones, rawhide and hooves, the majority of antler is harvested in the most sustainable manner one can possibly imagine, because no animals need be killed in the process.

In case you're not from Wisconsin, Minnesota, or one of those big square states out west and consequently didn't know this, antlers are not the same as the horns on a cow, who is stuck with the same set for life.

Although antler is also made of bone, bucks of all of the above species actually shed their antlers, or "racks", every year, and pretty much abandon them where they fall, after which they promptly begin to acquire a new and usually more impressive set. Sort of like iphones.

Harvesting these discarded racks consists mostly of wandering around the woods until you find a set, which is not as easy as it sounds. In fact, it is so difficult that some people are now training "shed dogs" to assist in the hunt. In order to get there before the local rodentia do, shed gathering (also known as "clinting" for no good reason) is done between December and February, and often requires tromping around in sub-zero weather on snowshoes, which is not everyone's idea of a fun time.

Because harvesting is so labor-intensive, antler dog chews are absurdly expensive, but when you factor in how long they last and how clean, odor-free and safe they are, they really are a great bargain.

In fact, one could make a strong argument for dispensing with the nylon and rawhide and pig parts and dried penises altogether and making antler pieces the *only* chewing option available for your puppy right from the get-go, in which case you'll want to buy a couple, because, like snowflakes, no two are identical and variety is good for puppies as well as people.

You do need to toss them when they finally are gnawed down to a size that could be swallowed whole, but it will take awhile, especially if the puppy is working on several at once.

Antler chews get 5 stars from Amazon's dog owning customers, with the exception of those who thought that for eighteen bucks they were getting a whole bag of them instead of just one.

Soft Toys

Unfortunately, there are no really "natural" alternatives in the soft toy department short of picking up actual roadkill, which is a little more natural than most of us are comfortable with.

There is an argument, however, for choosing stuffed toys that at least vaguely resemble what might actually be found in nature, though— in addition to being more "culturally respectful", dogs often innately prefer them. The best are made of sturdy material, well-sewn, and have few appendages to be chewed off and swallowed. (Tags should be cut off with a scissors.)

But you do need to bear in mind that no matter how well-made, stuffed toys are not designed as chew toys by definition—they should always be used in an interactive manner to some degree, and under supervision. When a puppy starts to seriously chew on or rip into a stuffed toy instead of playing with it, common sense should dictate that it's time to pick it up and replace it with a "real" chew toy like a bone or an antler – failure to do this teaches the puppy that destroying items made of cloth and stuffing is acceptable behavior, and it's *not,* unless of course you want your couch cushions to meet a similar end.

Toys that suffer small "accidental" tears caused by sharp puppy teeth should also be picked up immediately. (At the risk of pointing out the obvious, using a needle and thread to sew up a small hole before the first irresistible-to-puppies wisps of polyester stuffing appear will stop the process in its tracks and extend the life of the toy significantly. Your sewing skills really don't matter here, and it only takes a minute.)

That said, buying well-designed stuffed toys right from the get-go will actually lessen the chances that they will be destroyed.

In addition to durability, the best dog toys are designed with an understanding of the canine instinct to eviscerate small fuzzy animals.

And the manufacturer that literally owns this market is Kygen. They make several lines of plush toys designed with smaller stuffed squeaky toys that fit *inside* bigger stuffed toys, and they are nothing short of brilliant. The little toys may be easily removed, leaving the big one intact, by all but the dumbest of dogs after a little helpful instruction from the owner, who will then spend the rest of his life sticking them back in so that his dog can pull them out again. No matter, Goldendoodle puppies adore them…in fact, puppies and dogs of nearly all breeds and ages adore them.

The undisputed winner here is surely **Kygen's Hide-a-Squirrel**. Essentially a fuzzy gray tree stump with three removable squeaky stuffed squirrels inside, it is Amazon's #1 best-selling dog toy and yes, Virginia, it is indeed the one boasting 676 reviews and counting. Even *more* astonishing is the fact that over 80% of reviewers gave it 5 stars, which is probably some sort of record. And because it speaks directly to their DNA, dogs just universally love it. It actually comes in 4 sizes, but since most people ultimately upgrade to the "ginormous" size (which boasts no less than *five* removable squirrels) you might just want to start there.

If a Goldendoodle puppy could only have three personal possessions,

two good-sized chunks of antler and a Hide-a-Squirrel

would probably serve him well.

Since that's clearly not gonna happen, the next toy worth buying is **Kygen's Platypus**, another Amazon best-seller and part of its Egg Baby series.

Using the same principle as Hide-a-Squirrel, the squeaky eggs (which are remarkably sturdy) are gleefully removed from the Platypus by the puppy, then tossed around and played with until you put them back in, after which the whole process is repeated endlessly until the puppy gets tired, at which point you trade it for a chew bone so he'll go lay down and leave you in peace for awhile. There are actually several toys in the Egg Baby series, and Harvey the Hedgehog is another good choice. *These are all 4 star toys.*

If you get tired of stuffing little toys back into big toys and want to add a couple of less-interactive ones, **Ethical's Skinneeez** line is pretty cool.

Because the bodies of these plush critters have no actual stuffing, the "eviscerating gene" doesn't automatically kick in, and the long skinny shape is extremely attractive to puppies, who'll immediately toss them around and shake them. (This is obviously another DNA-based thing…as anyone who's watched a dog destroy a stuffed animal knows, the "tossing and shaking" behavior naturally appears *after* the toy is gutted.)

There's a Skinneeez skunk, a squirrel, a fox and a raccoon among others, all fairly realistic — unfortunately this realism coupled with their flat shape may cause the uninitiated to mistake them for roadkill, but that's really their only downside. They're also all under ten bucks. *Skinneeez get 4 stars from Amazon's customers across the board. (Although apparently somebody's dog actually managed to swallow one whole and had to have it surgically removed, after which the owner posted warnings all over the internet. This should not be a problem with the 24 inch model.)*

A couple more stuffed toys worth adding to the pile are all made by Coleman, the sporting goods company. All exhibit the "durability at a reasonable price" that's Coleman's stock in trade.

The **Coleman pheasant** is popular with dogs mostly because of its cool squawky squeaker, as is the **Coleman duck**, which actually quacks. (Even toy breeds are attracted to these "game birds", which is a little surprising.) Their neoprene **Water Sport Duck** is great for teaching puppies to retrieve out of water in a lake or backyard pool. Last but not least, **Coleman's Super-Sized Trophy Bear** is a sturdy and immensely popular "cuddle toy" for puppies of all ages with a good track record for longevity. *This last one is another dog toy with over a hundred Amazon reviews, and over two thirds of them are 5 stars. For some reason Coleman just got it right, and dogs instinctively love this bear. All of Coleman's stuffed dog toys are rated highly by customers, though—usually rating 4-5 stars across the board.*

Interactive Treat Toys

There is a last category of interactive toys which are fairly new to the market, and these are "treat toys". Unlike the interactive stuffed toys, the owner doesn't have to do much here— once it's filled, the dog simply interacts with the toy without a lot of input from anyone else. They are based on the premise that, unlike a grazing animal that just needs to put his head down, a canid is hard-wired to *work* for his food.

The fact that dogs think these toys are lots of fun and will often choose their food ball over a dish of food indicates the designers may be on to something. (Some trainers are now recommending these as the primary "dog dish", and many suggest their use to prevent or alleviate separation anxiety as well as food-bolting.) Usually designed in the shape of a ball or cube with a hole for the food to fall out of when rolled, these will keep dogs entertained for anywhere from 10 minutes to an hour.

Two of the most popular are the **OurPets IQ Treat ball**, and **Kong's Wobbler**. Both are dishwasher-safe, which is good.

Kong's Stuff-a-Ball is one of the few made of rubber, which is harder to clean but quiet enough to allow you to watch TV in the same room.

The **Buster Food Cube** is another popular one, but its squarish shape makes it even louder than the hard plastic balls, especially on tile or hardwood floors. It's probably worth it to get a couple different shapes and switch them out just to keep things interesting. *Overall, this bunch rates 4-5 stars from Amazon customers.*

Obviously there are tons of dog toys out there, and while this will get you started, you'll no doubt keep adding to your Dood's collection as you go along. If you try to remember that he's a full-fledged card-carrying member of the genus *Canidae* and not a little person in a dog suit, and always read the customer reviews to check for safety and durability before you bring anything into the house, you'll do fine.

The most important thing to keep in mind, though, is that there is no amount of dog toys, no matter how "interactive", that can take the place of human attention.

Dog toys are all meant to be used by people

as a fun way to interact with their dogs, NOT to entertain dogs left alone.

Because of the way they're hard-wired, any dog would rather play fetch with a plain old stick in the company of one of his human pack members than be left alone with a boxful of expensive dog toys.

Collars, leads and tags

The collar and tag is part of a dog's basic "wardrobe" – in fact, unless he's wearing a life jacket or a service dog jacket it's probably his *whole* wardrobe, and he should wear it at all times unless he's in the tub. Some experts advise against leaving a dog unattended in a crate with a collar on, but if you actually examine any modern crate you'll be hard-pressed to figure out how a dog can get his collar stuck anywhere in there, so this may just be outdated advice. Show dog owners never leave collars on their dogs, but that's really mostly about saving coat.

Puppy Collars

To start out, you'll want a **flat nylon puppy-sized collar with a matching 6-foot lead**. (Your breeder should be able to tell you which size is appropriate for your particular size of Dood.) The choice between a traditional "buckle" collar and the kind with a plastic snap is entirely up to you, but bear in mind this is a temporary collar, because your puppy is going to outgrow it in short order. Just pick a bright color that complements his coat.

You'll also need a tag with his phone number on it, and these can (and should) be made up on the spot at any major pet supply store like Petsmart *before your puppy arrives*. (In fact, if you are picking up your puppy, which you should do if at all possible, you should bring it along and attach it to his collar before he leaves the breeder's property.) Some people are paranoid about putting the dog's name on the tag as well, but if a puppy is lost, it's probably less traumatic for him if the person who finds him can actually call him by name. Even if he's microchipped, a simple phone number (your cell phone is probably best) is most likely to get him home the fastest.

.When shopping for collars you'll notice a dizzying array of "training" collars out there on the same rack—martingales, slip collars (referred to as "choke" collars by people who don't like them), prong collars and head collars (the ubiquitous Gentle Leader is the best known), but if your puppy is reasonably tractable (as most Goldendoodles are) and you actually take the time to train him to heel early he may never need any of them, and they'll all be the wrong size anyway.

Check cord

In addition to the 6 foot nylon lead, what you will also absolutely need right out the gate is a 5/8 inch 20-foot, 5/8 inch **cotton web training lead**, also called a "check cord" or "drop lead", depending on the trainer's area of expertise.

This will allow your puppy some freedom to romp in areas that are open but not entirely fenced, like parks and beaches, as well as being a critical tool for teaching him to recall in your backyard. (Actually, with a check cord, you can practice the recall lots of different places, which is a very good idea.).

Check cords are infinitely safer than the ubiquitous "retractable" lead, which appeared like a nasty virus back in the 1980s and which too many pet owners now use and all experienced trainers wish would vanish from the earth.

Besides literally *teaching dogs to pull*, which is stupid, these leads are downright dangerous. (The manufacturer of the FlexiLead actually suggests that to "reduce the risk of finger amputation" you remove your rings and wear sturdy gloves…it's right on their website, honest to God.)

As if *that* isn't bad enough, if a retractable lead is accidentally dropped (which it will be sooner or later), it will immediately and loudly retract, and then the poor puppy will find himself being chased by a noisy chunk of plastic banging along right behind him no matter how fast he runs! Nine out of ten puppies will panic in this situation, for which you can hardly blame them, and the results can be lethal. Even if you can manage to get to the puppy and the damned leash before he gets hit by a car, the damage to his leash-training will be extensive, to say the least. (On the other hand, if you drop the check cord, you can casually scoop it back up, and odds are good the puppy won't even notice.)

To avoid these and other possible disasters, here's my advice:

- **DO NOT BUY A RETRACTABLE LEASH FOR YOUR PUPPY.**

- **DO NOT ACCEPT ONE AS A GIFT.**

- **DO NOT PUT ONE ON YOUR PUPPY UNLESS SOMEONE ACTUALLY HAS A GUN POINTED AT YOUR HEAD.**

- **DO NOT STAND ANYWHERE NEAR A DOG ATTACHED TO ONE.**

The retractable leash is probably the *worst* thing that ever happened to leash-training.

Once your puppy gets bigger, you'll want to replace the 5/8 inch cotton web lead with a stronger nylon one (LL Bean makes the best ones), and you can buy them in lengths up to 50 feet. They are a great investment.

Books

If Amazon's *"Customers who bought this item also bought..."* is any sort of a guide, most people buy a handful of books on puppy-training and general dog ownership while they are killing time waiting for their puppy by ordering crates and dog beds and antlers and Hide-a-Squirrels. *But which ones should you buy?*

This can be extremely confusing, especially for the poor novice dog owner, as the various philosophies of dog training rival maybe only organized religion in both sheer number and intolerance for opposing opinions among their respective adherents. (For that reason alone, reading the reviews will only confuse you more.)

So let's make it easy:

If you are only going to buy one book on dog training, that book should **be *Mother Knows Best: the Natural Way to Train Your Dog* by Carl Lea Benjamin.** Written back in 1985, it's been selling steadily ever since and it's now also available on Kindle.

What sets this book apart? Simply put, *Mother Knows Best* is to dog training what *The Art of French Cooking* is to cooking, and Carol Lea Benjamin is no less than the Julia Child of dog training— the person who first introduced dog owners to the idea of "natural training" nearly thirty years ago. No one does it better.

In addition to teaching you in clear and simple steps how to actually train your dog, Carol Benjamin teaches you to *enjoy* him. She makes natural training *fun* for both the dog and his owner, rather than an unnatural chore.

Mercifully lacking the endless autobiographical material and "case histories" that seem to plague nearly all training books, Ms Benjamin spends a little time explaining her philosophy and then jumps right into a practical "curriculum" for a typical 8 week old puppy. The section on Etiquette for Puppies includes a housebreaking schedule, broken down hour-by-hour.

It really is the only training book you will ever need, unless you want to add ***How to Survive Your Puppy's Adolescence,*** which you might as well break down and buy at the same time, since you'll need it in only a few short months, anyway. Not surprisingly, it's written by the same author.

Assuming you want to keep your Goldendoodle as healthy as you possibly can (and who doesn't?) the other book worth buying right out the gate **is *Dr Pitcairn's New Guide to Natural Dog Care.***

Written by the world's foremost authority on natural and alternative veterinary medicine, this book offers some important insights into why modern dogs now suffer from so many chronic health issues and what you can do to avoid them. Newly revised, it now includes a chapter on environmental toxins and dogs that's a real eye-opener. Read it with an open mind and try to incorporate as much of it as you realistically can into your dog's care, even if you don't plan to make him home-cooked organic meals. The section on homeopathic and herbal remedies for minor problems will save you enough to pay for the book several times over…and you'll have avoided giving your dog a lot of unnecessary antibiotics to boot.

Another book worth buying, especially if you're thinking of cooking for your dog rather than feeding commercial dog food, is ***Home-Prepared Dog & Cat Diets: the Healthful Alternative* by Donald R Strombeck DVM PhD.**

The recipes are surprisingly easy, inexpensive and backed by a lot of hard science. If you find the idea of home-cooked food for your dog appealing but are at all worried that it may result in nutritional deficiencies, this book is a must-have. Dr Strombeck is Professor Emeritus at UC Davis School of Veterinary Medicine and is a recognized authority in canine nutrition. At 366 pages, it's packed with information; it's also *very* expensive, but you can usually buy a used copy on Amazon. It's worth knowing that much of the information in the book, including a lot of the recipes, can also be found online at http://dogcathomeprepareddiet.com.

If you're a compulsive reader, another book you might want to consider adding to your library is Stanley Coren's ***How to Speak Dog***, which expands upon the guide to understanding dog language introduced in *Mother Knows Best*.

And last but not least, you REALLY need to order a copy of ***My Seizure Dog*** by 7 year old Evan Moss. His seizure alert dog Mindy does happen to be a Goldendoodle, but that's not the only reason you need to buy this book...this is one very cool kid!

In the DVD department, **Cesar Millan's *People Training for Dogs*** is available on Amazon and worth owning. Like most of his books, this is not a "training manual" (by his own admission, Cesar Millan is not a dog "trainer"), but rather explains the psychology behind effective dog training.

Anyhow, this list should be enough to get you headed in the right direction, so you might as well pull out the plastic and start ordering so you'll have everything disinterred from its annoying packaging and assembled by the time you get your puppy.

And when the bills for all this stuff start coming in at the end of the month you'll immediately understand why the initial cost of the puppy really doesn't matter much.

CHAPTER FIVE:

Off to a Good Start

(or...surviving the first few days and nights and beyond)

The most important year of any dog's life is without doubt the first one. In fact, much of his future success in life depends upon what he learns not only in the first year, *but in the first 4 months*.

Puppies start learning very early from their mothers. If you want a well-balanced and well-trained dog (and who doesn't?) you'll want to continue this learning process with your Doodle puppy right away, rather than waiting until he's old enough to go to formal training classes, by which time you'll already have problems to "fix".

Remember, Goldendoodles are highly intelligent and if you do not train your puppy he will train himself, which rarely works out well for anybody. Virtually all the "problems" (like jumping, food aggression, inability to walk on a leash) with which professional trainers have to deal really involve *retraining* some poor dog who was forced to train himself due to a lack of leadership on his owner's part when he was little and cute. Here's an example:

The dog who jumps on everyone who walks into the room was simply never taught how to appropriately greet a human when he was little, so he came up with his OWN greeting.

As with children and spouses, it's a lot easier and more effective to teach a dog what we DO want him to do than to only try to teach him what we DON'T, because in the latter case he won't have an appropriate alternative behavior with which to replace the unwanted one.

If you don't want a dog to jump up on his hind legs and lick your face to greet you when you walk into a room, exactly what *do* you want him to do - sit, lie down, roll over, stand on his head? He's got to do *something*.

Now, it takes a total of maybe 20 minutes to teach even the most dim-witted 8 week old puppy the *sit/stay command*. If a dog knows that command, once he even starts to think about jumping up, he can be given the sit-stay command and be rewarded with praise and a pat on the head instead of a knee in the chest and yelling… or even worse, his best-beloved person *ignoring* him while he gets more and more desperate to have his existence acknowledged.

Whoever came up with the breathtakingly stupid idea

that *ignoring* an unwanted behavior will cause it to disappear

obviously never had children.

It's also kinder. The saddest cartoon ever is the one where two dogs meet and one says "My name is No No Bad Dog—what's yours?"

So the training begun by his mother should be continued seamlessly by you the minute you have your hands on your new puppy. Reading both *Mother Knows Best* and *How to Survive Your Dog's Adolescence* all the way through before you bring him home will give you all the confidence and tools you need to do it right. The clock starts ticking the minute you actually pick up your puppy, so let's start with that.

When is the best time to pick up your puppy?

Odds are you won't have a lot of leeway when it comes to picking up your puppy—most breeders have a "pick-up weekend" based on what they feel is the optimal age for the pups to go their new homes. Usually with pups the size of Goldendoodles, this is between 7 and 9 weeks. So you need to find out when you're supposed to pick him up and clear your calendar well in advance.

But under NO circumstances should you buy a puppy from a breeder who will let them go before 7 weeks. Puppies taken from their litters before this time will often have problems getting along with other dogs throughout their lives and in addition often lack "bite inhibition", which they learn from their mothers and siblings.

Is it OK to Have a Puppy Shipped?

At the risk of alienating a lot of well-intentioned breeders, the answer is NO.

For the better part of the last hundred years, buying a puppy meant looking for breeders pretty close to home, visiting them, finding one you were comfortable with, and then driving over to pick up the puppy as soon as it was old enough to leave its mom and littermates. *For a wealth of reasons, this "buying local" method is still by far the best.*

But in the internet world we now live in, buyers more often select a puppy online from a breeder halfway across the country whom they've never met, purchase the puppy without ever visiting the breeder's home and/or meeting the puppy or his parents, and then have the poor little guy shipped cross-country when he turns eight weeks old as if he were a cappuccino maker. We're now all so used to online purchasing and having everything delivered that no one seems to think twice about this whole process, or whether or not it is actually in the best interest of the puppy himself. IT IS NOT.

For a multitude of reasons that can have both short-term and long-term negative effects on the individual dog *and* the future of dogs in general, it is far better for a puppy to be picked up rather than shipped.

The first, of course, is that it's far safer for the puppy.

Think about it for a minute— you're willing to trust your puppy's very LIFE to the same guys who regularly lose your luggage???

It should not come as much of a surprise to learn that the airlines lose puppies, too. In fact, according to the US Dept of Transportation, between 2005 (when airlines were required to actually turn in reports for the first time *ever*) and 2011, US airlines killed, injured or lost 224 pets. Delta led the pack with 70, followed by Continental with 69, Alaska Airlines with 50, American Airlines with 45 and United with 24.

Close to 90% of the deaths reported were dogs, and lest you think that these were perhaps elderly or ill animals or bulldogs, which is what the airlines would like us to believe, the 2000 Samoyed National Specialty Winner, a four year-old prime specimen of a dog, died in the cargo hold of a flight from Orlando to CA while his owners were in the cabin of the same plane.

And as awful as that sounds, it's probably much worse.

Those figures only include dogs traveling as excess baggage when their owners are in the cabin. **They DO NOT include "incidents" involving any of the thousands of unaccompanied puppies shipped each year as cargo from breeders to their new owners —like yours! — because the airlines are not required to report those.**

How many of these puppies shipped "unaccompanied" are killed or injured? Because they do not need to be reported, no one knows the exact number, but according to the ASPCA, Air Transportation Association data puts the estimate at around *5,000 per year*, or roughly one in every 100 puppy shipped. This would include the 7 puppies that died of apparent overheating on a single American Airlines flight from Oklahoma to Chicago O'Hare in August 2010, as well as Maggie May, the Westie pup who was crushed to death in 2008 by a baggage cart on the tarmac at Atlanta's Hartsfield enroute to her new owner.

Although the airlines claim that the cargo holds are pressurized and air-conditioned, temperatures ranging from below freezing to 115 degrees have been recorded in the crates of shipped dogs, often because the plane was delayed on the tarmac. (When a Continental flight bound for Denver was delayed for 3 hours in Philadelphia, 3 Samoyeds in the cargo hold were found dead on arrival.) What sorts of injuries are recorded? United was recently sued when a dog's eardrums were punctured during transport—the owner received $410.50 in compensation. (Compensation was based on the weight of the dog.) And any dog that dies enroute to or at the vets' office rather than being found dead in its crate when they take it off the plane is listed as an "injury" rather than a death in the incident report.

So why do breeders assure puppy buyers that shipping puppies is perfectly safe, when the numbers indicate pretty clearly that it is NOT?

That's easy….*you* didn't know any of this until right now, did you? Odds are, *neither does your breeder.*

Because they make a lot of money shipping dogs, the airlines obviously don't advertise the risks, or the number of dogs and puppies lost each year, so most breeders remain blissfully ignorant until the awful day one of their own puppies dies enroute.

The commercial breeders DO know, but for them, it's simply part of the cost of doing business online. Shipping puppies sold via the internet is the best thing that ever happened to puppy mills—instead of selling them wholesale to brokers, they can now sell them at retail directly to the consumer, who thinks he's buying from a responsible breeder. *They're making more money than ever.* What's the loss of a couple of puppies compared to that? They simply write them off as business losses.

In fact, puppy mills would be out of business in short order

if the airlines simply banned the shipping of puppies under the age of a year,

because it is absolutely critical to their continued existence.

Aside from the very real physical risks, there is also a lot less *psychological stress* if you pick up your puppy yourself directly from the breeder, because he will know he has "permission" to be with you — his care is simply being transferred from one higher-ranking pack member than himself to another, which happens in the wild all the time.

On the other hand, there's really no natural equivalent to a puppy being put in a crate and driven to an airport by one person, shifted around innumerable times, subjected to highly toxic lead-laden jet fumes and a noise level that requires ear protection for humans, and then ultimately taken out of the crate after all this by a person *he's never seen before* at the other end. He has nothing in his DNA to cope with the stress of that.

Besides being the most popular week to ship puppies, the eighth week also marks the beginning of the first "fear" period in canine development—check out the chart at the end of this chapter.

The period between 8 to 12 weeks is when fear of loud noises develops,

and *anything associated with fear at this stage*

will be a fear stimulus throughout the dog's life.

If a puppy is subjected to shipping when he is going through the first fear period, the potential for long-lasting trauma is extremely high. Because no one has any idea exactly what may have frightened the puppy during shipping, there is no way to "undo" it with a program of desensitization. Some trainers believe that the fact so many puppies are now routinely shipped to their new homes explains a lot of the noise fears (hence the exploding popularity of "thunder shirts") and separation anxiety problems as well as the free-floating anxiety they now see in dogs.

If you think about these in terms of what a puppy may have experienced being shipped in the cargo hold on an airline during the first fear period, the theory has merit. How do you think your luggage gets so scuffed up???

The fact that many puppies apparently handle being shipped as well as they do is a credit to the adaptability of the canine psyche, but that's hardly an excuse for putting a puppy through the experience simply because it's more "convenient" for the new owner.

So if you want to keep your puppy safe, give him the best possible start in life and avoid creating any phobias you'll have to identify and figure out how to deal with later, arrange to pick him up yourself …your personal convenience is really *not* the most important factor here. Being responsible for a dog for the next 15 years is going to be pretty inconvenient at times, and this is as good a time as any to get used to it.

Does this limit you to breeders near your home? *Of course not.*

If you've selected a responsible breeder six states away, talked at length with the breeder via phone, seen photos and videos of the parents and litter in their environment (not just cute "posed" puppy shots!), and it's just too far to drive, for heaven's sake just *fly in and pick him up.*

Flying in an underseat pet carrier is not stressful for a puppy at all because the cabin is pressurized, air-conditioned and he is never more than 3 inches from human feet— most will sleep the whole way, even on a cross-country flight, with no need for sedation.

In fact, for reasons unknown, puppies are less likely to get airsick than carsick, assuming they're inside the cabin. (If he gets squirmy mid-flight, he probably needs to relieve himself. Simply carry him to the loo right in his bag and spread out a piddle pad on the floor, which you'll of course have tucked into the pocket of the bag. When he's done, pop him back into the bag and go back to your seat. If you forgot the piddle pad use paper towels.)

If you use air miles or shop around for a deal, you can often pick up your puppy for less than the average cost of shipping, which is usually between $350 and $400.

Most airlines charge a fee of around $100 to bring the puppy into the cabin with you, which is irritating on principle but a great deal when you consider the alternatives.

On the other hand, if the breeder does not ENCOURAGE you to fly in or drive to their home to pick up your new puppy, but "prefers" to ship, find yourself a new breeder, because that's the hallmark of a puppy mill.

Substandard breeders actually count on the fact that you will find it more "convenient" to have the puppy shipped, because that way, you won't see the God-awful conditions under which he was raised, or how many dogs they have or how many puppies they are cranking out.

Planning Your Pick-Up Trip

Whether you drive or fly, try to arrange it so that the puppy spends his first night away from his littermates in his new home rather than in a Holiday Inn somewhere along the way.

As everyone who remembers *Lady and the Tramp* is aware, the first night is going to set the tone for what follows, and what you'll have to do to keep a homesick puppy quiet in a hotel room probably won't make the next night any easier.

If you have a long drive it's best to stay at a hotel close to the breeder the night before. That way you can pick up the puppy early enough the next morning to make it home that evening, where his new setup will be waiting for him. (If you can't make the drive home in one day, it's really better to fly in and pick him up— less stress all the way around.)

In addition to a crate, you'll want to pack a "puppy pick-up bag" with the emergency supplies you will almost certainly need for the trip. This should include:

- His collar (with tag attached) and a leash

- A baggie of whatever food he's used to

- A bottle of water and a small bowl

- A big roll of paper towels

- Several plastic grocery bags

- Bonine (half a tab will help a lot if he's carsick)

- An antler to chew on

- A soft toy or towel you can rub on his littermates and/or mom

If you can manage the trip without an extraordinary number of small children and elderly relatives the whole thing will be easier, but two people are better than one— it's best to have a person sitting *next* to him on the ride home rather than sticking him in the back all by himself, where he's much more likely to put up a racket. You're also much more likely to know when he wakes up and has to go so you'll be able to pull into the nearest gas station or rest stop ASAP.

In that regard, if you have to stop to let the puppy out, do try to avoid the "official" dog-walking areas at a rest stop if you can – that's where all the dog germs are! It's far safer to find a less-used grassy area at a service plaza.

Housetraining

Once you've arrived at home, *begin your housetraining routine immediately*. Take the puppy out of the car directly to the area of the yard (or sidewalk if your in the city) that you plan to use to for him to relieve himself, tell him to "hurry up". It's good to choose a not-too-stupid phrase and stick to it so your puppy will learn to relieve himself on command—and for Heaven's sake don't use "good boy!" or it will come back to haunt you!

Praise him lavishly when he goes, *walk him around a little to sniff and explore afterwards* and then bring him into the house and directly into his rendezvous area, where he can get a drink of water and a meal. (A small meal is best if it's late, but no matter how late it is, you don't want to put him to bed hungry.)

Give him time to explore and play a little inside, and as soon as he looks like he needs to go again, take his paw and ring the bell and then take him right out the door that you intend him to use directly to the area you want him to use (this will now be the second time he's been there), and praise lavishly again when he goes. If he starts to relieve himself in the house, say "Oops, outSIDE!" with sufficient volume to stop the flow, scoop him up quickly and take him out to the appointed area to finish (using his paw to quickly hit the bell on the way out), so you can praise him again. Here's the magic key to housebreaking:

The more times the puppy does it right,

the faster he'll "get it" and let you know he has to go.

The more mistakes he's allowed to make because you're not paying attention

the longer it will take. It's that simple.

It's also good to keep in mind that the average age for a puppy to be really reliably housetrained is 6 months or so, although most Goldendoodles are reliable way before then. ("Reliably housetrained", by the way, means the dog understands that he is not to eliminate inside, and will hold it until someone lets him out.)

Assuming you're feeding him at the same times each day, actually *writing down* the times when your puppy has a bowel movement and urinates for a couple of days can help a lot, because it allows you to be proactive. Although this sounds a little OCD, it really *does* help—once you realize that your pup always has a bowel movement 20 minutes after he eats, you can get him outside at the right time; if you have no idea, you're going to have more accidents. You'll also realize how many times in a single day a puppy pees, which is illuminating, to say the least. Use this information to make up a schedule. (If you're *really* OCD, you'll no doubt design a nifty spreadsheet, but a pen and paper will work just fine.)

Having a bell hanging from the door speeds housebreaking

because a puppy will learn to ring a bell way before he'll learn to bark at the door.

This will avoid puddles in front of the door, which are a good indication the puppy is learning faster than you.

This is also a good time to point out that you'll get farther faster if you always let the puppy explore and play outside for a little bit *after* he has relieved himself in his designated area. If he is always brought inside immediately after he goes, he'll figure that out in a hurry, and it will take him longer and longer to relieve himself so as to stretch out his time outside. Puppies are smart.

Also, young puppies do not generally completely empty their bladders all at once, which is why so many people complain that the puppy went outside and "did his business" and then came inside and promptly made another puddle on the floor. A puppy may have to squat twice or even three times before he's done, so it pays not to be in a huge hurry when he's outside.

Anyhow, continue this "playing-exploring-going outside" routine until it's time for the humans to cash it in and go to bed, remembering to cut off his water supply after 7PM.

(Giving him unlimited access to a big bowl of water 24/7 is not a great idea, by the way—young puppies will drink until they are tired, not until their thirst is satiated, and a puppy can drink a *lot* of water before he gets tired!)

Tuck the puppy in for the night in his little crate in your room (right next to the bed is best at first) with his blanket that smells like home, a stuffed toy for company and his antler chew in case he needs to relieve some stress by chewing a little, and try to get some sleep. He should settle in after some cursory whining, which you will respond to by cheerfully telling him to "go to sleep" rather than by letting him out. If he's tired out and hasn't had water after 7 PM, he may sleep all night, or he may have to get up at 2 AM. If he does, take him outside (don't forget to ring the bell!), let him relieve himself but not play, and tuck him right back in his crate. (Note: *don't* turn on all the lights or he'll think it's morning and he'll want to play. Nightlights are good if you don't want to run into furniture on the way out.)

As soon as he makes any noise in the morning, take him directly outside, ringing the bell on the way. (If he walks pretty well on a leash, there is an advantage to snapping it on and leading him quickly out the door, because he'll learn the route to the door with his feet. If he's not leash-trained, it's best to carry him, because he can't learn two things at once.) Have your slippers and robe next to the bed and your jacket and snow boots right by the door if need be. DO NOT STOP to go the bathroom yourself— you're a grown-up and should be able to hold it for a couple minutes, while your puppy surely cannot.

The week following should be more of the same, except he'll use his "big crate" for naps during the day, and assuming you don't let him "tank up" on water in the evening he should start making it through the night. This is the week when you want to be sure someone is home pretty much 24/7.

Crate-training

Although a necessary skill to learn, being alone in a crate is not "natural" for a puppy, nor is it self-rewarding behavior, so you'll want to use treats for this. Crate-training is best started when he's tired out from 10 or 15 minutes of running around outside and ready for a nap. Pop him into his crate, using a little treat as "bait" if you need to bribe him in there, give him an antler chew, close the door, and leave the room. If he falls asleep, leave him in there undisturbed until he wakes up, then take him immediately out to his exercise area.

If he's clearly not tired and barks and howls and you're sure his bladder is empty, *tell him "no barking!" and ignore him until he stops.* Immediately letting him out of his crate when he kicks up a fuss is a bad idea, because that rewards the behavior, and even the most dim-witted puppy will quickly learn that barking and whining is the way to avoid staying in his crate.

Once he's quiet for a while (even a minute or two will do it if that's all you can get between tantrums), you can praise him and let him out, because now you've rewarded him for *not* fussing. Run him around until he's really tired this time and try again.

Needless to say, crate-training is much easier if the puppy was already familiarized with the crate by the breeder. (Breeders who take the time to do this are worth their weight in gold. It also makes the ride home a lot easier.)

Giving Him Time to Recharge

It's not uncommon for the puppy to spend a lot of Day One or Day Two sleeping quite a bit and maybe seeming a little "off" – if he's eating OK and doesn't have diarrhea or a fever, odds are it's just a stress reaction and he needs the time to recharge his little batteries. (Not surprisingly, this is more common in puppies who've been shipped, which is a lot more stress than being picked up.)

On that note, you will want to take your puppy's temperature on his first full day home, so you have a baseline for what's "normal". (It'll probably be somewhere around 100.5—101.5, but like people, there is natural variance from dog to dog.) That way, if you need to take his temperature because he's throwing up or seems ill, you'll have something to compare it to. And it's often the first question the vet will ask if you call, so it's good to be prepared.

Once your puppy has settled in (which should take no more than a couple of days), you're ready to begin the training program laid out in Chapter 3 of *Mother Knows Best*. Hopefully, you will have read the whole book while waiting for your puppy, so you'll understand the basic philosophy of natural training. And do try to remember that for a puppy, praise is a better reward than food, and correction (which is critical to training a dog or a child) is not he same as "punishment", no matter what the dolphin trainers say. If you want to train a dolphin, get a dolphin.

One last caveat – although all your friends and relatives will be anxious to meet the new puppy, it's best to wait a few days until he's had time to decompress and recharge his batteries before introducing lots more new people into his life. Goldendoodle puppies are innately social and love meeting new people, but no matter how much the puppy enjoys the attention, being charming is a lot of work, so make sure his immune system is up to it.

Taking Him Out in the Big World

In order to have a well-socialized Goldendoodle, any trainer will tell you it is absolutely *imperative* that he be exposed to new people, places and dogs within the first four months of his life. Without it, he can become shy of strangers and fearful of strange dogs and new places, which several trainers report is the major problem they see in the breed.

On the other hand, your veterinarian will no doubt warn you that it is unsafe to expose your puppy to new places, people and dogs before he has "completed his puppy vaccination schedule", which probably won't happen until he is 4-5 months old, when he gets his rabies shot. And that's *way* too late to start taking your puppy out in the big world for the first time.

This leaves the poor owner, who understands the critical need for socialization but certainly doesn't want his puppy to contract a potentially deadly infectious disease in order to get socialized, caught in the middle, not knowing what to do. Luckily, there is a simple solution here.

When you take your puppy to the vet for his puppy check-up,

simply ask to have a "serum antibody titer" run.

Vets can now buy in-house titer kits very reasonably, and these will tell you within minutes if your puppy is protected against Distemper and Parvo. The average price for having them run is about $30. (If your vet is not aware of this in-house option, a blood sample will need to be sent to an outside lab. Hemopet, which is the best lab to send it to, charges $45 for a parvo and distemper titer, and your vet will probably tack on a few dollars more for the blood draw.)

With MLV (modified live virus) vaccines like those in puppy shots, immunity begins about 5 days after vaccination, so if it's been at least a week since his last vaccination, the titer should accurately reflect his immunity level. If the results show your puppy has adequate immunity, he's good to go pretty much anywhere.

It's interesting to note that in England, puppies are generally vaccinated only twice rather than 3 times as is done here—once at 8 weeks and then again at 10 weeks, after which they are considered immunized and safe to go out and about in the world for socialization. (This abbreviated schedule is recommended by the RSPCA, in fact.) And they use the *exact same vaccines* used in the US!

Now, as your vet is legally bound to point out, your puppy still won't be protected against rabies, which is admittedly deadly to man and beast. But in all honesty a puppy's risk of exposure is just about nonexistent because the US has been free of canine rabies for years, and the only way dogs in the US now contract rabies is from direct contact with rabid skunks or raccoons. Statistically, your puppy is probably more likely to be eaten by an alligator (don't laugh- this is a real risk in some parts of the country!) than he is to contract rabies at Petsmart before he's had his first rabies vaccination.

Where to take your puppy?

A well-trained puppy, especially one as cute as a Goldendoodle, can go *lots* of places as long as they're on a leash. They can go to soccer games, art fairs, and many outdoor markets. Most parks and downtown "pedestrian" areas are dog-friendly, and some outdoor cafes allow them. Petsmart welcomes leashed dogs, as do many other pet shops. In Florida, dogs are often seen riding in carts in

Lowe's and wandering around the garden section.

And then, of course, there are dog parks. These large fenced areas give dogs a place to run and play and socialize with other dogs, and most well-socialized dogs love the experience. For many urban dogs, it's the only place they can safely burn off energy. Although some trainers don't recommend them for puppies, dog parks can be a great experience as long as the owner exercises some common sense. Most dog parks now have a "big dog" area and a "little dog" area, and when a Goldendoodle is a puppy, he should be taken to the latter, where there is less chance he'll be frightened by big rowdy dogs.

And of course you should be taking him for walks around the neighborhood on a leash from Day One even if you have a fenced-in back yard.

Dogs familiar with their own neighborhood who know their human and canine neighbors

are much less likely to panic and get hopelessly lost if they find themselves accidentally loose, which will happen sooner or later no matter how careful you are.

The important thing is not *where* you take your puppy, but that you *do* take him lots of different places, because it's absolutely critical for his socialization. Dogs who are not exposed to what animal behavioralists call "novel stimuli" in the first 3-6 months of life will never be really comfortable away from home as adults, and this can be crippling for the dog and a pain in the butt for the owner.

So take him as many places as you can, and practice some basic on-leash obedience work in as many different places as you can, so he learns to be well-mannered everywhere he goes. And remember to bring clean-up bags!

The other thing you want to do with your puppy in the first 4 months is take him on lots of car rides. If the first and only car trips a puppy experiences in the first 8-11 week "fear" period are to and from the airport, the odds of his developing chronic "car anxiety" and carsickness go way up, because that is the only association he'll make with riding in the car.

Because of this, it's *really* important to take him for short little car trips to somewhere *fun* during this period so he will make positive associations *and* realize that he'll get to come back home again. If you live in Manhattan, take him for short cab rides in a carrier bag for as long as he'll fit in one.

Have Crate, Will Travel...

Dogs like vacations, too. A well-trained Goldendoodle with a folding wire crate can be taken on most family vacations and is welcomed by many hotels, B&Bs, National and State parks, private campgrounds and more. To find out which ones, check online before you make your reservations—googling "pet-friendly travel" will bring up lots of helpful websites.

When vacationing with your dog, you might also want to consider vacation rental properties (which rent by the night or week) instead of hotels, as many are pet-friendly and come with fenced yards. And because they come with kitchens, you don't have to worry about the dog barking in a strange hotel room every time you go out for meals. For lots of reasons, pet-friendly vacation rental properties are the best thing that ever happened to dog owners. VRBO is a great website to check in this regard – all listings with a paw print are pet-friendly. Even if they only accept pets under 20 pounds, you can often get around that by explaining that your dog is crate-trained and will be left in his crate any time he is left alone.

And if you are staying with family or friends, a well-behaved crate-trained dog is much more likely to be welcome than one who isn't.

And When He Just Can't Go Along...

However, no matter how well-behaved your Dood may be, there are bound to be some times he just can't go along.

For example, if you are flying and your dog doesn't fit under the seat in a soft-side carrier, it's really safer and less stressful for him to leave him home than to check him as baggage and hope he ends up in the same city you do. Even if you're driving, funerals are another event where even the best-trained Dood might not be welcome. Weddings can go either way, but destination weddings in exotic locations are usually not dog-friendly.

In those cases, you have three options—you can A) leave him with friends, B) hire a pet sitter, or C) take him to a boarding kennel. Each has its advantages and disadvantages.

If your puppy is young (like less than 4 months or so), you may want to consider leaving him with friends he knows, because a boarding kennel will be pretty traumatic and he'll be lonely staying home alone with a pet sitter, unless you can find someone to stay at your house full-time. Geriatric dogs (who sleep a lot anyway), or dogs who live in a multiple-dog household, may prefer to be left at home with a sitter coming in a few times a day, especially if it's only for the weekend. Young energetic dogs will probably be safest (and have the most fun!) at a boarding kennel.

If you choose option C), be sure and do your homework first. Most boarding kennels now have websites, and you can see what their rates are and if you like the place before you even call. Some even have webcams so you can check on your dog. It's still a good idea to physically visit the kennel before you commit to it, though. As with breeders, you want to steer clear of any place that does not encourage you to visit, or won't let you get past the office to see where the dogs are actually kenneled.

If you find a kennel you like and use it exclusively, you may find your dog is actually happy to go there—luckily, dogs often have a very different idea of what constitutes a "vacation" than people do, and social dogs like Doods can find a kennel situation, where there are lots of new dogs to run and play with, pretty exciting. One of the things you want to find out is whether the kennel has secure "play areas" and scheduled exercise periods as well as individual runs. If it does not, your dog will be safe, but he'll be bored silly.

Also check to make sure the kennel accepts titers in lieu of annual vaccinations. Some do and some don't. Most will still require bordatella (kennel cough) vaccination, and all will require an up-to-date rabies certificate.

What to Expect in the First Year

For a canine, most of their physical and psychological development takes place in the first year. In the space of 12 short months, a Goldendoodle will grow from a blind and helpless little slug weighing less than a pound to a physically and sexually mature animal that may weigh 80 pounds or more. This rapid growth is biologically "expensive", and during this period his immune system and his brain may not always be able to keep up, which needs to be taken into consideration, especially in regards to vaccination and toxic anti-parasitics as well as training. Within a space of a few months your adorable puppy dashes headlong from roly-poly toddlerhood (that's usually when you pick him up) to gangly puberty and then without even stopping for breath charges into full-blown adolescence, at which point he appears to have forgotten everything he knew a few months earlier.

Virtually all of the critical phases of canine development take place within the first year.

These phases are, like so much else, hard-wired into his DNA and were necessary to survival in the wild, even if they seem less critical (and often counterproductive) in a domesticated suburban companion. Knowing what is occurring at various stages will help a lot in maintaining your sense of humor.

As long as you are consistent and firm in your training, and willing to correct and reinforce when needed as adolescence strikes, both you and your Dood will make it through just fine. It's also good to remember that if you can just get through the first two years, the next ten or twelve are pretty easy sledding.

CHAPTER SIX:

Feeding Your Dood Right

(or...Ignorance is NOT always bliss)

Feeding the family dog is a LOT more complicated than it used to be.

Even a decade ago, most people did no research at all before they bought dog food—they either fed what the breeder recommended for the life of the dog, or they fed whatever food they fed their previous dog.

Now, if the breeder's dogs are healthy and long-lived, or if the owner's previous dog lived a long and healthy life, both these methods still have much to commend them in the "common sense" department.

Unfortunately though, what now happens all too often is that somewhere along the way, the new owner will no doubt run into someone who explains to them why the food that they have been feeding with great results is actually *poisoning* their poor dog, and why they should immediately switch to a "healthier", and often much more expensive brand. (Not surprisingly, the dog foods recommended are often sold through multi-level marketing plans, so if someone recommends a particular brand of dog food, it's always good to find out if they are making money recommending it!)

The new owner, lacking confidence, will start feeding this new food, which may or may not actually be better for their dog, because they figure this expert surely knows a lot more than they do.

These self-styled "dog food experts" also abound on the internet, and several maintain websites that "rank" various brands of dog food. Unfortunately, very few of them appear to have any related academic credentials, and although they certainly mean well, a lot of the information provided is inaccurate, and in some cases can actually endanger your dog's very life.

The two notable exceptions are Dr. Richard H. Pitcairn, who has a veterinary degree from UC Davis and PhDs in both immunology and microbiology from Washington State, and Donald R. Strombeck DVM PhD, a gastroenterologist and Professor Emeritus at UC Davis Vet School. Both of them strongly advocate cooking for your own dog at home and both have written widely on the subject, including recipes that will provide the necessary nutritional balance. Both of their books are on the book list in Chapter Four

So What's the Best Food to Feed?

This one's a no-brainer. There is no doubt that if you really want to feed your dog only fresh, high-quality food without having to worry about the quality or source of the ingredients, or contamination during manufacturing, or what god-awful chemicals might be in there, your ONLY real option is cook it at home yourself.

Surprisingly, even for a large dog, this is much easier than one might expect and will cost no more, and often much less, than buying high-end commercial dog food. There are lots of books on the subject on Amazon, with lots of recipes. In fact, Dr Strombeck has a bunch of them right on his website (www.dogcathomeprepareddiet.com) if you don't want to buy a whole book. If time is a factor, you can easily cook up a week's worth in an hour or two and freeze it in 7 separate containers.

If you eat organically yourself and want the same for your dog,

cooking for your dog is the ONLY way to go,

because the word "organic" is used pretty loosely in the dog food world.

One of the most alarming trends in dog food is what's called *green-washing*, which is no more than a marketing trick to make the ingredients (which are often the exact same ingredients found in less-expensive foods, as you will see) simply sound more appealing by using words like "organic", "human-grade" and "natural", which is perfectly legal. Consider yourself warned.

Genetically Modified dog food? You betcha!I

If you want to avoid GMO ingredients, you're pretty much in the same boat. Considering that well over 75% of the corn, soybeans, canola and sugar beets produced in this country are now genetically modified, they are virtually impossible to avoid unless you cook your own food. (This is a relatively new situation, by the way—the first genetically modified crops started appearing in 1996 and have grown exponentially since then.)

And because, unlike most other developed nations, at present *there are no Federal laws requiring labeling for GMO ingredients in either human or dog food in the US,* you'll have to take any dog food company who claims to use only non-GMO ingredients entirely at their word.

Even worse, a "grain free" dog food may not even be GMO-free, if the meat source has been fed GMO feeds. Although it was not supposed to happen, new research from a large 10 year study in Norway shows that the Bt toxin (an insecticide genetically engineered to produced by the plant itself in many of Monsanto's GMO crops to make them insect-resistant) appears to travel right through the food chain. And a recent Canadian study found Bt toxin in the blood of 93% of pregnant women tested.

Can GMO products adversely affect a dog's health? *Very likely.*

That same Norwegian study published in 2012 showed that *in every species tested,* animals fed GMO corn got fatter, showed immune system changes and were less able to digest proteins due to changes in their digestive systems when compared to the control animals. (If you plan to cook for your dog, it's worth knowing rice, oats, barley, potatoes and wheat are also not, at present anyway, genetically modified. Several of Dr. Strombeck's recipes actually include pasta.)

And last but not least, if you cook for your dog yourself, you won't have to worry about whether or not your dog food has been recalled because of contamination by salmonella or e-Coli or deadly aflatoxin or something, which happens a LOT more than people think.

These recalls due to food-borne pathogens have become at least as common in dog food as they have in the human food chain, and for the same reasons.

Dog Food Inc....or...the trouble with having an open mind is that your brains may fall out.

What most people do not realize about American pet food is that it's a lot like American human food—in other words, it's Big Business. In 2010 alone, pet food sales in the US amounted to around 18 BILLION DOLLARS.

And although few people realize it, most of the dog food brands out there are in fact

owned by only a small handful of the same multinational corporations we all know and love.

Some of them own their own dog food manufacturing facilities, while others subcontract production out to huge "contract manufacturers" you've probably never heard of (and some of whom have been shown by FDA to have appallingly low standards for basic hygiene.)

Here's a rundown of who currently owns which well-known dog food brands, admittedly incomplete and subject to change at any given moment due to corporate mergers:

- **Mars, Inc.** – *Owns the Pedigree, Royal Canin, Kal Kan, Waltham and Nutro brands.*

Products in the US are manufactured in 16 Mars-owned plants around the country. It also contract manufactures the *O' Roy* brand for Walmart. Mars owns the Waltham Centre for Pet Nutrition in England, a state-of-the-art canine nutritional research facility, and is currently building one in the US.

(And, yes, this is the same Mars that makes M&Ms. Mars also bought the Wm. Wrigley Jr. Co in 2008 for $23 billion in a cash deal. That's a lot of chewing gum.)

- **Nestle Purina** — *Owns the ProPlan, ProPlan Selects, Purina ONE, Purina ONE Beyond, Purina Dog Chow, Puppy Chow, Mighty Dog, Beneful and Alpo brands.*

In the US, Purina products are all produced in one of Purina's 13 company-owned and managed manufacturing plants. Purina does not contract manufacture for other companies. According to the company, all of their dog food ingredients are sourced entirely from the US, although they are not GMO-free.

Ralston Purina, founded in 1894, merged with Swiss-based Nestle back in 2003, although the Nestle Purina Pet Care Division, including their (also state-of-the-art) canine nutritional research facility, is still based near St Louis, MO and is open for tours.

- **Proctor and Gamble** — *Owns the Iams and Eukanuba brands, and Natura's Innova, Evo, California Natural, Healthwise, Mother Nature, and Karma brands.*

Some of their products are manufactured at company-owned facilities (according to the company all Natura products are produced at the P & G-owned Natura plant in Nebraska), while others (including Iams and Eukaneuba) are contracted out. Proctor & Gamble, of course, also makes many well-known cleaning products. They used to make Pringles but sold them to Kelloggs recently for $2.7 billion.

- **Colgate-Palmolive** — *Owns the Hill's Science Diet, Prescription Diet and Nature's Best brands, which are contract-manufactured.*

Longtime manufacturers of toothpaste, dish soap and a gazillion other personal care products, they also now own the Tom's of Maine brand, which they purchased for $100 million back in 2006.

- **Del Monte** — *Owns the Nature's Recipe, Milk-Bone and Kibbles N Bits brands. Del Monte also does contract manufacturing of various private label dog foods.*

Other than pet foods, canning industry giant Del Monte mostly produces canned fruits and vegetables now that they sold their Star-Kist Tuna brand to Dongwan Enterprises, a South Korean company, for $300 million.

- **Diamond Pet Foods Inc** — *A pretty small fish compared to the first five, Diamond owns the Diamond, Diamond Naturals, Chicken Soup for the Dog Lover's Soul, Kirkland, and Taste of the Wild brands, and does contract manufacturing for Dick Van Patton's Natural Balance, Wellness, 4Health Pet Food, Canidae and Solid Gold.*

Diamond only owns manufacturing facilities for dry food and contracts out its canned foods, so some of these brands (including those owned by Diamond itself) also offer products produced by other contract manufacturers like Simmons. It's worth noting that foods produced by Diamond have been involved in several recalls in the past few years and at least one of its plants has been cited by FDA for quality-control deficiencies of a fairly appalling nature.

- **Simmons Pet Foods Inc** – *A giant in the poultry processing industry, Simmons is the second-largest employer in the state of Arkansas after Tyson. Its pet food division is probably now the largest contract manufacturer and private label producer of dog food in the country and produces canned foods for most of the dog food industry, with the exception of Purina.*

Simmons bought embattled contract manufacturer Menu Foods in 2010 for $239 million (after Menu suffered huge financial losses is the "tainted wheat-gluten" scandal that killed untold thousands of pets), which added several more dog food factories and a lot of long-term contracts with big-name dog food companies (like Iams) to Simmons's holdings. As their website states: *"In a world obsessed with brand names, ours is conspicuously absent. You brand is our brand, and we wouldn't have it any other way."*

Other contract manufacturers of both canned and dry dog foods whose names you've likely also never heard but which manufacture foods for well-known brands include the following:

- **CJ Foods** – *makes Blue Buffalo and Burns Pet Health canned foods*

- **Ohio Pet Foods** – *makes Blue Buffalo and Life's Abundance dry foods*

- **Chenango Valley Pet Foods** — *makes Drs Foster & Smith, Back to Basics* **Blue Sky** – *makes Solid Gold.*

- **Crosswinds Industries**—*makes Nature's Logic*

- **American Nutrition**—*makes Natural Balance*

- **Ainsworth**—*makes Dad's, VF, Rachel Ray's Nutrish*

For the record, Blue Sky is actually the contract manufacturing division of *Merrick Pet Care*, the dog food division of *Tejas Industries*, a family-owned Texas corporation whose holding include a nearby rendering plant that formerly operated under the name *Hereford Bi-products*. Merrick also manufactures and sells dog food under its own name.

The list of companies that produce their own dry foods in their own manufacturing facilities is far more limited, but includes the following ones, none of whom appear to have run afoul of the FDA in the quality-control department:

- **Nestle-Purina**— *as mentioned above, Purina manufactures all its Purina-branded products and its new ProPlan Training Treats in its own plants, the only one of the "giants" to do so.*

- **Champion Pet Foods**—*a Canadian company that owns and manufactures the Acana and Orijin brands at its own plant in Canada.*

- **Central Garden & Pet Company**—*a California company that produces the Breeder's Choice Pinnacle and Avaderm brands at its company-owned Irwindale, CA plant.*

- **Fromm's**— *a Wisconsin-based company that manufactures its Fromm's dry foods at its company-owned Mequon WI plant.*

In other words, with very few exceptions, dog food branding has become a shell game, and it's pretty hard for the average consumer to figure out where a brand of dog food is actually made, or who actually owns the company.

The problem with this is that because of green-washing, consumers often think they're

buying from small companies who use

only "carefully hand-selected wholesome" ingredients, when they're not.

Instead, they're paying a premium price for the *illusion* that their dog food is made in a sunny kitchen full of cheerful elves mixing up vats of healthy meats and fresh colorful veggies from the local health food store, when odds are good it's made in a humongous totally mechanized factory (some of which are state-of-the-art and some of which are pretty awful) that may also manufacture much cheaper brands, using many of *the exact same raw ingredients*.

Yup, that's right—*the exact same ingredients*. Why is that? Because..........

It is the *contract manufacturer* who purchases the ingredients,

NOT the company whose brand name is on the bag.

For example, chicken meal is all purchased by the ton by the contract manufacturer from rendering plants and trucked in. It is frankly unlikely to be "carefully hand-selected", no matter what the pretty bags or company websites say. And every company they contract manufacture for is getting the same chicken meal.

Another major problem with commercial dog food is that the labeling requirements are pretty loose. There are really no rules for terms like "all-natural", "organic", "holistic", or "human-grade", which represent the fastest-growing segment of the dog food market. Basically, you can call your dog food "Good Earth's Holistic All-Natural Organic Blend" even if it's made from recycled Twinkies and there's no law against it.

In fact, no dog food that meets the national nutritional guidelines can qualify as USDA 100% certified organic, because all of the vitamin and mineral supplements required to meet the guidelines are not available in organic form.

This makes all those websites that "rank" different brands of dog food pretty much useless, because they are all based on what the company itself says about their products and what's in them, *which is written by professional marketing guys who've probably never been to the plant and which simply may or may not be true.*

In some cases, these ratings may be *worse* than useless.

Here's an appalling example:

One small company, which invariably receives "5 stars" on all the dog food rating websites, was recently sent a warning letter by the FDA. Why?

A random check of their products revealed that the meat in their "Lamb and Rice Dog Food" was really not lamb at all, but rather according to FDA analysis was *"bovine material"*.

For their "Grain-free Duck Pet Food", *"analytical sample results did not detect the presence of duck in the product."*

FDA did not specify what actually *was* in the food, just that it was *not* duck, which is a little scary if you think about it. And this is one of the most expensive dog foods on the market!

It should also be noted that although the company was cited for "adulteration" by the FDA, these products *were not recalled*, presumably because they did not pose a danger to animals or humans. And their 5 star ratings are STILL up there on the "dog food rating" websites.

Several other small companies boasting 5 star ratings from these websites have their dog food made by contract manufacturers who've received warning letters from FDA within the last two years citing them for salmonella contamination detected in their products, and/or detailing serious deficiencies in their manufacturing processes in areas ranging from temperature control and sanitation to failure of their raw ingredients to meet the nutritional specifications listed. Although these letters are all archived deepthe bowels of the FDA's website and technically available to the public, odds are the average consumer will never be aware of their existence.

Meat and poultry meals ALL come from rendering plants,

no matter how dog food companies try to spin that unappetizing fact.

The reason is simple: although rendering lard can actually be done in one's kitchen (assuming you have a big pot, access to the fat of a freshly slaughtered hog and don't mind the smell), rendering whole fresh animal *carcass*es into safe and usable meal requires literally millions of dollars in high-tech equipment if one does not wish to run afoul of the EPA.

Farmers do *not* render their own chicken meal—it *all* comes from rendering plants. Chicken meal is not "carefully prepared from whole chicken breasts" like the kind you buy at Publix, no matter how much people *want* to believe that. (There's really no tooth fairy, either.) Making dog food is a lot like making any other modern processed meat product like chicken nuggets, hamburger, sausage and hot dogs—decidedly unappetizing. (Think pink slime.)

But the biggest danger in commercial dog food lies not in the

admittedly unappetizing "sourcing" of ingredients

or the possible long-term adverse effects on the immune system from

genetically modified ingredients,

but rather in the possibilities of *adulteration and contamination*,

because these two can kill your dog within days.

Over the past 10 years alone, adulterated and contaminated dog food has actually *sickened and killed thousands of pets* who ate the products before they were recalled.

And in the case of e-Coli and salmonella, this contamination has the potential to do the same to people who come in contact with these dogs. (In April 2012, a rare form of salmonella linked to contaminated dog food produced at a Diamond plant in Gaston SC sickened over a dozen people in 14 states, including a 4 month old baby.)

In 2007, adulteration of imported wheat gluten (an ingredient routinely used in many human and animal foods) with melamine caused kidney failure resulting in illness and death in thousands of pets across the country. Because the manufacture of so much dog food is outsourced, one single contract manufacturer who purchased this contaminated ingredient, Menu Foods, was responsible for the recall of *nearly 60 different brands*, including 5 of the 6 top-branded dog food companies in the US.

As with human food, because of the way commercial dog foods are sourced, manufactured, and packaged, contamination by food-borne pathogens (like salmonella or e-Coli) can occur at any point in the process, *even if the manufacturer has good quality control.*

The only real defense against this (in both the human and canine food chain) is to constantly test for adulteration and contamination at every point in the process, and if it is detected, to quickly identify the source of contamination and/or the ingredient containing it, immediately shut down the plant producing it, notify customers and remove all contaminated products from retail shelves ASAP if they've gotten that far.

Not surprisingly, this gets a whole lot easier if the company whose name is on the bag actually controls the entire process.

Companies that purchase their own ingredients, manufacture food in their own plants and

control the sale of it have the best chance of getting a product off retailer's shelves in a hurry

if it's found to contain a potentially harmful pathogen.

As became appallingly obvious during the dog food recalls of 2007, companies that outsource the purchase of ingredients as well as the manufacturing and packaging of their foods simply cannot do that—in fact, it turned out that some of them did not even know what ingredients were really in their own dog food!

So… if you don't want to cook your own dog food, the safest option is probably to buy a brand from a company that purchases its own ingredients and manufactures its foods in its own facilities, and whose quality-control standards are such that they've not received any warning letters from the FDA concerning violations in the last few years at least. And the company should allow the public to tour their manufacturing facilities.

Buying dog food from a company that won't allow you to see where it's made

is like buying a puppy from a breeder that won't allow you to visit:

Odds are, there's a good reason for it.

So how, exactly, do you determine if a company actually purchases its own ingredients and manufactures its own food? *The easiest way is to call the company and ASK them.* Every dog food company has a phone number on its website and its product labels. If you ask the questions, they'll pretty much have to answer them.

The most important question is: *"Do you own your own manufacturing plants? If not, what is the name and address of the company currently manufacturing your dog food?"* Another good question is: *"Are all of your ingredients sourced from the US?"*

If they hem and haw, don't know, or flat-out won't tell you, for Heaven's sake *don't buy their food*.

It's also important to note that although a company may manufacture all its own dry dog food, it may *not* manufacture its canned foods or dog treats, many of which are imported (usually from China), and they rarely volunteer that information

So What About Dog Treats?

Basically, they're worse. If the number of annual recalls is any indication (which it is), commercial dog treats in general seem to be much more susceptible to contamination than dry or even canned dog food.

In particular, given its symbiotic relationship with food-borne pathogens, the idea of drying poultry into jerky is really stupid, which is probably why no human culture has ever eaten it. *To keep your dog safe, don't buy dog jerky treats AT ALL, and don't try to make them yourself, either.*

With few exceptions, most dog treats are imported

or contract-manufactured in the US with ingredients imported from Asia,

mostly because it's cheaper.

The whole "dog treat" business is sheer anthropomorphism anyhow. In general, dogs in the US have gotten a lot fatter as the treat market has grown, and overweight dogs are way more prone to health problems.

No matter what the "foodie" trainers say, it's far better for a dog's *health* if he works for praise rather than for constant food rewards… and he'll be a lot more reliable, too. (Drug detection dogs have been traditionally rewarded with a quick Kong toss, so odds are your Dood can cheerfully execute a simple sit-stay without having to bribe him with treats.)

. Probably the *safest* thing to do in the treats department is to just buy your dog a box of little organic crackers made for people (wheat is one of the few grains not genetically modified, just for the record), or bake your own dog biscuits, which is really easy. A pocketful of Rice Chex cereal is a time-honored training treat for young puppies, and they are little enough so you don't have to wait forever for the puppy to chew them.

If you need something really spectacular to reward your dog with (like after a grooming session), just buy some beef jerky *made for people*, for Heaven's sake.

Made entirely in the US, Jack Link's is hard to beat, and you can buy it at virtually any checkout counter in America, including the one at your local gas station. But even then, dehydrated meat should only be given to a dog in little teeny-weeny pieces because without the 80% water that comprises fresh meat, you're giving the dog a lot of protein.

And giving him constant food rewards just for being *adorable* is a bad idea on many levels—Lord only knows what the dog thinks he's being rewarded for, but odds are it won't improve his overall behavior. (Just for the record, that focused intense stare most people read as "begging" is actually *demanding* in dog language, and giving in to a dog's demands for food will not raise your status in his eyes.)

What about "Raw Feeding"?

In the world of dogs, probably nothing is more controversial than raw feeding. The whole concept began with a book by an Australian veterinarian named Ian Billinghurst back in 1993 called "Give Your Dog a Bone". His BARF Diet™ is now commercially produced and is sold on his website, barfworld.com. (*I swear I am not making this up.*)

Although raw feeding proponents maintain such a huge presence on the internet it seems like practically everyone is doing it, surveys show that actually only around 2% of dogs in the US are actually raw-fed.

No Hard Science ... Yet

Besides what might be called the Yuck Factor (many people are just not comfortable finding old dog-hair-covered chunks of raw chicken backs under the couch), the main problem with raw feeding is that *virtually all of its health advantages are anecdotal.*

To date there has never been a single controlled scientific study

to either support or debunk the claims of raw food's

nutritional superiority over cooked food.

Proponents of raw diets claim that enzymes critical to digestion of protein are destroyed by heating. This is absolutely true. But dogs, like most protein-based animals, produce their *own* digestive enzymes, so this is really sort of a dumb argument.

In fact, one of the few digestive enzymes canines do *not* produce is amylase, which allows for the digestion of raw plant matter. Dogs just can't get any useful amount of nutrients from raw grains and veggies, although they're great for people.

As far as destruction of the protein itself goes, controlled laboratory studies have shown that the protein levels in fish is reduced by a whopping 1.5% after heating for 10 minutes at 266 degrees, which represents some seriously overcooked fish.

An egg (one of the most complete animal-based proteins on the planet) contains 6 grams of protein cooked or raw. The *digestibility* of the protein in that egg, however, goes from 51% if consumed raw to a whopping 90% if cooked, which would appear to be an argument for cooking it.

The same is true of many vegetables and grains like corn (which for unknown reasons people suddenly believe is indigestible to dogs). Once cooked, the digestibility of corn, and the bioavailability of its nutrients, goes up to over 90%. (Raw corn, like all other grains, is pretty indigestible, but you probably already know that. And GMO corn has its own problems.)

In case you're curious, the digestibility of various foodstuffs is determined by measuring the nutrient levels of what goes into one end of the dog and comparing those numbers to the nutrient levels of what comes out the other end using *spectrophotometric analysis*. The difference is the percentage of digestibility. This is obviously not something the average dog owner can do at home.

But Isn't Raw Feeding More Natural?

As far as raw food being the "natural" diet for canines, that's pretty hard to argue with since the species has never managed to master the art of cooking, but it's also worth knowing that wolves in zoos, who are generally fed commercial dog food, live several years longer on average than the oldest recorded wolf in the wild. This may or may not actually have anything to do with nutrition, but it's a fact nonetheless, and at the very least it would indicate that cooked food doesn't *shorten* their lives.

All that said, anecdotal evidence indicates that a lot of dogs apparently thrive on a raw diet. The truth is, dogs apparently can thrive on *lots* of different diets—it's one of their strongest evolutionary advantages as a species.

But raw feeding (whether prepared at home or purchased commercially) has one HUGE disadvantage, and its importance cannot be understated, especially in the US:

Cooking kills food-borne pathogens that can pose a serious health risk to PEOPLE.

Alhough most healthy adult dogs appear less susceptible to them, food-borne pathogens like salmonella, E.coli, and campylobacter do sicken and kill thousands of people each year in the US alone. These three pathogens are ubiquitous in raw chicken—according to the CDC, probably three-quarters of the chicken sold in grocery stores is carrying one or another of them, and thanks to widespread antibiotic use in the poultry industry, many strains are now antibiotic-resistant. (In fact, new research indicates that some 85% of human urinary tract infections are caused by E.coli from chicken.)

No matter how carefully raw meat is handled prior to feeding, studies have shown that dogs fed a raw diet shed these pathogens in their saliva, urine and feces. As this presents a clear health hazard to humans who may come in contact with it, neither the FDA nor the USDA recommends feeding uncooked meat to household pets. Because they visit hospitals and nursing homes, where compromised immune systems abound, Delta Society, one of the nation's most-respected therapy dog associations, will no longer allow raw-fed dogs in its PetPartners Therapy program. Bottom line with raw feeding is this:

It may indeed be perfectly healthy for dogs, but raw feeding presents a serious and well-documented potential danger for the humans they may come in even casual contact with—especially babies, children, the elderly, and those with autoimmune disease or immune systems compromised by chemotherapy.

In a litigious society like ours (and where it seems like every third person you run into has an autoimmune disease) that alone should give one pause.

Actually FEEDING Your Goldendoodle

Now that you have the facts about the production and marketing of commercial dog food, you should have sufficient confidence to decide whether to stay with the food he's on, to change to another brand you're more comfortable with, or to cook for your dog yourself. (The last choice is still the safest and healthiest.)

Whatever you decide, this is something you'll want to do slowly by mixing the foods incrementally, or you will have "digestive upset" as sure as God made little green apples, and you'll have to clean up the results. And probably for the first couple weeks you'll want to stick with what he's used to eating, because there have been enough major changes in his short life already.

So the next step is actually getting your puppy to EAT. An awful lot of Goldendoodles are reported to be picky eaters, much to their owners' collective distress. This tendency is probably inherited to some degree from their notoriously picky Poodle ancestors, since the average Golden Retriever would eat gravel if you put it in his bowl. Not surprisingly, F1b Doods seem to be pickier as a rule than the F1s, and dogs with Mini or Toy Poodles behind them are generally pickier than those bred from Standards. But genetic tendencies aside, exactly how picky a dog ends up is largely owner-determined.

What typically happens is that the owner comes home with his new puppy and a bag of *the exact same food he's been eating since he started on solid food,* and the first time it's offered the puppy won't eat it. In fact, he looks at it like it's some sort of toxic waste you've put in his bowl to poison him.

There is no way to overstate this:

What you do in the next 48 hours will determine whether you have a picky eater for life,

or a dog who'll cheerfully and enthusiastically eat anything you put in his bowl.

Think about this carefully for a minute— besides his mother's milk, this particular food is *all your puppy has ever eaten.* In his limited experience, that's what food IS…he has absolutely no framework for "liking" it or "not liking" it.

Odds are, he's not eating because his system is stressed from changing homes, which means his level of stress hormones like cortisol are elevated. The first thing a dog's instincts tell him to do when this happens is to keep his tummy empty— it's hard-wired into his DNA from much earlier times, and is a logical part of the fight-or-flight response. Whether one ends up fighting or fleeing, it's easier to do it on an empty stomach. (In fact, man is probably the *only* animal that actually eats as a response to stress, or while traveling. And you can see how well *that's* worked out for us!)

If your puppy refuses a meal, simply pick up the dish after 10-15 minutes

and wait until his next scheduled mealtime,

at which point you simply offer him the exact same meal again.

And for Heaven's sake do not add anything to "tempt his palate", which is anthropomorphism at its worst. Dogs have spectacular olfactory capabilities compared to ours, but it is now known that they have significantly fewer taste buds. This should not come as a big surprise to dog owners…I mean, really—this is a species that collectively views a dirty cat litter box as an all-you-can-eat buffet. Gourmands they're not.

Once you start changing foods to get him to eat, you allow the puppy to initiate a game called "what do I feel like eating today?" and *it will never end*, because when it comes to this game, dogs play to win. It will also lead to other behavioral problems.

In the world of canines, the *alpha* controls the food,

which is what the "picky-eating" game is REALLY about.

The pack's alphas eat what and when they want, and pack status is what is being tested here. Unless a dog is simply not hungry or is actually ill, picky eating is generally about *control*, not taste. This is also why keeping food down all the time so the dog can eat whenever he feels like it is not a good idea. A dog who thinks he is in charge of his own food will almost always expand the battle for dominance into other areas…growling over food and then possessions invariably comes next.

Missing a meal is not going to hurt a healthy puppy – the canine is by definition a "stuff-or-starve" predator and in the wild, food for cubs does not appear on a rigid schedule. The reason we keep our puppy on a schedule is because it makes housebreaking much easier, not because it's critical to his metabolism.

(Clearly, if the puppy appears lethargic, is vomiting and/or has a fever, you need to call the vet…you do need to exercise some common sense here.) But odds are, if a puppy doesn't eat, the next time you put the same food down, he *will* eat it, because he's probably now hungry.

Switching Foods

The other big mistake you'll want to avoid is changing dog foods on a regular basis. Unless your dog food brand has been recalled or you've lost confidence in the company, you can really feed the same food forever, with the exception of maybe switching from puppy to adult formula. (Even then, it's best to stay with the same brand and just switch formulas.)

Although humans think it's the spice of life, variety is just not a big deal for dogs, and it upsets both their psyches and their stomachs. If your Dood is eating his food, is not too fat, has nice firm stools and his coat is thick and shiny………don't switch foods just for variety's sake or you could regret it.

For some reason (probably because of all the experts on the internet!) as soon as a dog starts scratching, the owner assumes it's because he's "allergic" to something in his dog food and will immediately switch to another brand. This is usually a mistake.

Veterinary literature over the years has shown that 90% of dog allergies

are caused by reactions to something *other than food.*

If your dog is scratching a lot, before you change dog foods you should probably run a flea comb through him nose to tail, because according to veterinary data, that's the #1 reason dogs scratch.

If there are no fleas and no flea dirt (a dog can scratch for hours after a flea bit him and jumped off or died, especially if he's allergic to flea saliva) then you need to next look at his environment for the possibility of a contact allergen—the stuff you are washing your floors or his bed with might be a good place to start! Many a puppy has stopped scratching when his owner stopped using a chemical-laden Swiffer on the floor. (Floor-cleaning products should be the first thing you look at if his underside is itchy or reddened.)

What else causes itchiness?

Generally speaking, pollen, mold, dust and environmental toxins, which include all the stuff we spray on our furniture, floors and in the air, as well as the neurotoxins we squirt on him to keep fleas at bay. Statistically, both inhalant and contact allergens are nine times more likely to cause a reaction in dogs than allergens in his food.

Recent vaccinations are also a possibility—we now know that all reactions to vaccines are not immediate anaphylactic ones, but may be more subtle and delayed.

So anyway don't keep switching foods – if your dog IS predisposed to allergies, constantly introducing new novel proteins can actually increase the odds of a food allergy developing, and you will have done more harm than good.

Although it is baffling to us, a dog who's a good eater will be absolutely thrilled when you put down his bowl, even if he's been eating the exact same food for 15 years. (It's one of the great things about dogs.) Adding a dollop of yogurt or a handful of cut-up cooked chicken to plain old kibble will totally knock him out. And contrary to what the dog food companies would like us to believe, some fresh unprocessed food (also known as "table food") is good for everybody, including us. Cooked (even canned) carrots or green beans or pumpkin or sweet potato are also good choices, and dogs can utilize all the good vitamins and phytonutrients in bright-colored vegetables if they're cooked.

How much should you feed?

This is probably the most important question of all.

The answer here is simple– if you want your dog to live a long and healthy life, you need to feed him enough to keep him lean, *and no more*. Most American dogs are NOT lean, by the way – in fact the obesity rate in dogs increased from 44% in 2002 to 51% in 2011, which is alarming on several levels.

An Important Study

In a groundbreaking study led by researchers at Nestlé Purina and including scientists at Cornell, the University of Illinois, Michigan State University and the University of Pennsylvania (published in the *Journal of the American Veterinary Medical Association* back in May 2002 if you want to read the whole thing) 24 pairs of Labrador retriever siblings between 6 and 8 weeks of age -- matched by sex and weight-- were selected, with one of each pair assigned to eat 25 percent less of the same food than its sibling.

The dogs were a part of the study from the time they were weaned until they died, and their health was closely monitored throughout their lives. The study lasted 14 years. The median age of dogs in the reduced-diet group, the researchers found, was 13 years -- 1.8 years longer than the median age of dogs fed a normal diet. (That would be over 13 years longer for a person, just to put it in perspective.) And they were healthier for their entire lives.

Leanness is especially critical in Goldendoodles, because they are descended from two breeds predisposed to canine hip dysplasia (CHD). And how much you feed your dogs has a lot to do with whether or not a dog develops it.

.In the study, in the control group of "well-fed" dogs, 16 had CHD at 2 years of age, and 8 were normal.

However, of the 24 dogs in the "restricted diet" group, only 8 had CHD and 16 were normal!

The reduced diet was also found to reduce the risk of developing osteoarthritis, which generally is one of the most common sources of chronic pain in dogs.

Only six of the 24 dogs on the reduced diet developed osteoarthritis of the hip by age 10, while 19 of the 24 control group dogs did.

And for the dogs on reduced rations who did develop CHD, the odds of developing concurrent osteoarthritis decreased by 57%.

If that isn't a strong argument for keeping your Dood lean, nothing is.

Roly-poly fat puppies are not healthy puppies,

any more than roly-poly fat kids are healthy kids.

If your puppy is not lean (this means he should have a waist when viewed from above, a tuck-up when viewed from the side and although you shouldn't be able to see his ribs you should be able to feel them clearly enough to count them) he is headed for health problems no matter what his breeding.

But when it comes right down to it, the most important thing to remember about feeding your dog is not to obsess about it. Dogs are notoriously allelemenetic in their behaviors, and if *you* obsess about what your dog is eating, odds are so will he. And if you really think about it, dogs have managed to thrive on man's leftovers for millennia, which is also worth remembering.

.

CHAPTER SEVEN:

The Holistic Goldendoodle

(or...how to raise a healthy dog in a toxic world)

OK, you might as well be forewarned:

This is NOT your standard boilerplate "Breed Book Health Chapter" by a long shot.

For one thing, it's 45 pages long , which could be a record, and pretty technical. (But this is important stuff., so plow through it. Strong coffee may help.) And at no point does it say things like "Your vet will know which shots your puppy needs", or "consult your veterinarian about which flea preventative is best for your dog".

Instead, it assumes you are an intelligent person who wants to take responsibility for your own dog's health. It also assumes that you want to make the best choices for your dog *based on the most current scientific research available,* which an unfortunate number of clinical vets do not appear to possess.

Given what is now understood about immunology, the decisions you make for your puppy right out of the gate regarding things like vaccinations will determine to a large degree how healthy he remains throughout his life, regardless of the genetic hand he was dealt. And if your Dood is already an adult....well, read this chapter anyway, because when it comes to healthy choices, it's never to late to start!

From the standpoint of overall health and longevity, the Goldendoodle should have one huge advantage over both his "parent" breeds – what geneticists call *heterosis*, or hybrid vigor. In fact, this hybrid vigor is one of the reasons a lot of people decide to get a Goldendoodle in the first place!

Yet in recent years owners are beginning to report more of the same allergies, autoimmune diseases and even cancers that are plaguing purebreds, which is more than a little alarming. What's going on?

Part of the problem is that there are more and more backcrossed Goldendoodles being produced in an effort to improve the hypoallergenic and non-shedding qualities, as well as in an effort to bring down size. These dogs, designated as F1bs and F2bs, are most commonly the result of crossing an F1 Goldendoodle with a purebred Poodle, or in the case of an F2b, crossing an F1b back to a Poodle.

But as is often the case with any deliberate breeding strategy designed to genetically cement (or "fix") a particular trait, backcrossing is a double-edged sword. The tradeoff here may well be in reduced immune function, because the danger in backcrossing is that it reduces the genetic diversity gained through the original crossing of two unrelated breeds pretty rapidly, especially in the genes of the DLA complex, which are involved with immune recognition.

Understanding the DLA genes

Three of these DLA (which stands for "dog leukocyte antigen") genes, all located on canine chromosome 12, regulate the recognition of foreign antigens and evoke an appropriate antibody response. Why is it critical that you understand what they do?

Virtually all autoimmune diseases in dogs identified to date

have been associated with specific alleles in these three Class II DLA genes.

They are also under what is called *high linkage disequilibrium*, which means they are inherited as a "block" rather than individually. This three-gene block is called a *haplotype*. A dog inherits one DLA haplotype from each parent. In virtually all autoimmune diseases studied to date, *homozygosis* (where a dog inherits identical haplotypes from both parents) increases the risk of disease.

Now here's where it gets sticky for the Goldendoodle. No less than 10 autoimmune diseases have been identified in the Standard Poodle, which is a breed with little diversity in the DLA genes. In fact, a recent study revealed that out of a possible 14 haplotypes identified in the breed, over 90% of Poodles from both the US and UK shared a *single haplotype*, (that would be DRB1*01501/ DQA1*00601/DQB1*02301 for the chronically curious) and around 50% of them are actually homozygous for it. Because they inherited an identical copy from both parents, these dogs can only pass that haplotype to 100% of their offspring.

Given that, one doesn't have to be a rocket scientist (or even a geneticist) to figure out that repeatedly backcrossing a Goldendoodle to another Poodle significantly increases the odds that some of the resulting puppies are going to end up with the exact same DLA haplotype (and resulting immune problems) as your average purebred Poodle, and gains made through hybrid vigor will be lost. Each successive backcross increases the odds of that happening.

The good news is that even with autoimmune diseases which have been clearly linked to a particular haplotype or single allele in the DLA genes, the presence of that haplotype or allele *only increases risk*, it doesn't guarantee the disease will develop, as would happen with a classical genetic disorder.

And hybrid vigor is NOT a panacea for all ills that may befall a dog. Good health, in dogs as well as people, most often involves both genes and environment (that's what that whole "lean dog study" was about), and *understanding the interplay between the two* is critical to keeping your Dood healthy, whether it is genetically blessed or not.

Understanding Disease and Heritability

There are basically five different kinds of diseases (or *disorders*) in dogs, some of which are highly heritable, others which are far less so and some of which are not heritable at all. (This is worth knowing because in general, hybrid vigor has the greatest positive effect on traits with low rather than high heritability.) While we're pretty much stuck with the genetic hand the dog was dealt on the first bunch, many of the others can be largely avoided through the choices we, as responsible owners, make for our dogs. Here's a brief rundown:

Classical genetic disorders.

Although a lot of diseases are heritable to varying degrees and may "run in families", true genetic disorders are actually rarer by comparison, and are almost always single gene disorders.

A *single gene disorder* is caused entirely by the action of a single *mutated* gene (called an allele or allelic variation) inherited from one or both parents, and there are no other genetic or environmental factors involved. Contrary to what you may read in the media about some new "cancer gene" or "autism gene", *genes do not cause diseases.* Mother Nature is not a Nihilist—genes are simply the recipes for specific proteins or enzymes needed for an organism to survive and reproduce. It is when a particular gene *mutates* (usually through an error in copying during meiosis which alters the "recipe" for that gene) and the mutated form of that gene is passed to the next generation that a genetic disease may result. Or the mutation may be totally benign or even advantageous—gene mutations are responsible for evolution, after all, and without them we'd all still be swimming around in the ocean and breathing through gills.

If the mutated disease-causing allele is *dominant*, inheriting one copy from either parent is all it takes to be affected— the FGF4 mutation associated with short-legged dwarfism would be an example here, as dogs with only one copy of the gene variant have short legs.

If it is *recessive*, as with Type II Von Willebrand's Disease (which causes abnormal bleeding due to insufficient clotting factor in the blood), a dog must inherit one copy of the causative gene from each parent in order to be affected. A dog who inherits just one copy will be a "carrier" and will pass that gene to half his offspring, but will not be affected himself because the normal, or "wild-type" allele inherited from the other parent can perform the job of that gene—in this case producing clotting factor—by itself.

Although these are often the easiest genes to identify, cures for single gene disorders are usually rare to nonexistent, and gene testing both parents prior to breeding is the only way to avoid them. Like Von Willebrand's, PRA (which causes irreversible blindness in many breeds of dogs) is another recessive genetic disease, and like VWB, also occurs in both Golden Retrievers and Poodles. The good news is gene testing is available for both these diseases.

Diseases like these are considered *100% heritable*, which means if you inherit the causative gene mutation(s), you are going to get the disease. Period.

Whether or not the immune system is robust, or whether or not a dog's parents are of the same breed or two different breeds won't change that one iota, so there is no advantage provided by hybrid vigor at all.

And although this argument is the one most often used by purebred dog enthusiasts to dismiss the advantage of hybrids, the truth is most of the disorders that plague modern dogs are NOT single gene disorders.

Pathogenic disorders.

Also called *infectious diseases*, these are caused by invading pathogens, most commonly viruses and bacteria. Lyme disease, Leptospirosis, Parvo and Distemper would all be examples of pathogenic diseases—the first two are caused by invading bacteria, while the last two are viral.

A dog's resistance to these "bugs" (many of which are pretty ubiquitous in the environment) is largely dependent on the ability of his immune system to identify them and mount an appropriate response after exposure. On the surface, the heritability of infectious diseases is pretty much 0%, because whether or not you get one is entirely dependent on environmental exposure. In other words, no matter what his genetic makeup, if a dog never crosses paths with the distemper virus, he simply cannot contract the disease we call Distemper.

On the other hand, the immune system has a LOT to do with how well the body deals with foreign pathogens when they do cross paths.

This is because although the two terms are often used interchangeably, *infection* and *disease* are two different things from an immunological standpoint. Infection, which is the invasion by and multiplication of a foreign pathogen upon exposure, may or may not progress to disease, depending upon the body's ability to halt that multiplication before it gets out of hand and causes damage to the host. This ability to halt the proliferation of foreign pathogens is what we generally refer to as *disease resistance*.

Innumerable studies in both plants and animals in recent years have demonstrated that diversity in the immune-regulating genes of both the Major Histocompatability Complex (the DLA complex in dogs) and the various cytokine loci confer resistance to everything from potato blight to HIV. In fact, this theory of *heterozygote advantage*, which won a Nobel Prize for Doherty and Zinkernagel back in 1996, has become the cornerstone of modern immunology.

Not surprisingly then, resistance to infectious disease is one area where F1 hybrids have huge advantage, because hybridization produces genetic diversity in the offspring.

Environmental disorders.

This bunch, which has gotten a fair amount of press in recent years, are not influenced by genetics much at all, because diseases caused by exposure to environmental toxins both natural and manmade are pretty dose-dependent.

In other words, no matter what your genetics, exposure above one level will cause sickness, while exposure above another level will result in certain death. (Lead and mercury poisoning famously fall into this category, as well as exposure to radiation and most chemical herbicides and pesticides.)

This occurs because the immune system is primarily designed to recognize live pathogens—it has little or no ability to mount an immune defense against toxins or inorganic "toxicants". Essentially, we're talking about poisons here.

And because the body's ability to excrete poisons is limited, the effects of most are cumulative – in other words, exposure to small amounts over a long period of time can have the same effect on the body in the end as a lot of exposure all at once. In general, the less exposure to toxins an organism is exposed to, the better its chances of long-term survival. The greater the exposure, the greater the chance of serious illness and death.

What falls into this category? *A LOT of stuff, unfortunately*. In the "naturally-occurring" department we have toxic heavy metals like mercury and aluminum (which are used as preservatives and adjuvants in many canine vaccines), uranium and lead, as well as the "true" toxins (such as the post-synaptic neurotoxin *a-Cobratoxin* unique to cobras) produced by various snakes, insects, and plants and the icky little microorganisms called *endotoxins*.

In the "man-made" department we have ionic radiation (most commonly from x-rays) and somewhere in the neighborhood of around 60,000 man-made chemicals, most of which are toxic at some level of exposure.

These range from ethylene glycol, the killer ingredient in antifreeze, to BPA found in plastics, to synthetic neurotoxins like those found in flea and heartworm preventatives. In fact, according to the EPA, of the 3,000 high-volume production chemicals (meaning over a million pounds of each is produced in or imported to the US each year) *over 40% of them have never even been TESTED for toxicity*.

Environmental disorders can manifest in many ways, the most well-known of which are cancers.

So this one is the exception to the rule— although the heritability is pretty much zilch, hybrid vigor cannot help much here, either. The only real defense is to avoid unnecessary exposure to toxins insofar as possible in the first place, which is the owner's responsibility.

Nutritional disorders.

Nutritional disorders arise when the dog's diet is deficient in one or more essential amino acids, vitamins, or minerals. In general, people probably obsess a lot more about possible nutritional deficiencies than they really need to, given that close to 50% of America's dogs now suffer from obesity.

Because dogs fed a homemade diet are generally given a vitamin/mineral supplement and all commercial dog food is formulated to contain the minimum daily requirement of nutrients, nutritional deficiencies in American dogs are now pretty rare, with the possible exception of Vitamin D, which can be "cooked off" in processing if the manufacturing plant is not careful about temperature. (Companies which do not maintain their own research facilities and have no in-house population of dogs on which to test their product are especially vulnerable here, because the *only* way to determine if a dog food contains the necessary levels of bioavailable nutrients when it comes out of the bag is to periodically run periodic blood levels on dogs actually eating it.) The good news is that dogs, like people, can manufacture all the Vitamin D they need if they're simply exposed to sunlight. The bad news is that dogs, like their owners, are spending a lot more time indoors than Mother Nature had ever imagined they would, but this is clearly something the owner can control.

Nutritional disorders rank pretty low in the heritability department, and so it's probably not surprising that the ability to utilize nutrients is increased with hybridization—what are called *feed conversion rates* are increased in hybrid offspring.

This means hybrids both grow faster and pack on fat easier than purebreds eating the same amount and type of food. This is a real advantage if you're raising beef cattle, but when it comes to dogs...*not so much.*

Since lean dogs live longer and are significantly less susceptible to hip dysplasia, the average Dood owner really needs to worry more about overfeeding and excess nutrition resulting in too-fast growth and weight gain than to worry about nutritional deficiencies. Because of this, Goldendoodle puppies destined to be medium-to-large-sized dogs should be fed a diet specifically designed for larger breeds, whether commercial or homemade.

Immune System Disorders.

This group, which comprises the last category, are probably the most complex of the bunch, but they all share the same common cause—*dysregulation of the immune system.* To quote our government's very own National Cancer Institute, from whence most of this information originated: "When the immune system malfunctions, it can release a veritable torrent of diseases and disorders."

This torrent can be broken down into three major categories, according to the nice folks at the NCI:

- **Allergies**.

An "allergy" is an inappropriate or exaggerated immune response to common substances that are not generally harmful. The most common allergies in dogs are flea bite dermatitis, caused by an exaggerated reaction to flea saliva, and atopia (often called atopic dermatitis), which is caused by a reaction to environmental allergens. Together these account for about 90% of itching and skin problems seen in dogs.

Atopic dermatitis in dogs is actually the canine version of hay fever, and is often triggered by the same things.

In both species, IgE antibodies (whose original function is protection against parasites) coat mast cells, where they sit waiting for contact with the parasite proteins for which they are sensitized. If encountered, the mast cell releases histamines which will attempt to destroy the invader. (This is why dogs with healthy immune systems are rarely bothered much by fleas, by the way.)

In allergic animals, the whole system is oversensitive and histamines are released inappropriately in response to innocuous substances such as pollen, mold, and dust mites. *In dogs, however, rather than being concentrated in the linings of the respiratory system, these mast cells are concentrated in the skin, with the greatest number found in the face and feet.* This is why dogs respond to allergens by scratching, rubbing their faces on furniture and chewing on their feet, rather than wheezing and sneezing like people.

It's worth noting (again!) that food allergies, which is usually the *first* thing owners suspect when a dog is itchy, actually account for only 10% of allergies in dogs. And about 80% of dogs with food allergies also have *atopy,* which accounts for the high failure rate in treating food allergies by diet manipulation alone.

As with autoimmune disease, susceptibility to allergies, which tend to run in both human and canine families, is linked to genes that control immune function. What causes the oversensitivity in some genetically susceptible individuals and not others ? Environmental triggers.

It is now pretty well understood that over-vaccinating a puppy can over-stimulate the immune system, and the AVMA does not recommend it for that reason.

Old Friends

And one of the most recent and intriguing possibilities for the recent rise in allergies in both children and dogs is the "Old Friends" hypothesis, which is admittedly *weird*, but actually makes sense as more is learned about the mechanism of immune response.

It has also long been known that, like autoimmune diseases, allergies and asthma are primarily diseases of the developed world. In developing countries, an array of parasites both protozoan and helminthic are a normal part of life and drinking water.

And in countries where children are exposed to parasites from birth,

allergies and asthma are virtually unknown.

As a country moves toward western-style modernization, parasitic infections among children decrease and allergies invariably increase almost in direct proportion. It has also been noted that in developed countries, children who grow up on farms or with pets are far less likely to develop asthma and allergies than children who grow up without animals around them. This is believed to be because where there are animals there are generally parasitic organisms of one sort or another.

Scientists now believe that neither of these observations is coincidental, and that early exposure to various parasitic organisms (the "old friends" with whom man has coexisted for millennia) may well be necessary for the proper development of the immune system. Could the same be true in dogs?

Although no one's yet done any similar studies on dogs in developing countries, any vet who's been in practice in the US for many years can tell you that allergies and chronic autoimmune disorders in dogs have increased significantly in their practices over the last few decades. What has changed?

Well, obviously, the dog has largely moved out of the barn and into the house. And as recently as thirty years ago, acute viral and bacterial diseases (like distemper and parvo) and parasite infestation were common, and made up a large portion of any vet's day-to-day practice.

Today, with no less than 25 different vaccines for dogs now available and the introduction of extremely effective systemic wormers like ivermectin back in the 1980s, these acute viral and bacterial diseases are now rare, but they've been replaced by allergies along with cancers and chronic disorders of the immune system.

Because of that, many forward-thinking vets now believe that a case can be made for the Old Friends hypothesis here as well, and suspect that keeping dogs on a year-round regimen of systemic wormers and anti-parasitics even when it's not necessary may well be contributing to the explosion of canine allergies as well as unnecessarily increasing his toxic load.

- ## Autoimmune Disorders

Autoimmune disorders are the result of the immune system's inability to distinguish between antigens produced by foreign pathogens and healthy tissue. Unable to determine the difference between "self" and "non-self", the immune system begins to attack its own tissue, resulting in what we call autoimmune disease.

Autoimmune disorders are the fastest-growing group of diseases in dogs,

especially among purebreds.

All autoimmune diseases recognized to date in dogs and humans have one thing in common—they all are associated with genes that regulate the immune response.

In dogs, these genes are gathered in a distinct region on canine chromosome 12. An identical region exists in all species of mammals and birds and is known as the major Histocompatibility Complex (MHC).

As noted earlier, the MHC of the dog has been designated the "dog leukocyte antigen' (DLA) complex. The DLA complex is divided into four regions, containing Class I,II, III, and IV genes.

A strong association between autoimmune disorders and the DLA class II genes has been shown for a number of canine disorders to date, including diabetes, hypothyroidism, Addison's disease, autoimmune arthritis, immune-mediated hemolytic anemia, chronic granulomatous meningoencephalitis (called PDE in pugs) and most recently chronic canine inflammatory liver disease.

Unlike single gene disorders, where a copy of the causative gene pretty much guarantees the disease, dogs with particular DLA haplotypes have been shown to have significantly increased *susceptibility* to these autoimmune diseases, especially when they have inherited the haplotype in a "double dose".

The main function of the MHC (DLA in dogs) is self/non-self recognition. The immune system must be able to identify every foreign protein that invades the body, whether it is on a bacteria, virus, fungi parasite, etc, as being "non-self", and to recognize every protein that is part of itself and not react immunologically to it.

As genetic variability is lost in the DLA, not only does the immune system

lose the ability to mount an appropriate response,

but the ability to differentiate between what is self and what is non-self

becomes more and more tenuous.

Although there are well over 140 different haplotypes spread across the canine world, most breeds have (quite inadvertently through selection for specific traits) now been reduced to only a very few, many of which are unique to a particular breed.

The fact that F1 hybrids are therefore likely to inherit an entirely different haplotype from each parent explains why they are in general more disease-resistant and less susceptible to the autoimmune diseases that plague their parent breeds.

- Cancer

In the final analysis, cancer really represents a catastrophic breakdown of the immune system. As cells constantly reproduce throughout the body, errors naturally occur, and it is the job of specific cells of the immune system to constantly seek and destroy these aberrant cells by recognizing the antigens they produce as "non-self" invaders. When this surveillance system fails, tumors form and cancer results.

It has long been recognized that genetic susceptibility to cancer may be due in part to inherited variation on MHC genes. In fact, in recent years, several specific HLA gene alleles have been associated with either susceptibility to, or protection from, various types of cancers in humans, including breast cancer.

The fact that different breeds of dogs are predisposed to different cancers pretty much reinforces the theory that cancers have a genetic component. By some estimates, purebreds have a cancer incidence rate nearly twice that of mixed breeds — fully 60% of Goldens die of cancer, for example, mostly hemangiosarcomas and lymphosarcomas. This indicates that genetic diversity is probably advantageous here as well.

Since even cancer susceptibility appears polygenic rather than caused by single gene mutations, a dog whose genes are a blend of two breeds is simply less likely to inherit all the genes (including those in the DLA complex) necessary for susceptibility to a cancer that may plague one of its parent breeds.

But the key word here is *susceptibility*. Cancer, like all disorders of the immune system, clearly has a genetic component, but the heritability is nowhere near 100% on any of them, even where a specific DLA haplotype has been identified that clearly increases risk.

Like allergies and autoimmune disorders, cancer is primarily a disease of the developed world, and that indicates some fairly strong environmental factors at work, which act as "triggers". For example, it is known that rabies vaccination can trigger a particularly lethal form of sarcoma at the injection site in both cats and dogs.

In other words, genetics may indeed load the gun....

but environment pulls the trigger.

By virtue of its genetic diversity, the immune system of a hybrid dog should be in pretty good shape genetically, but even the best immune system can be overwhelmed by environmental factors *that are totally within the owner's control.* Keeping your Goldendoodle healthy is not only the job of your vet....IT'S YOURS.

Choosing the Right Vet is Critical

The time to find a vet is *before* you bring your puppy home, and since this will be your puppy's Primary Care Provider, you want to put some thought and energy into finding the best one you can, not just the one who is closest or recommended by a dog-owning friend. You'll need to check out websites, make some phone calls and ask some questions.

As with breeders, all vets are *not* created equal –common sense should tell us that *somebody* graduated dead-last in class back at vet school, and also that the lucky recipient of that dubious distinction is unlikely to have a plaque displayed in his office commemorating it.

Likewise, some vets continue to keep up with current research in their field while others appear to have never cracked a book or read a scientific journal since the day they left vet school. You need to shop around to find one from the first category.

How can you tell who's who? As a general rule, vet practices that offer cutting-edge procedures like laser and stem-cell therapies are more likely to be run by vets who are keeping up with what's new in veterinary medicine, so that's certainly something to look for.

But the easiest way to tell if a veterinary practice is up-to-date

is by simply asking about their vaccination protocols.

For many years, vaccinations were administered annually whether the dog needed them or not, and no one thought much about it. Odds are your previous dogs were vaccinated annually, and with the old "5-way" and "7-way" combination vaccines. (A lot of "expert" advice on the internet still recommends this, by the way.)

All this changed back in 2003, when the American Animal Hospital Association, the American Veterinary Medical Association, and most veterinary teaching hospitals changed their vaccination protocols based on new research. All now recommend what are called the "core" vaccines for all dogs, with any others added only where necessary, and based on a dog's individual risk. Absolutely *none* now recommend annual vaccinations.

However, it is absolutely amazing how many vets in clinical practice around the country seemed to have missed the memo ten years ago. You do NOT want to take your puppy to one of those guys, because we now know this sort of vaccination regime can compromise his long-term health and well-being.

Although necessary to protect a puppy against infectious disease,

vaccines can be one of the triggers for autoimmune disorders.

So let's talk about vaccination here, because unless you're well-informed yourself, it's going to be pretty hard to figure out if a prospective vet is!

ALL the statements in boldface below were copied *verbatim* from the 2011 Vaccine Policy of the American Veterinary Medical Association, just so you know…read them very carefully.

Revaccination of patients with sufficient immunity does not necessarily add to their disease protection and may increase the potential risk of post-vaccination adverse events."

Exactly what are these adverse events?

"Possible adverse events include, but are not necessarily limited to, failure to immunize, anaphylaxis, immuno-suppression, autoimmune disorders, transient infections, long-term infected carrier states, and local development of tumors."

And when it comes to triggering autoimmune disorders, over-vaccination is clearly one trigger you do not *need* to pull. Here's why:

"Unnecessary stimulation of the immune system does not necessarily result in enhanced disease resistance, and may increase the potential risk of post-vaccination adverse events."

That's a pretty strong argument for not administering extra vaccines your puppy does not need. But how do you and your vet figure out if your dog actually needs another vaccination in order to be protected? Here's the AVMA again, with the answer:

"Due to the emergence of newer and improved antibody tests, serological assays are being used to determine immune status and establish vaccination protocols for animal patients."

These serological antibody assays are commonly called "titer tests" (that's pronounced like "tighter" just so you don't embarrass yourself) and they use a simple blood sample. Traditionally, vets have sent these out to an independent lab, which could end up costing over a hundred dollars and meant you had to wait at least several days for results. However, there are now at least two companies that sell in-house tests kits so vets can run titers inexpensively right in their offices and have the results in 15-20 minutes. The cost of in-house titer testing currently runs between $30 and $50 in most parts of the country, and is worth every penny.

As titers are accepted as valid by both the AVMA and the AAHA, any vet who still thinks they are "unreliable" and automatically re-vaccinates without running them has probably been out of vet school for more than 10 years and hasn't been keeping up. So "Do you routinely run titers in your practice?" is also a good question to ask.

But don't dogs need "booster shots"?

That's another outmoded theory. Aside from rabies, the "core" vaccines your dog needs are now all *modified live or recombinant vaccines* and according to all scientific evidence do *not* need to be boosted in order to be effective. *Killed vaccines*, which do require a "booster", have not been used in decades for these diseases.

According to the 2011 AAHA Guidelines (which any vet should have read) the newest research has shown that *a single dose* of a modified live vaccine administered to a dog over 14 weeks of age will both "prime" the immune system *and* provide immunity for several years.

Being immune is a lot like being pregnant—it's an either/or sort of thing. You cannot make an already immune dog *more* immune by "boosting" it— the dog either has immunity against a disease or he does not. And a dog with an antibody titer is immune. (Actually, because of what's called "cell memory", a lot of dogs who display an inadequate titer have demonstrated immunity when challenged, but most vets and owners prefer to err on the side of caution here.)

The ONLY reason puppies get a series of puppy shots

is because of possible interference from maternally derived antibodies,

not because the vaccines themselves need "boosting".

Here's what happens: Puppies display "passive immunity" for those diseases to which their mothers were exposed—either naturally or through vaccination. These maternally derived antibodies, passed primarily through colostrum in the first 48 hours of life, can last anywhere from 5 to 16 weeks, depending on the puppy. Puppies under 5 weeks are usually completely protected.

However, for each puppy, there is about a week when there are still sufficient maternal antibodies to destroy the attenuated antigens in the vaccine, but not enough to fight off the disease itself if the puppy is exposed. This period is called the "window of vulnerability".

At 6 weeks, only 37% of puppies are protected by a vaccination given at that time—the other 63% still carry enough maternal antibodies to prevent the vaccine from working. Some of those puppies may have high enough maternal antibody levels to protect them if they are exposed to the disease itself over the next couple of weeks, while others may not.

Because the vet does not know which puppies are protected, a second vaccination is generally given to all puppies only because it is frankly cheaper than running titers on all of them.

Now, if you read the stuff from the AVMA carefully, you don't need more than three functioning brain cells to figure out that the poor guys in the 37% who *were* protected by the first vaccine are the ones at risk for adverse effects from over-stimulation of the immune system when they get the second round.

This is why many breeders and vets now believe that where the risk of parvo and distemper is not high, the first shot not be given until 8-9 weeks, when around 80% of puppies will be protected by it.

By 12 weeks, over 95% of the puppies in a litter will have outgrown their maternal immunity to the point where they will be protected by vaccination. (In fact, research in the UK indicates that the new "high-titer" vaccines now used there and in the US provide protection for nearly all puppies by 10 weeks.)

By 16 weeks, maternal immunity is no longer a factor, and every puppy who can seroconvert will do so and be protected by vaccination.

So it should be pretty clear that if a puppy misses one of the shots in the series for some reason, there is no earthly reason to give him "extra" shots to get to some magic number *as long as the last one given produced a titer or was administered at 16 weeks or later.*

Once the puppy goes to his new home, the owner can elect to have titers run BEFORE any subsequent shots are automatically administered.

Because this is hands-down the SAFEST approach for the puppy from both a "short-term protection" and a "long-term immune function" standpoint, all vets should offer this option, although few actually do.

To be on the safe side, titers should be run 5-7 days after the last vaccination. If the puppy does *not* have a positive titer, it means he was one of the puppies with a high level of maternal antibodies at the time the vaccination was given and the shot "didn't take." In that case, the vaccines can be re-administered to protect him.

On the other hand, if he *does* have a positive titer, the 8-week shot "took" and there is no logical reason to increase his risk of adverse reaction by giving him vaccines he does not need. (Remember, immunity is a lot like pregnancy— there is no such thing as "more immune"!!)

And if your puppy has a positive titer at 10 or 12 weeks, you can take him out and about for socialization without worrying about waiting until he's "completed his puppy shots" at 16 weeks. How cool is THAT?

And that way his vaccination protocol is designed *for his individual immune response,* rather than representing a "one-size-fits-all" approach that can lead to autoimmune problems down the road. The vet you choose should be on board with that philosophy.

Aside from unnecessary revaccination, the other danger to a puppy's immune system and overall future health is from the sheer NUMBER of different vaccines given, especially if they are given all at the same time, or in a combination (*polyvalent*) vaccine. Here's the AVMA's advice on the subject:

"Vaccines, including polyvalent products, should be selected to include only those antigens appropriate for the specific risk of the patient, thereby eliminating unnecessary immune system stimulation and thus lowering potential risks of adverse events. Veterinarians should be aware of the risk of "endotoxin stacking" with the use of multiple Gram-negative vaccines."

What does this mean? The more vaccines given at one time, the greater the risk of over-stimulating and thus damaging the immune system. This includes a single shot that contains multiple antigens – the above-mentioned "polyvalent products".

Endotoxins are intracellular toxins found in gram-negative bacteria, and are found in all vaccines (although they are generally present in highest numbers in vaccines that protect against bacterial diseases like leptospirosis). When released, endotoxins produce a powerful inflammatory response in the system, and "endotoxin stacking" by combining vaccines makes it worse. Common symptoms of what is essentially toxic shock can include both fever and lethargy, which are all too common in puppies after vaccination.

In a recent large study on adverse vaccine reactions in dogs published in the JAVMA, the two greatest risk factors were found to be the size of the dog and the number of vaccines given at one time. In fact….

Research showed *each additional vaccine* given to a dog weighing less than 22 pounds increased the risk of adverse reaction by 27%!!!!

The size part makes perfect sense because *all dogs get the same vaccines*, no matter what their size or age. That's right— your 15 pound Goldendoodle puppy will receive *exactly the same vaccine* as an adult Newfoundland weighing 150 pounds! It's amazing how many people logically assume there are different vaccines for different sized dogs, but unfortunately, that is just not the case.

This means that proportionally, a puppy's immature little system has to deal with 10 times the amount of antigen (that's the viral or bacteria component) as well as 10 times the *endotoxins, adjuvants, carriers and preservatives* as a large adult dog. These include a fair number of toxic substances including (but certainly not limited to) aluminum, formaldehyde, and mercury. And obviously, the more vaccines a puppy is given at one time, the more of these toxic substances he is exposed to at one time.

And the worst part of this is that many of these vaccines protect against diseases for which the dog is at little or no risk in the first place.

Plain old common sense should tell us that an animal would never experience this sort of "all-at-once" exposure in nature, and no immune system is designed to handle it. Sort of like flying in the cargo hold of a 727, the possibility of vaccination as it is now too often practiced just never occurred to Mother Nature when she was designing the canine immune system.

Not to put too fine a point on it, but if the vet you are considering using as your puppy's primary health provider doesn't know any of this, he needs to take a brush-up course in Immunology 101 *and you need to find a different vet.*

The days when being a responsible dog owner meant taking your dog in to the vet for his "yearly shots" without even knowing what on earth the dog was being vaccinated against or whether he even needed another vaccination at all are OVER. *Keeping your puppy healthy means you have to do your homework.*

No state, county or city in the US actually requires vaccination for anything other than rabies. *It's amazing how many people do not know this.* Now, most training classes, boarding kennels, day care facilities and even groomers require more than that, but it's not the "law". So let's see what he needs to be both protected from life-threatening diseases *and* welcome in most canine establishments.

Understanding "Puppy Shots"

The most important thing to understand is that all so-called "puppy shots" are not the same.

Depending on the vet, if you do not specify, a "puppy shot" may be a DP, a DHP, a DHPP, a DA2PPVL, a DA2PPV+CV, or the mother of all combos— the dazzling DA2PPVL+CV, which many vaccine experts wish would simply vanish from this earth.

And those are just from *Merck's* personal Vaccine Buffet. If you throw in the various offerings of Pfizer and Merial (which is really the animal products line of pharmaceutical giant Sanofi), you are pretty much guaranteed to be lost in the Alphabet Soup of canine vaccines forever.

The whole thing is further complicated by the fact that in the last few years there have been a rash of mergers in the pharmaceutical world— for example, Intervet became part of Shering Plough, which then merged with industry giant Merck, and all animal vaccines formerly made by those three companies (including the Galaxy and Proguard vaccines) are being relabeled under the Nobivac brand.

Fort Dodge was bought out by pharmaceutical giant Weyeth, which recently merged with Pfizer, which markets the Vanguard line of animal vaccines, but then Pfizer announced in 2011 that it planned to sell off its Animal Health division completely, so who knows where they will end up.

What all this means is you can't just assume your new dog is getting the same vaccinations your last dog got, or that your vet is using the same vaccines he used to use. And If this is starting to remind you forcibly of the Wonderful World of Dog Food, you're not alone….

So let's try to sort this mess out so you'll know what your puppy needs and what he really doesn't need so you'll know what to ask for…and remember, YOU can specify which vaccines you want your dog to get.

The Four "Core" Vaccines

Back in 2003, after years of study, the Association of Animal Hospitals came up with a new vaccination protocol for veterinarians. At that time they decided to recommend only FOUR vaccines for all dogs, which they designated "core vaccines". Certain other vaccines could be given only as necessary if a dog is at particular risk, while some are not recommended at all. (Some combination vaccines routinely given to puppies actually include these "non-core" and "not recommended" vaccines, which is why you need to read this part carefully.) Presumably all vets got this memo.

All 4 core vaccines can be covered in two "shots" – the DHP and the Rabies shot.

Although the core vaccines can be given separately, three of them are usually combined in the puppy shots, while rabies vaccine is always administered as a single shot. Here's the breakdown of the DHP and what's in it:

Distemper (that's the "D")

First described by Edward Jenner (the smallpox guy) back in the 18th century, distemper is an old disease. Primarily affecting puppies under 6 months of age, canine distemper is rarely seen in the US today outside of shelter populations, and many vets in practice today have never seen a single case. But prior to the 1960s, when widespread vaccination of dogs really took off, it killed roughly *half the puppies* born in the US in any given year.

Distemper begins with an upper respiratory infection (often characterized by a thick greenish discharge from the nose and eyes) before progressing to the nervous system, where it can cause seizures and even death. Because it is caused by a virus, the only treatment for distemper is supportive. And it's a pretty horrific disease—without supportive treatment, close to 90% of puppies who contract it will die. Even *with* supportive treatment, a puppy's odds of survival are not all that hot, and those who do survive often have lifelong neurological and ocular damage.

The reason all dogs still need to be vaccinated for what is now a pretty rare disease is because both wild animals (in 1994, a third of the lions in the Serengeti died from canine distemper) and shelter populations provide a constant "reservoir" for the virus. The virus is spread primarily through direct contact and is not particularly hardy in the environment. For this reason, puppies from shelters and commercial breeding operations (i.e. purchased through pet stores and online brokers) are at higher risk than puppies from small private breeders. But dogs adopted or purchased from these places can shed the virus for weeks if they've been exposed, putting all unvaccinated dogs who come in contact with them at risk.

The distemper virus, which is a close cousin of the human measles virus, has been shown to deplete the body's store of Vitamin A – in fact, the symptoms of distemper closely resemble the symptoms of serious Vitamin A deficiency. In one study, ferrets who were Vitamin A replete were shown to be completely resistant to challenge with the distemper virus. For this reason, a teaspoonful of old-fashioned cod liver oil a couple days before a dog is scheduled for a distemper vaccine to boost his Vitamin A levels might lessen the chance of reaction and certainly can't hurt.

Canine Infectious Hepatitis (that's the "H")

This is another disease that's rare in the US since widespread vaccination began in the 1960s—in fact, it's so rare *there hasn't been a single case of it* recorded in dogs in this country in the last 20 years at least and probably longer. (Why it was included as a Core Vaccine is frankly a total mystery.)

Caused by the CAV-1 (Canine Adenovirus- type 1) virus, infectious hepatitis primarily attacks the liver, kidneys, spleen and eyes- symptoms can range anywhere from relatively mild with spontaneous recovery to death within hours, with mortality most likely in puppies. The CAV1 virus is highly contagious and is spread primarily through ingestion of urine, feces and saliva of infected dogs. The virus is considered hardy and can survive in the environment for 6 months or more.

Somewhat oddly, modern vaccines do not actually contain the CAV-1 antigen, as early vaccines using it produced pretty severe side effects like corneal opacity (blue eye), which is also one of the symptoms of the disease. However, it was discovered that vaccination against CAV-2 (a similar virus but which only causes a mild self-limiting respiratory infection) also protected dogs against the more serious CAV1, and that antigen is now used instead.

So, if your dog is given a "3-way", he's actually protected against both canine infectious hepatitis (CAV1) and the milder CAV2, which means the DHP "3-way" actually protects against 4 diseases.

Since the risk for puppies in the US contracting canine hepatitis is low to non-existent and the risk of adverse reaction is statistically higher than the risk of contracting the disease (especially if the puppy weighs under 22 pounds at the time of vaccination), the CAV2 antigen is usually the one that is left out of the initial puppy shots by many holistic vets and breeders, who opt for the DP combination instead.

Parvovirus (that's the "P")

"Parvo" is a word that strikes terror in the hearts of breeders everywhere, and with good reason. The parvovirus attacks the rapidly dividing cells in the digestive tract, which is where the virus does the most damage, causing vomiting and bloody diarrhea. Untreated, 80% of affected puppies will die, usually of dehydration. With the best supportive treatment, maybe 75% will survive, but it's going to cost a breeder untold thousands of dollars to try and save a litter, and a quarter of them probably won't make it no matter what they do. *Fear of parvo is the reason so many breeders limit visitors when they have a litter.*

The virus first appeared in dogs back in the 1970s, and prior to development of a vaccine, thousands of dogs of all ages across the US died a pretty horrific death. Today, because of widespread vaccination and because the virus is ubiquitous in the environment, parvo is primarily a disease of puppies between 6 weeks and 6 months of age.

The *bad news* about parvo is that unlike distemper, the virus is extremely hardy in the environment, spread through the feces of infected dogs and picked up by human shoes. Once in the soil, it can live for up to 9 months outdoors, and actually longer if the ground freezes during that time.

The *good news* is parvo is actually pretty easy to kill indoors. A simple solution of water and chlorine bleach at a ratio of 30:1 will effectively kill it. (And anyone who bred dogs back in the 1970s probably still remembers that 30:1 translates to 4 ounces of bleach to a gallon of water.)

The truth is, out of the whole bunch, parvo is really the virus a puppy in the US is most likely to come in contact with. Unlike distemper, it is not confined to shelters, pet shops and puppy mills. Because it is so ubiquitous in the soil, unprotected puppies are at risk anytime they leave their own fenced yard.

Until you know for sure that your puppy is protected by running a titer, his feet really shouldn't touch the ground off your property, *even in the vet's office.* Bring him in his crate and keep him in it except when he's on a newly disinfected examining table, because the last dog who walked through the waiting room may have tracked it in on his paws. That dog may be vaccinated and therefore immune, but your puppy may not be. Remember, parvo is not an airborne virus — it is spread through feces, and clings to surfaces that it comes in contact with, like paws and shoes.

Now, since the 3-way DHP combination vaccine will take care of all the recommended core vaccines except rabies, one would logically think all vets would administer it. They don't.

For some unfathomable reason, many clinics in the US routinely use the CHPP combination instead, which includes parainfluenza, a non-core vaccine that protects against a second mild self-limiting respiratory infection. This would be fine except that each added vaccine increases the risk of adverse reaction in a dog under 22 pounds by 27%! (And many Goldendoodle puppies are under 22 pounds when they are getting vaccinated.)

So, assuming your vet does not even carry the DP (which most do not), be sure and ask for the 3-way DHP instead of the 4-way DHPP.

Rabies

The last of the 4 "Core Vaccines", this one is always given as a single shot and is never a component of a combination vaccine. Because rabies poses a public health risk to humans, it is the only canine vaccination required by law in all 50 states.

However, because it is a killed vaccine and has a higher level of adjuvants and endotoxins than an MLV, it is also the cause of a LOT of serious vaccine reactions in dogs, so what we want to do is vaccinate our dogs to protect both them and us and to comply with state laws, but not over-vaccinate or vaccinate earlier than needed for protection and thereby increase the risk of adverse reactions.

Unfortunately, most people have little or no knowledge about the rabies virus, the disease it causes, actual risk to their dog or the laws in their state, and so there is an appalling tendency to over-vaccinate for rabies. Understanding both the disease and the relative risks of contracting it will help you make better decisions for your Dood.

Rabies is a particularly nasty viral disease first described back in 2000 BC. It can technically infect any warm-blooded vertebrate, although it is common in some (like canines) and virtually unheard of in others (like rodents).

Rabies is *zoonotic* and is passed from animals to other animals or humans through saliva (or rarely through actual tissue in the case of organ transplants), but *cannot* be transmitted through feces, urine, or blood. The virus is not hardy in the environment and becomes noninfectious when it dries out or is exposed to sunlight, usually within minutes or at most a few hours. (Simply petting or handling a rabid animal does not automatically constitute exposure, at least according to the CDC...who knew?)

Once it enters a new host, usually through a bite, the virus travels through the peripheral nerves (which can take weeks or even several months depending on where the bite occurred) until it reaches the central nervous system, at which point it causes acute encephalitis and is almost always 100% fatal, usually within days of symptoms appearing. In humans who've been exposed, the rabies vaccine can be successfully administered as a prophylactic prior to the appearance of symptoms, usually in a series of 5 shots. Unvaccinated dogs who have been exposed are generally euthanized.

How prevalent is it? Rabies kills around 55,000 people a year, mostly contracted from dog bites, with the overwhelming majority of rabies cases occurring in Africa and Asia. A hundred years ago, the US averaged about 100 human deaths from rabies every year, and nearly all were the result of dog bites. Once widespread vaccination, that changed radically, and in 2007 the CDC declared the US to be officially free of canine rabies, a "vaccine success story" by any measure. But in spite of that, there were 59 cases of rabies in dogs and 2 rabies cases in humans reported to the CDC in the Continental US in 2010. *This is because there are several other strains of rabies besides the canine one.*

Carried by wild animals, these strains can be transmitted to both animals and humans, and until we figure out how to eradicate those strains, dogs will continue to need rabies shots. (It's worth noting that there are almost *five times* more cases of rabies reported in (free-roaming) cats than in dogs every year, the only species for which incidence is actually rising. So what are the risks of your Doodle puppy contracting a "wild animal" strain of rabies before he's had his first rabies shot? It all depends upon where you live.

The following map (which changes little from year to year) shows the incidence of confirmed rabies in dogs in the US in 2010....all 59 of them. Each dot represents one case.

156

In humans, virtually *all cases* of rabies contracted in the US are caused by bites from infected bats, and rabid bats have been identified in most states, making rabies pretty much of an equal opportunity disease for humans from a geographical standpoint. *(It's also good to know that your odds of contracting rabies from a bat in the US are somewhere in the neighborhood of one in 155 million- you actually have a better chance of winning the lottery. Or being elected President.)* Dogs, on the other hand, are unlikely to contract rabies from bat bites— in fact, there are exactly ZERO "bat-to-dog" rabies cases recorded by the CDC over the years. Go figure.

Instead, both dogs and cats are nearly always infected by bites from rabid skunks, raccoons and foxes, with skunks leading raccoons by a margin of two to one and foxes barely in the money.

And for unknown reasons, the incidence of rabies in raccoons is limited almost entirely to states along the Eastern seaboard and Texas, while the incidence in skunks is greatest in the Eastern states from Maine to Georgia and in a vertical band through the Midwest extending from Minnesota down to Texas, with a few scattered on the Pacific coast. Not surprisingly, if you look at the map, you'll notice the incidence of rabies in dogs and cats occurs primarily in those areas as well.

Contrary to popular belief, squirrels, chipmunks, rabbits, rats and mice are NOT carriers of rabies in the US, and pose no rabies risk to an unvaccinated puppy. (Good to know that we've been worrying unnecessarily about backyard squirrels and chipmunks all these years, huh?)

Now, that pretty much confines his risk to areas where these skunks, raccoons and foxes are found (in other words, *outdoors*) and then only in those parts of the country where they carry the rabies virus.

A dog cannot "catch" rabies from casual contact.

The only way a puppy *could* conceivably contract rabies is if he were allowed out unsupervised (in other words off-leash) in a state where rabid animals are found and happens to get bitten by a rabid one in the "furious" late stage of the disease, so it makes sense to avoid letting your puppy run loose in parks, landfills and around dumpsters prior to vaccination if you live in one of those states. But you'd have to be a total *dunce* to do that anyway for a wealth of other reasons...I mean, just *think* about it— statistically, a loose puppy is about a million times more likely to get hit by a car than he is to contract rabies from being bitten by a rabid skunk or raccoon that just happened by *at that very moment*.

And even if you *are* a total dunce, the statistics are still weighted heavily in a dog's favor— remember, there are over 75 million dogs in America, and between 50-70 total cases of rabies in dogs per year. Do the math.

Given all this, it's pretty obvious there is no reason your puppy needs to get his first rabies shot on the same day as his other puppy shots at 12 or 14 weeks, because his risk of contracting rabies is so low. *It is simply not necessary and will seriously increase his chances of an immediate or delayed vaccine reaction, so don't let anyone talk you into it.*

What About the Law?

Ah, the Law. Now that you understand the actual risks or lack thereof, you can safely wait the recommended 3-4 weeks needed to give his immune system time to recover after his last puppy vaccines before getting him his first rabies shot and still not run afoul of most state and municipal rabies laws. And extensive research has failed to turn up anyone who's ever gone to jail (or even been fined) for waiting until their puppy was 6 months old before having him vaccinated for rabies. He just can't get a dog license until he has proof of rabies vaccination.

In most states the first vaccine is a "one-year vaccine", so a second will need to be given a year after the first in order to comply with most licensing laws, although according to the CDC, a dog is considered immune to rabies 28 days after a single rabies vaccine. (That's a year after the first, not when the dog turns a year old , by the way.)

And thanks to a lot of lobbying by concerned vets and owners, all subsequent rabies vaccinations are now good for three years in every single state. This is an improvement over the old "annual rabies vaccine" laws, but it's still probably overkill—most immunologists and vaccine experts agree that a rabies vaccination provides immunity for at least 5 and probably 7 years. (In fact, there is an ongoing research study at the University of Wisconsin designed to prove exactly that, so that state rabies laws can be changed. For more information on it, Google the Rabies Challenge Fund. And feel free to donate while you're on the website, because as one might imagine, the entire study is being funded by private donations rather than by the pharmaceutical companies that manufacture and sell rabies vaccines.) To reiterate:

The risk of your puppy contracting rabies from a wild animal is statistically very, very low. NO state requires annual rabies vaccination any more, so do not allow your vet to do so.

And NEVER allow the rabies shot to be given within 3-4 weeks of any other vaccination, or within 4 weeks of spaying or neutering.

Other suggestions from vaccine experts for decreasing the chance of a rabies vaccine reaction include:

- *Using a "clean" (i.e. containing the least number of adjuvants) vaccine*

- *Giving the homeopathic remedy lyssin 30c (anyone can purchase this online) the day before and within 2 hours after vaccination may lessen the risk of reaction.*

- *Always delaying vaccination on a dog who is, or has recently been, ill, especially with GI problems.*

- *Delaying vaccination when the dog is under stress or has recently changed homes.*

- *Adding probiotics to the dog's diet for a week or two before and after vaccination*

Many assume the only adverse reactions to rabies vaccine are immediate acute reactions (anaphylaxis), but delayed reactions to rabies vaccines may occur up to 45 days later, and so no one associates them with the recent vaccine given. Reactions to rabies vaccine include:

- *Behavior changes such as aggression and separation anxiety*

- *Obsessive behavior, self-mutilation, tail-chewing, shredding bedding*

- *Pica- eating wood, stones, earth, stool*

- *Destructive behavior, shredding bedding*

- *Seizures, epilepsy*

- *Fibrosarcomas (cancer) at injection site*

- *Autoimmune disease (like immune-mediated hemolytic anemia)*

- *Chronic gastrointestinal problems*

Any previously unseen behaviors or health problems occurring within a month or two of rabies vaccination should probably be viewed with suspicion.

If your Dood reacts adversely to the rabies vaccine in spite of all efforts to be careful, it's good to know that in the following states at least, he can get a Medical Rabies Waiver from his vet. This is *critical* because if a dog has reacted adversely to rabies vaccine once, odds are the next time will be worse.

States with Medical Rabies Waivers as of 2012:

Alabama, California, Colorado, Connecticut, Florida, Illinois, Maine, Massachusetts, Missouri, Oregon, New Hampshire, New Jersey, New York, Vermont, Virginia, Wisconsin

If your state does *not* currently have a Medical Rabies Waiver Form, or if your county or municipality still requires annual rabies vaccination, visit the **Rabies Challenge Fund** website to see how you can help change these dangerously outdated laws.

Non-Core Vaccines

The AAHA Guidelines consider some vaccines to be "non-core vaccines", or optional, based on the individual dog's lifestyle, environment and risk of exposure. These include parainfluenza, bordatella, Leptospirosis, Lyme disease, and a rattlesnake vaccine. Because, like the rabies shot, all these vaccines are made with *killed* rather than *modified live* antigens and therefore require adjuvants, the risk of adverse reaction is by definition higher. So before you let your puppy automatically be given one or even several of these, let's see who really needs them.

Kennel Cough (Parainfluenza and Bordatella)

Along with the CAV2 virus already used in core vaccines to protect against its Hepatitis cousin, the parainfluenza virus and bordatella bronchiseptica bacterium are primarily responsible for *Canine Infectious Tracheobronchitis*, more commonly known as "kennel cough".

Although not a life-threatening or even particularly serious disease (it's usually self-limiting even without treatment) kennel cough is highly contagious, so training classes, groomers, doggy daycare, boarding kennels all generally require proof of vaccination. Even though the vaccines available are not long-lasting or effective against all the strains out there (lots of dogs who are current on the kennel cough vaccinations still end up with kennel cough), your dog is likely to need proof of vaccination against kennel cough to be welcome in most doggy venues.

The intranasal versions (which are literally squirted up the dog's nose) are the least reactive, and the most popular is probably Intra-Trac3, which includes CAV2, parainfluenza and bordatella.

Of course, if your puppy was vaccinated with the popular "4-way" DHPP vaccine instead of the 3-way DHP, he's already covered for CAV2 and parainfluenza (which is the second P) and in the interest of not over-vaccinating you should request that bordatella be administered as a single intranasal vaccine.

Lyme Disease

As anyone who's had it can attest, Lyme disease in humans is a serious and often debilitating chronic disease. Because of that, a lot of people automatically assume it's the same for dogs and that their puppy needs to be vaccinated against Lyme, especially if he lives in an endemic state. However, the most current data available indicates this may not be the case at all.

Also caused by the spirochete *borrelia bergdorferi* and transmitted primarily through the saliva of infected ticks, the symptoms of Lyme disease in dogs differ from those in people, and are for the most part far less devastating. In addition, symptoms usually occur much later (according to Cornell's Baker Institute up to 2-5 months after a bite by an infected tick) and the classic Lyme rash is almost never seen.

Symptoms in dogs most commonly include low grade fever, lethargy, loss of appetite and shifting lameness. These usually resolve within 48 hours after treatment with oral doxycycline, which should be continued for a full 4 weeks due to the slow replication rate of *borrelia bergdorferi*. Puppies should be treated with amoxicillin to avoid damage to the enamel on developing teeth, and probiotics should always be given after the course of antibiotics to restore normal gut flora.

But more importantly, based on nationwide test results,

it is now estimated that over 95% of dogs infected with the Lyme spirochete

never develop any clinical symptoms at all.

At this point, no one really knows why this is the case, but in humans, research has shown that chronic Lyme is associated with—big surprise!—a particular allele in one of the Class II HLA genes, so it's not much of a stretch to postulate that resistance to Lyme is associated with the Class II DLA genes in dogs…in other words, there's likely a genetic predisposition to susceptibility to this particular bug, and not surprisingly, some breeds appear to be particularly susceptible. In some purebreds, Lyme can cause serious kidney disease.

Most experts recommend asymptomatic dogs with a positive Lyme titer have a blood panel drawn and an auscultation to preclude the possibility of sub clinical cardiac or kidney involvement, and because of the "lag time" between exposure and the development of symptoms, some vets feel that it is prudent to treat Lyme-positive dogs with doxycycline simply to err on the side of caution.

And much like rabies, Lyme risk is entirely geographical.

In 2010, 95% of the reported cases of Lyme came from 12 states, with another

4% coming from California. All other states combined accounted for the other 1%.

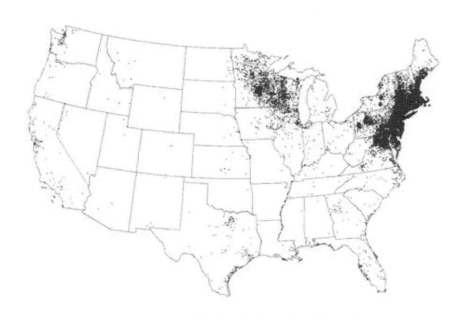

And even in Lyme endemic states like those in the Northeast, around 90% of healthy dogs have positive Lyme antibody tests. That's why those maps that show incidence of tick-borne diseases are so scary—they are not showing actual disease *incidence* so much as *exposure*. (And it's good to remember that those maps are brought to you by the manufacturers of Lyme vaccines and the companies that sell the snap-test kits….all of whom have a financial interest in selling more of their products.)

So why not vaccinate your puppy against Lyme "just to be on the safe side", in case he's one of the 5% who will develop symptoms after exposure? *Because it may not be the "safe" side at all.*

Serious questions have been raised about the safety of the Lyme Vaccine.

Testing on Lyme-vaccinated dogs with chronic inflammatory autoimmune arthritis (which does not typically occur in dogs naturally infected with Lyme) and other autoimmune diseases has revealed the presence of *vaccine-strain*, rather than wild-strain, Lyme. This raises the alarming possibility that *the vaccine itself is causing the problems*. (Not coincidentally, the human Lyme vaccine was pulled from the market when similar reports started coming in.)

At this point in time, the safest universally-recommended defense against Lyme is simply the prompt removal of ticks. After a tick attaches and begins to feed, spirochetes residing in the midgut of the tick begin to migrate into the salivary glands and from there into the host, which can take up to 12 hours. Because of that, there is actually little chance of infection during the first few hours of tick feeding, although it rises exponentially after that. So as long as you remove ticks promptly, the odds of a dog becoming infected with Lyme are pretty low.

And if you're *still* worried, you can always give your Dood a single capsule of doxycycline, which is an old drug and long-proven safe for adult dogs. Why?

A large randomized double-blind placebo-controlled human study conducted in an endemic area of New York determined that a single 200 mg dose of doxycycline administered within 72 hours after a tick bite could prevent the development of Lyme disease. Efficacy was determined to be around 87%, which is coincidentally about the same as most Lyme vaccines, but without the risk of adverse vaccine reaction. How cool is that?

It's also worth knowing that currently, the University Of Wisconsin School Of Veterinary Medicine, (located in a Lyme-endemic state) neither recommends nor routinely administers the Lyme vaccine, which should tell you something.

Lepto

Another non-core vaccine, this is one that a lot of vets try to scare clients into buying based on a "Lepto outbreak" in their area. *This is unfortunate*, because like the rabies vaccine, the lepto vaccine is one of the most likely to cause life-threatening adverse reactions (anaphylaxis) in dogs. Unlike rabies, however, the lepto vaccine is neither required by law nor even necessary for *any* dog, no matter what the local risk at any given point in time.

Really.

Called Rat-Catcher's Yellows in earlier times, Leptospirosis is an old disease that's been around for a long time. It is caused by infection with the water-borne spirochete *leptospirosa*. Over 200 different strains (or *serovars*) of lepto have been identified to date, at least eight of which are known to cause Leptospirosis in dogs. The most current vaccines protect against FOUR of them.

On top of that, because it is a killed vaccine, two doses must be administered within weeks of each other to elicit an immune response (which effectively doubles the chance of reaction), and the most recent evidence suggests protection may only last 6-8 months. Combine that with the risk of adverse reaction, and the whole "lepto vaccination" picture is not particularly impressive.

So what is the real risk of your dog contracting Leptospirosis?

Probably pretty low.

A survey of the Veterinary Medical Database between 1983 and 1998 turned up a total of 340 reported cases. Even assuming that represents some serious under-reporting, putting those numbers into the framework of a canine population of maybe 50 million dogs during that 15 year period, it's not exactly what you'd call an epidemic.

Although Lepto is zoonotic, direct transfer from people to dogs or dogs to people (or even dog-to-dog) is pretty much nonexistent in the US. Instead, because the lepto spirochete is aquatic (it can survive up to 2-3 weeks in fresh (not salt) water, damp soil or mud) it is primarily transmitted through drinking or inhaling water containing the urine of an infected animal. For this reason, lepto outbreaks tend to be clustered in small geographic areas, and are most likely to occur after flooding and overwhelmingly during September, October and November. Hunting and herding dogs, who are much more likely to drink out of stagnant ponds and such, are at highest risk.

So how serious is Lepto if the dog actually contracts it?

Like Lyme, it varies greatly from dog to dog.

Some infected dogs may be totally asymptomatic, while others become pretty violently ill within days, with high fever, and/or vomiting, excessive thirst and reduced dark-colored urine, generalized pain and often jaundice, because if not treated promptly, Lepto can attack and damage the liver and kidneys and cause death. On the other hand, if diagnosed and treated promptly with common garden-variety antibiotics (usually a combination of amoxicillin and doxycycline) response is good and mortality in healthy adult dogs is low.

There is no data on the actual incidence of asymptomatic dogs testing positive for Lepto in the US as there is with Lyme, but a large human study in Nicaragua in 1999 revealed that over 70% of those testing positive for Lepto were totally asymptomatic; canine studies in Germany revealed a similar pattern in dogs. Once again, resistance to the disease may well be a function of the individual immune system.

So, assuming you decide not to routinely vaccinate your dog against Lepto, what do you do if your vet tells you there has been an outbreak in your area—are you stuck with vaccinating? *Luckily, the answer is no.*

At least three separate human trials

have shown that 200 mg of our old friend doxycycline administered once a week

will prevent Leptospirosis with over 95% efficacy.

And unlike the vaccine, which is only effective against 4 of the 240 strains, *doxycycline will protect against all of them*, and will also prevent shedding of the organism in the urine, which is a definite plus with a zoonotic pathogen. Given the fact that most vaccines—including rabies!—only have to produce an efficacy rate of 80% or better for FDA approval, doxycycline's 95% is pretty impressive.

In fact, the CDC recommends that Americans traveling to parts of the world where Leptospirosis is endemic begin a regimen of one 200 mg dose of doxycycline weekly, starting 1-2 days before arriving and continuing for the duration.

However, be apprised that most vets are not aware of the use of doxycycline as a prophylactic for Leptospirosis, so you may have to download and print the information from the CDC and maybe the original NEJM publication (which is easy to find online) yourself and bring it along to support your case. Given the high possibility of adverse reaction to the vaccine, it's probably well-worth the effort.

Coronavirus, Giardia, Canine Influenza and Rattlesnake Vaccines

In the interest of not wasting anyone's time this section will be mercifully brief—the first one is another "vaccine in search of a disease" and any vet who actually recommends Corona vaccine ought to be viewed with suspicion.

The second two are not recommended by anybody except the pharmaceutical companies that manufacture and sell them. In other words, they all pretty much failed the AAHA's benefit/risk test, and there's no reason to risk overstressing any poor dog's immune system for this bunch.

The need for the last one, on the other hand, is entirely based on where you live and the number of rattlers your Dood is honestly likely to encounter, because a rattlesnake bite can kill a dog. Hunting dogs and Search and Rescue dogs working in rattlesnake country where the possibility of getting to a vet in a big hurry is problematic both fall into the "probably want to consider this one" category. Because a lot of dogs do have an adverse reaction to it though, even when it's really needed the rattlesnake vaccine should always be administered by itself and never within 3-4 weeks of any other vaccines to lessen the risk.

Now that we've pretty much beaten the whole vaccine issue to death, let's move right on to the *other* area where you really need to educate yourself, because as with vaccination, the choices you make here from puppyhood on can have a long-term influence on your Dood's lifelong health and longevity. And that would be...

Parasites...Internal and External

Ok, let's face it, nobody likes parasites. We don't even like to *think* about parasites. And luckily, now that we have all these monthly pills and "topicals" we can easily protect our dogs with, we really don't have to think about them at all. *Think again.*

There's a growing body of evidence that all this stuff we've been merrily popping down our dogs' throats and squishing between their shoulder blades every month may, like over-vaccination, also be contributing to a lot of the health issues we're now seeing in dogs—everything from food allergies to autoimmune diseases to seizures.

Heartworm Preventatives? Not So Much.

The biggest problem is that way too many owners erroneously view monthly heartworm and systemic flea and tick products are "preventative medicine" and routinely give them on a monthly basis year-round with little or no further engagement of the thought process.

This is unfortunately incorrect on several levels. None of these products actually **prevent** fleas, ticks, heartworm or anything else from entering your environment or attacking your dog, nor are they really **medicines,** although the manufacturers certainly market them that way. (As their manufacturers are quick to point out, a couple of the avermectins also used in humans are in fact approved as drugs by the FDA, but when those exact same chemicals are sprayed on cotton fields, they mysteriously become insecticides and are regulated as such by EPA…go figure.)

Technically, these products are heartworm and flea **treatments**, not preventatives, and marketing them as "meds" really borders on the unethical. They are in reality simply insecticides that kill the parasites that happen to be on (or in) the dog at that moment. Some of the flea and tick products also contain a hormone disrupter that prevents parasites from reproducing or maturing normally, but again, they don't prevent the flea or tick or worm from attacking your dog in the first place.

And like most insecticides, they are all *neurotoxins*—that's how they kill bugs. We count on the fact that the neurotoxins used are ones that do not readily cross the blood-brain barrier in mammals. But the key word here is "readily". According to their own manufacturers, exposure at high levels will produce all the classic symptoms of neurotoxicity (tremors, ataxia, seizures and coma), which would indicate that they *are* indeed capable of permeating the mammalian blood-brain barrier, wouldn't it?

Unbelievably, the effects of chronic low-level exposure to avermectins

has never been clinically studied in dogs *at all.*

The longest clinical trial appears to be a 24 month study on ivermectin (the active ingredient in Heartguard) performed decades ago…and that was *on rats.*

And since these insecticides all end up in the liver sooner or later, it's probably NOT a coincidence that seizures and chronic liver problems started becoming a lot more common back in the 1980s, when all these systemic neurotoxins became part of the average American dog's daily life.

And if that isn't enough to give you pause, a growing body of scientific evidence now indicates that, along with the "beneficial bacteria" we now call *probiotics*, and ingest intentionally, exposure to some of these parasites may also be necessary for the proper development and regulation of the immune system!

To understand why, we need to know a little something about parasites, so here we go...

Protozoa, Ectoparasites and Helminths—Old Friends?

A parasite is simply an organism that lives on or in a "host" and gets its food from that host. They come in three basic varieties:

- **Protozoan parasites** are the smallest, often found in water, and anyone who's suffered "Montezuma's Revenge" in Mexico has probably crossed paths with a few of them. In dogs, coccidia and giardia are the most common. Dogs naturally carry small numbers of these protozoa in their gut flora- it is only when the system is stressed and the ecosystem of the gut is thrown out of balance that they actually cause symptoms, the most common being diarrhea.

- **Ectoparasites** are parasitic insects or arthropods with external skeletons and include fleas, mites and ticks. As far as we know, these are not particularly beneficial to anyone except the companies that make a lot of money trying to keep them off our pets, although it's entirely possible that knowledge could change in the future.

- **Helminths,** which are parasitic worms (earthworms are not helminths) make up the last category, and are currently of great interest to immunologists. This group includes both flatworms (of which the tapeworm is best-known) and nematodes (roundworms) like ascarids, whipworms, pinworms, hookworms and *dirofilaria immitis*, commonly known as heartworms. Why are helminths suddenly interesting? Well, here's where it gets downright weird.

Recent genetic research has shown that in the millions of years of evolutionary coexistence with their mammalian hosts, helminths have been a major selective force on the development of the *interleukin (IL) genes*, especially a subset responsible for the production of *cyclokines*, which are involved in the regulation of the inflammatory processes of diseases like Crohn's, celiac disease, allergies, asthma, rheumatoid arthritis, and MS. (This goes a long way toward explaining why these problems are all for the most part limited to so-called "developed" countries, which scientists have known for years.)

In numerous animal studies, deliberate controlled helminth infestation has been shown to be protective against all of the above, as well as type 1 diabetes *and food allergies.*

These studies bolster the "Old Friends hypothesis", which postulates that after millennia of co-evolution mammalian T-regulator cells can only be fully effective after stimulation by microorganisms and parasites with low pathogenicity.

In addition to being protective against the development of allergies and autoimmune disease as was found in animal studies, recent FDA-approved human clinical trials at places like Mt Sinai medical School and the University of Wisconsin have shown that controlled infection with helmiths can actually *reduce the symptoms* and in many cases *reverse the damage* already caused by autoimmune diseases as varied as Crohn's, asthma, autism and MS.

(If you're interested, you can find out more about this by simply googling "helminthic therapy", which in spite of its intrinsic weirdness is rapidly gaining credibility in mainstream medicine –in fact, the MS trial at UW was funded by a grant from the CDC. It's probably not a good idea to do this while you're eating, though…).What does this mean for our dogs?

Well, because the avermectins are "broad-spectrum", which means they pretty much kill all the nematodes they encounter (some of which may be beneficial), keeping our dogs on a year-round monthly heartworm program when it's not necessary may *not* be the best thing for their immune systems. And they don't kill flatworms like tapeworms– prazyquantel is most effective for that.

But wait a minute…

Don't we test for heartworm before beginning monthly treatment because giving him Heartguard can kill the dog if he's already infected? That's another misconception. *Although once true, that information is simply 30 years out of date.*

The new monthly heartworm prevention medications are safer to use than the older diethylcarbamazine-based programs. (Anyone remember daily Filaribits?) DEC could cause serious illness and even death in a patient given the medication while harboring heartworm microfilaria. So preventing this occurrence was the original reason for heartworm testing prior to putting a dog back on Filaribits every spring. But Filaribits are no longer even available, and the newer monthly insecticides such as ivermectin rarely if ever cause serious reactions if given when microfilaria are present in the bloodstream..

In fact, they are commonly used along with melarcomine (Immiticide) *as part of the heartworm-eradication treatment* for dogs testing positive on a snap test. (Although slower, long-term use of Frontline Plus and doxycycline alone has been shown to be effective in eradicating heartworm infection in asymptomatic dogs that test positive for heartworm.)

Whether or not a dog is on heartworm treatment year-round, testing once or twice a year is still a very good idea. Here's why:

Although the manufacturers do not go out of their way to advertise this fact,

no insecticide is 100% effective against heartworm even if administered year round.

A percentage of dogs (maybe up to 1%) will test positive even when they've been on heartworm meds monthly for years. (A heartworm test cannot come up positive until 6 months after exposure, because the test can only identify adult heartworms, not microfilaria.)

So basically, the real goal of "heartworm prevention" is really prevention of *an infestation of adult heartworms,* which can occur in spite of a monthly heartworm program and which can endanger a dog's health if left untreated for 6 months or more. A heartworm snap test run twice a year is the "failsafe"; and it's totally nontoxic.

Flea and Tick Prevention

Unlike helminths, there is no evidence at present that fleas and ticks serve any purpose other than to drive us crazy. Both are *ectoparasites*, which means they have a hard external skeleton. Both have been around longer than man and his canine buddy and both will undoubtedly be around long after we're gone, because they are both unbelievably tough and highly adaptable. The real frustration has always been trying to find something that will poison them *without* poisoning us and our dogs.

For the last several years, once-a-month topical insecticides looked like the answer, but that premise is starting to be questioned—and by the EPA itself, no less, a government agency usually frustratingly slow to react when it comes to potential danger from pesticides.

Given that, the fact that topical insecticides (this includes ALL of them rather than a particular brand) are currently under investigation by the EPA should be enough to give one pause.

This investigation began after EPA received some 44,000 (that's forty-four thousand) reports of adverse effects to topical insecticides in 2008 alone.

And since let's face it, since hardly any of us even knew that adverse reactions to stuff like Frontline is supposed to be reported to *the Environmental Protection Agency* in the first place (or how to go about doing that), those numbers probably just represent the tip of the iceberg.

According to results of their preliminary investigation, the three systems most often affected were the skin, the intestinal tract and the central nervous system, with symptoms ranging from chronic skin problems, vomiting and diarrhea all the way to seizures, coma and death.

Until they discover exactly what it is about these topical formulas that is causing these problems, owners who want to minimize risk to their dog's health might want to err on the side of caution and consider some safer alternatives.

One of the best pieces of advice from EPA (and which honestly wouldn't occur to most owners) is to bathe the dog IMMEDIATELY if he seems to be showing any adverse (or even odd) symptoms at all after his monthly treatment, using mild shampoo and lots of water. In other words, the sooner you get that stuff off the dog, the better. Doing so may actually save his life.

And in the "your tax dollar at work" department, here is some more advice from our friends at the EPA, copied verbatim from their website:

Discuss with your veterinarian whether topical flea treatments are even necessary for your dog. (Note: If your dog doesn't actually HAVE fleas on him, the logical answer here is probably no. Killing fleas you don't have is a little like treating for malaria if you live in Duluth.)

Vacuuming on a daily basis to remove eggs, larvae and adults is the best method for initial control of a flea infestation. It is important to vacuum the following areas: carpets, cushioned furniture, cracks and crevices on floors, along baseboards and the basement. (Recent studies have shown that a plain old vacuum cleaner will remove around 95% of fleas in all stages from the indoor environment, which is about as effective as most of the toxic insecticides currently available. Needless to say, these studies have NOT received a lot of press from the multi-billion-dollar Flea Industry...)

Steam cleaning carpets may also help as the hot steam and soap can kill fleas in all stages of the life cycle. Pay particular attention to areas where pets sleep. (Like vacuuming, steam cleaning is every bit as effective as the hormone-disrupting Insect Growth Regulators found in many flea products and a lot less creepy.)

Wash all pet bedding and family bedding on which pets lie in hot, soapy water every two to three weeks. (That's pretty self-explanatory.)

Flea combs are very effective tools in the suppression of adult fleas. They allow hair to pass through the tines but not the fleas, removing fleas as well as flea feces and dried blood. Focus combing on those parts of the pet where the most fleas congregate, usually the neck or tail area. When fleas are caught, deposit them in hot soapy water to kill them. (If a flea comb reveals no fleas or little black granules of dried blood called "flea dirt", odds are you have no fleas in your indoor or outdoor environment, and no need to expose your dog to unnecessary neurotoxins.)

What the EPA clearly understands that most owners do not is that fleas and ticks are an *environmental* problem. What the monthly "preventatives" actually do is turn your dog into a four-footed toxic vacuum cleaner, gathering up any fleas or ticks that happen to jump onto him for a meal and either killing them outright or rendering them incapable of reproduction via toxins delivered through the animal's skin or bloodstream.

Unfortunately, this method by definition requires that the dog's skin or bloodstream be constantly infused with neurotoxic insecticides, some of which are harmful not only to the dog but to humans and the environment, and one of which has recently been linked to Hive Collapse, which is decimating the honeybee population in the US.

Natural Flea and Tick Repellants

Of course, the best way to prevent flea infestation in your home is to keep fleas the dog may encounter outdoors from jumping on him in the first place. That way they won't end up in the house. (The same is true of ticks, by the way.) What you need is a non-toxic flea and tick *repellant*.

The other advantage here is that you can spray down your dog when he leaves his own yard, which will help to keep your own yard flea and tick-free.

Essential Oils and Octopomine

And as it happens, Mother Nature has thoughtfully provided us with a fair number of them. They are found in many essential oils.

What these plant-based substances all do is interfere with the *octopomine neuroreceptors* of pheromone-driven insects and arthropods. Octopomine is sort of the insect version of adrenaline, and blocking the receptors for it causes quick death by CNS collapse. Insects are hard-wired to avoid these substances, all of which are aromatic. This is why they act as *repellants* as well as *insecticides*, and thus protect the plant from insect damage. It's an elegant example of Nature at her most brilliant. And....

Unlike most insectides, octopomine is not toxic to people or dogs

because mammals, fish and birds *don't have octopomine receptors.*

Clever.

Most of these substances have been used effectively for literally thousands of years without poisoning the planet, and really only fell out of favor in the last 30 years or so, when the big chemical and pharmaceutical companies decided they could do better.

Of course, as the toxicity of these man-made insecticides becomes more and more apparent, this is may well be another example of where "better is the enemy of good".

Along with others that may not smell as good (like neem oil and citronella, which a lot of people don't care for), the following more pleasantly aromatic essential oils have also been laboratory-tested and have been found to be both safe and effective in both repelling and killing both fleas and ticks:

- Cedar

- Lemongrass

- Peppermint

- Cinnamon

- Clove

All are FDA approved as human food additives, and are considered safe by the EPA when used as directed. (In other words, keep them out of the eyes and don't use them full strength on the skin)

Cedar oil, which has been used effectively for at least 3 thousand years as an insect repellant, is probably the overall winner here, as it's better than most at repelling ticks as well as fleas, although some owners claim peppermint oil is also effective on ticks. If you live in an area where ticks are a problem, that's worth knowing.

Non-toxic sprays and shampoos containing these essential oils are readily available commercially—you can find a wealth of them on Amazon if you search for "all-natural flea sprays" once you get there.

Most list their ingredients and you can sort of guess what they'll smell like based on that.

Barklogic, which gets good reviews, is primarily lemongrass and has a lemony aroma.

Vet's Best, another brand with good reviews, is peppermint and clove-y.

PetNaturals spray is a lemongrass/cinnamon combination that also gets high reviews.

Natural Chemistry's whole line of shampoos and sprays well and smell flat-out yummy.

There are lots more to choose from— just read the reviews and choose one that fits your needs. Remember that buying a product online that *doesn't actually list its ingredients* can be a little dicey, though — neem oil, for example, is a very safe and effective natural insecticide but smells a lot like burnt peanut butter.

Most of these companies make both a shampoo and a spray. If you are going to go this "non-toxic" route, you will need both.

Making Your Own Flea and Tick Repellants

Of course, you can also make your own natural flea and tick repellant spray by simply adding a couple tablespoons of essential cedar oil to a spray bottle of water, and then adding a teaspoon or so of any of the other bug-repellant essential oils you happen to like….truth is, it's hardly rocket science and it's a lot cheaper that way if you're a "do-it-yourself" type.

Here's a pretty easy "recipe":

Natural Flea and Tick Repellant

2 Tablespoons Cedar oil

1 Teaspoon Cinnamon oil

1 Teaspoon Clove oil

2 Teaspoons Vanilla extract

1 drop Dawn dish soap

12 oz filtered or distilled water

Mix together and shake well before each use. Cover eyes before spraying face.

Spray head, feet and legs and underside well. Rub into the fur with your hands.

Remember, you want to spray the dog mostly where fleas and ticks are going to jump on hitch a ride And adding a couple tablespoonfuls of cedar oil (along with a teaspoon or two of any other essential oils you feel like adding) to a bottle any shampoo will turn it into a safe and effective flea shampoo, although it's best to start with an unscented baby shampoo so you don't end up with something overwhelming. And always spray it on the inside of your arm before spraying it on your dog to make sure it's not irritating—if it is, pour out half, add more water and try again. And always keep it away from the eyes and mouth.

Now, unlike the once-a-month stuff, these sprays do have to be applied every day or two during the flea season, and you might want to spray your dog down again right before taking him for a walk in tick-heavy areas.

Besides insecticides that you actually put on or in your dog, the other major possibility for toxic exposure that the intelligent dog owner may want to consider is:

Lawn Chemicals

We all want a healthy, green lawn for our families to enjoy. But many people do not know that using synthetic lawn chemicals in your yard may increase your dog's risk of developing certain types of cancer.

A landmark 2004 study from Purdue University involving Scottish Terriers showed that dogs exposed to chemically treated lawns, specifically those treated with a chemical called **2,4-D** had a risk of transitional cell carcinoma (bladder cancer) 400% to 700% higher than that of dogs not exposed to these toxins.

An earlier study published in The Journal of the National Cancer Institute, a link was found between 2, 4-D and malignant lymphoma in dogs and non-Hodgkin's lymphoma in people, while a third study showed 2,4-D in the urine of dogs exposed to treated lawns.

This is probably not all that surprising when you consider that 2,4-D was one of the two primary components of Agent Orange, the jungle defoliant widely used during the Vietnam war and associated with cancers, reproductive issues and birth defects in humans and animals exposed to it.

Although most lawn care companies will try to convince you that their products are "safe for children and pets", there are a few things to consider before treating your lawn. First, they're only obligated to provide information on ***"Active Ingredients"*** in their products. This list leaves out the many ***"Inert***

Ingredients" also found in the products, many of which are known carcinogens or have documented health risks associated with them. One chemical that is often (amazingly) considered an inert ingredient is **2, 4-D** , the focus of the Purdue cancer study.

Dogs are at greater risk of exposure and potential side effects from lawn care chemicals because dogs do not wear clothing -- chemicals get on fur and are more easily absorbed into the skin. Nor do dogs wear shoes -- chemicals are absorbed through the paw pads and chemicals can be tracked into your home and they may be ingested when dogs lick their paws, as they often do. They also have a higher ratio of skin surface in relation to their body size, which gives them a proportionally larger surface area which can absorb toxins.

And dogs don't just walk on the grass, they roll in it, lay in it, sniff around in it and dig in it -- all opportunities to inhale, ingest and absorb more toxins than the average human would.

And last but certainly not least, in addition to walking on and playing in grass, Lord knows it's not uncommon for dogs to EAT grass while out in the yard, either intentionally or as part of all of the sticks and other things that they chew on while outside. *Chemically treated grass was never meant to be eaten.* Even if you don't treat your own lawn, it's good to remember when taking him for a walk that your neighbors might treat theirs. If you think your Dood may have been exposed to "toxic grass", hose off his feet (especially the pads on the underside) after you get home. That way he won't end up tracking the toxins onto his bed or ingesting it if he licks his paws.

In summary....

OK, now you know that a whole lot of how healthy your Dood ends up is really up to you, and the decisions YOU make for him from puppyhood on. Remember, *less toxins equal better overall health.* Choosing a more "holistic" vet who is up to date on immunology and understands the dangers of over -vaccination and overuse of insecticides and antibiotics will make things a lot easier, because you won't have to argue with someone trying to sell you what are often *totally unnecessary* toxins.

That said, in spite of all efforts, your Dood may find himself in need of emergency treatment at some point in his life, because of an accident or the ingestion of something not intended for ingestion. In these cases time is often of the essence.

Post the phone numbers for your vet, the nearest emergency clinic and the poison control center on the *wall* (rather than in your cell phone) so everyone in the house has access to it.

CHAPTER EIGHT:

Goldendoodle Grooming

(or...why people own shorthaired dogs)

No matter what you may have read on the internet, the Goldendoodle is universally considered by all professional groomers surveyed to be a *high-maintenance* breed, and this should be clearly understood before you commit to adding one to your household.

Breeders who "gloss over" the substantial grooming requirements of the Goldendoodle in an effort to sell puppies do potential owners and the breed itself a disservice, and actually contribute to the numbers of Doods finding themselves in need of a new home. (Sadly, along with "hyperactivity", inability to keep up with the coat is one of the most common reasons given when Goldendoodles are surrendered to shelters.) And to make things worse…

Much of the well-meaning information about Goldendoodle coat care on the internet

is either flat-out incorrect, or ridiculously optimistic.

In the "flat-out incorrect" department, for example, most websites state that the Goldendoodle's coat will grow 4-6 inches in length if not trimmed, when in fact, the coat on an untrimmed Goldendoodle can easily reach *ten inches*. (The only possible reason so few breeders know this is because so very few Doods are actually kept in full coat, which is a shame because it can be absolutely gorgeous.)

In the "ridiculously optimistic" department, a depressing number of breeders' websites claim that the Goldendoodle will need to be professionally groomed 3 or 4 times a year. Good luck with that.

And virtually all websites recommend using a slicker brush, which is the WORST possible grooming tool for this breed. (Or any breed, if it comes right down to it.)

This combination of disastrous advice is the major cause of the following all-too-common scenario:

The owner drops an adorable but shaggy Dood off at the groomers in the morning, with explicit instructions for a bath, a brush-out and a trim, but "not to shave him or make him look like a Poodle", a possibility the owner has already been warned about by breeders and owners everywhere.

When the owner comes back to pick him up in the afternoon, she's presented with an exorbitant bill by an extremely grumpy groomer (who tersely explains that the dog was "matted to the skin" and that was the best she could do, sorry) and a shaved-down dog who looks like a cross between a naked Poodle and Mamie Eisenhower with a mustache.

The disgruntled owner adds her voice to the legion of Goldendoodle owners badmouthing professional groomers.

Meanwhile the groomer, who's lost money by spending way too much time on a big matted dog who's not even table-trained, adds her voice to the legion of professional groomers badmouthing both Goldendoodles *and* their owners.

This animosity between owners and groomers has gotten so bad that an alarming number of groomers will no longer take any new Goldendoodle clients. At any price.

The real pity here is that this whole scenario could be easily prevented if all Goldendoodle breeders would do what all reputable purebred breeders of coated breeds have done for years: namely, show each new owner exactly what it takes to keep their breed's coat in good condition and properly groomed, give them a list of tools and products that work well on that specific breed, and explain the necessity of grooming *at least once a week*. Then professional groomers could do a great job in half the time even if the dog was only brought in once a *year* and everybody would be happy.

Since that's probably not going to happen any time in the foreseeable future, however, let's do the next best thing and honestly explain what's required to keep a Dood looking good, and exactly what the owner needs to do and what tools are required, whether they want to keep him short, long, or anywhere in between. The same principles apply whether they plan to employ the services of a professional or want to learn how to groom their Dood at home.

Since most owners are probably going to use a professional groomer, let's start there, because the basics are actually the same for both groups.

Avoid Disaster....Know the "Look" You Want

First off, if you are planning to have your Goldendoodle groomed professionally, you have to decide exactly what you want the end result to look like so you can clearly communicate that. Groomers really DO want to please their clients (it's better for business and the tips are more generous), but they are *not* mind-readers, and most do not keep a resident psychic on staff.

Bring a photo to the first appointment....with a caveat.

Many websites suggest bringing a good photograph of the look you want along with you when you drop the dog off, and this is actually pretty good advice, except for one problem—*nine out of ten Dood owners will bring along a photograph of a dog that to the groomer's experienced eye is pretty clearly several weeks from its last grooming appointment.*

Faced with these photos, many groomers have concluded that (unlike the rest of their clients, whom they perceive as sane) what the Goldendoodle owners really want are dogs who leave their grooming shops looking, well... *totally ungroomed*...which they just cannot get their heads around.

I mean, *think* about it for a minute—odds are pro groomers *became* groomers in the first place because they personally *like* the looks of sculpted, plush, sort of "frou-frou" dogs. Remember... these are people who actually think little bright-colored satin bows stuck onto various parts of a dog's head with teeny-weeny rubber bands are *cute,* and photos of shaggy dogs romping on the beach just don't do anything for them.

So for Heaven's sake find a photo of a *freshly-groomed* dog that illustrates the length and overall pattern you want. (Hint: these photos usually involve a dog actually standing on a grooming table.) Also make sure it's a dog with the same sort of coat that yours has—what works for a slightly wavy dog will be impossible to achieve with a curly one and vice-versa.

Unfortunately, unlike the Bichon or the Bedlington or the Dandie Dinmont, there is no immediately recognizable "official" trim pattern for the Goldendoodle to be found in the classic grooming texts, which seriously complicates things. This is mostly because they have no history of being exhibited at dog shows, which is where the various trims that different breeds sport evolved over the years.

That said, the one thing that *all* owners seem to agree on is that they do not want their Dood to "look like a Poodle", so let's examine that, because it clearly means different things to different people.

What Makes a Doodle Look Like a Poodle?

In the US, all the different Poodle trims involve varying amounts of plush body coat in various (and seemingly random) places, but all of them require a closely clipped muzzle and feet, with a "pompadour" on the top of the head ranging anywhere from a short rounded dome shape in the Sporting Trim favored by most pet owners to topknots of truly astonishing heights in the Puppy, English Saddle and Continental Clips required in the show ring. All are finished with a sculpted pompon on the tail. Although a well-groomed Poodle is a work of art (the best groomers are really topiary sculptors whose chosen medium is hair), collectively this is not a look *anyone* seems to desire in a Goldendoodle, and shaving the muzzle pretty much destroys the breed's characteristic expression.

On the other hand, if what is meant by a "Poodle look" involves more overall body shape rather than just the head, tail and feet, we have a different problem, because if both are clipped to the same length stem to stern with a 10 blade, it's going to be pretty hard to tell a clipped-down Goldendoodle from a clipped-down Poodle with a blocky muzzle. *That's just a fact of life.*

Because many of the physical traits of a Poodle tend to be controlled by dominant genes, the average Goldendoodle is built way more like a Poodle than a Golden retriever. Clipped short all over, both are revealed as square, leggy, lean breeds propped well up in front with a fair amount of tuck-up and rear angulation and the pretty typical lean heads seen on most pointing breeds.

f you do happen to like it, the clipped-down no-frills "sporting" look is far and away the easiest to maintain and probably best for people with allergies, because dogs in this clip can be bathed frequently with very little prep or finish work required. It's most popular with people who actually hunt with their Goldendoodles or spend a lot of time in and around boats. In fact, if this is the look you want for your Dood, you can skip a lot of this chapter....!

Virtually any groomer can take down a dog with a 10 blade, or you can buy a decent set of electric clippers and learn to do it yourself in no time flat, as there is not a great deal of artistry required—it's the canine version of the military buzz cut. However, this trim is not every owner's cup of tea, and has reduced more than a few to tears when a dog emerges from the grooming shop sporting it.

The "official" trim that actually comes the closest to what most Dood owners seem to want is probably the pet trim for the Soft Coated Wheaten Terrier, with the only real difference in the trimming of the top of the head, the ears and the tail.

To see what this looks like, just Google "pet wheaten images" and you'll find lots of examples. The Goldendoodle and the Wheaten have very similar coats, and the overall body proportions and angles very similar as well, which is why this works. The main anatomical differences are in tailset and earset—even the head proportions are similar, which goes to show you how much difference trimming can make!

The basic pet Wheaten trim can vary in length, depending upon the owner's wishes, but in all cases it involves a shorter "jacket" on the body (either clipped with a 4 blade or ideally scissored) blended into slightly longer hair on the underbody and the legs, which are scissored in a column straight down to the toes, without shaving the feet.

Any professional groomer should know how to do this trim—just be sure and tell them to scissor the head into a "Benji" trim rather than a standard Wheaten show trim, and to leave a plume on the tail.

Unless the groomer is completely inept, requesting a modified Wheaten trim will pretty much guarantee that your Dood does not end up being mistaken for a clipped-down blonde Poodle.

Plush vs. Shaggy

Of course, what *some* owners really mean when they say they don't want their Dood to look like a Poodle is simply that they don't want them to look overly "coiffed', because it is the shaggy, casually tousled appearance that attracted them to the breed in the first place.

In reality, this is a difficult look for the majority of groomers to achieve, and virtually *impossible* to achieve with just a clipper, which is what most groomers use. Even with a snap-on comb attachment that leaves the hair up to an inch long, all the hair will be the same length and the finish will be "plush" rather than shaggy.

No matter what pattern is used, the *only* way to achieve a shaggy rather than a smooth plush finish is by using a peculiar breed of scissors called a "chunker". In essence a one-sided thinning shears with very coarse teeth, they are also called a "texturing shears". Popular for some years with hairdressers, these are relatively new to the dog grooming world. Although just starting to catch on, groomers who know about them love them, as do their clients, because they truly are capable of producing a more natural, shaggy-dog look while still taking off needed inches of hair. If that's really the look you want, request that the groomer use a chunker. If they don't know what you're talking about, find one who does, because the results will be worth it.

How often does a Goldendoodle REALLY need to be taken to the groomer

... and what will it cost?

If you want to keep your Goldendoodle in a fairly short trim (maybe between one to three inches), most groomers agree he will ideally need to be trimmed every 4-6 weeks or so, although many owners can stretch it out to 8 weeks if they are religious about brushing. The Poodle coat spends more time in the anagen, or growth, phase than most breeds— this translates to a really fast-growing coat, and most Goldendoodles appear to have inherited that trait, especially the multi-generational ones.

If you do not want to brush your own dog at all but don't want to keep him really short, most groomers agree the Goldendoodle should be taken to the groomer's *weekly*, because that's the bare minimum of how often the average one needs to be brushed out in order to avoid matting.

Currently, the cost for having a Goldendoodle groomed runs between $50 and $100 per visit, depending on where you live. (Some groomers will give a discount to owners who bring their dogs in frequently, because it takes them significantly less time to groom these dogs, and groomers' fees are really based on the hours involved.) Spreading out the time between groomings rarely saves money in the long run, because the groomer will have to charge more if the coat has been neglected.

But any way you slice it, keeping your Dood short will quickly add up to hundreds of dollars a year and untold thousands of dollars over his lifetime if you plan to have him professionally groomed, so you need to factor that in before deciding to add one to your family.

Grooming Your Dood at Home

Can you do it yourself? Yes, absolutely. Anyone can learn to bathe and brush a dog. And if you have maybe two hours once every 4 to 6 weeks to put into the project, you can invest in two decent pairs of shears (one of which is the aforementioned chunkers) and learn to scissor your dog yourself to whatever length you prefer, which frankly is NOT rocket science.

Although your first efforts may produce less than stellar results, the soft wavy Goldendoodle coat is both forgiving of scissoring errors and grows back with astonishing swiftness, so you'll have lots of opportunity to practice your technique. (A do-it-yourself trimming guide follows the sections on brushing and bathing, because whether you have your dog trimmed professionally or do it yourself, that is the order that needs to be followed.) And all of the equipment needed to do the job will cost less than a single year's grooming bills.

The "Full Coat" Option

OR you can opt keep him in full length coat, in which case you can be prepared to literally stop traffic wherever you go. Although it also requires regular and thorough line brushing, which will take longer than brushing out a shorter coat (you can do it while you're watching TV), you will save thousands of dollars in grooming costs over the years. A dog in full coat will only need periodic "hygienic" scissoring of his feet, around his eyes and beneath his tail, which almost anyone can master.

If you have a particularly curly F1b or F2b dog, a full-length coat will tend to stand away from the body like a giant dandelion puff and probably isn't a great idea, but most F1 Doods that look pretty curly cut down would only display a slight wave if kept in full coat, because the weight pulls out the wave in dogs just as it does in people.

And although no one ever believes this, a longhaired dog of any breed that's *never* had his coat trimmed will actually tangle and mat way less than one who has, because the hair is allowed to maintain its natural growth pattern of different lengths, which is lost forever as soon as it is trimmed to all one length.

Lest you find this option impossible to believe, it's worth knowing that with the exception of the hygienic trimming described above, the Goldendoodle pictured on the right in the photo at the beginning of this chapter *never been cut down*. Murphy is a certified Search and Rescue Dog who swims regularly and works in the brush and snow of Utah's high country. At seven years of age, his body coat measures a full ten inches from the roots to the ends.

Whether you decide to have your dog trimmed by a professional, or plan to do it yourself, and no matter what length you wish to keep him at, the average Doodle still needs frequent and thorough comb-outs *at least once a week,* and some of them frankly need to be done daily, especially during the adolescent period when the coat is transitioning from puppy coat to adult coat. The frequency varies from dog to dog, but in general, softer coats with more curl will tangle and mat faster than straighter coarser ones, which can usually be managed with a thorough going-through once a week.

If mats never have a chance to develop, the process will be painless and relaxing and both you and your Dood will come to enjoy the grooming sessions. (A short daily grooming session will actually help to develop a strong bond between the groomer and the "groomee", and will make all other aspects of training easier.)

On the other hand, if you put it off, the combing out of snarls and mats will turn it into a long and painful chore for both of you, and *nobody* will enjoy it.

Using "the Right Stuff"

Whether or not you'll actually keep your dog mat-free depends to a large degree on how easy or difficult the job is. And that depends entirely upon having the right equipment. With "the right stuff", a thorough daily comb-out should not take more than 10 minutes tops for a well-trained Goldendoodle puppy and maybe twice that long for a large adult. And if you really truly do it once a day starting from the day he arrives at your home, your dog will be well-trained in short order!

The equipment and the grooming techniques that follow are probably different than what you may have used previously, or even different than what most pet groomers use. That's because they are the tools and techniques dog-show people use to groom *their* dogs…you know, the ones you see floating around the ring at Westminster with flowing silky coats. (Trust me, those coats have *never* seen a slicker brush, and they've never been brushed out standing on the floor.)

For years, the only place you could buy this stuff was from one of the big general supply booths at a dog show, but now, except for the grooming table and the spray bottle, pretty much everything else can be purchased online from www.BBird.biz in one fell swoop.

So without further ado, here it is….

The Quintessential Goldendoodle Grooming Supply List

- **A grooming table and post.** *There is no way to overstate this: the grooming table is the single most important piece of equipment needed here. Besides saving your back and preventing your dog from up and leaving right in the middle of the grooming session, every professional groomer on the planet uses a grooming table, and they unanimously complain about the fact that Goldendoodles are never table-trained, which makes grooming take a whole lot longer...and for which you, dear reader, will pay dearly in hard cash. You can buy one on Amazon with a grooming post and loop for under a hundred dollars.*

- **A PSI wood-handled poodle comb.** *If this were the ONLY grooming tool you owned, your Doodle would be mat-free for life. Regular use of this comb from the roots to the ends will ensure a "fleece" of matted coat doesn't form at the skin, which is almost sure to happen with a slicker brush.*

- **A Chris Christensen 16mm T-brush.** *Even though a poodle comb really will suffice, most people will feel the need to brush their Dood anyway. This brush is far and away the best one for the job. Well-made in Germany with smooth polished pins that won't damage the coat or scratch the skin like cheaper ones will, it has a smooth t-shaped wooden handle and an ergonomic shape that's far easier on the wrist than a traditional pin brush. It comes in two sizes—the large one works for most dogs, while the smaller "mini" is a better choice for their smaller cousins and puppies.*

- **A plastic spray bottle.** *As every dog-show groomer knows, brushing a dry coat is*

187

totally verboten if you want to avoid coat damage. Since damaged coats mat far more easily than coats that are not, it's well-worth the small effort involved in lightly misting the dog's coat each and every time you take a brush or comb to it— once you do get into the habit of doing this, brushing a dry dog will seem as wrong as driving off without fastening your seat belt!   As far as what to mist the coat with, plain water with a teaspoon of unscented conditioner added will work just fine. Adding a couple tablespoonfuls of cedar oil will also repel f\leas and ticks, so you can kill two birds with one stone here. A simple plastic spray bottle with a broad base can be purchased cheaply at any dollar store—it's a good idea to buy two, in case the sprayer stops working on the first one mid-dog. (This is one of the few places where there's no percentage in paying more than you need to.)

- **Detangler .** A silicone-based detangler applied to mat and allowed to dry before detangling will make the job easier. Chris Christensen's Ice on Ice spray works well., as does Silk Drops, which is made for people.

- **A guillotine-style nail clipper and a nail file or emery board.**   On a dog the size of a Goldendoodle, the guillotine will work far better than the scissors-type with a so-called 'safety guard'. They can be purchased at any pet store or from Amazon. If used correctly (instructions are included later on) they are not scary at all, in spite of their ghastly name. A sturdy nail file or emery board will smooth the nail after clipping and avoid inadvertent scratches from an exuberant dog. It's a good idea to buy a little container of Qwik-Stop at the same time, which will stop any bleeding immediately if you accidentally do cut a nail a little too short.

- **A box of cornstarch and a plastic parmesan cheese shaker.**   You can buy a box of cornstarch at any grocery store and the cheese shaker is another dollar store item.(You can also use cornstarch baby powder if you don't mind the scent, in which case you won't need the shaker.)

- **Coconut oil and a bag of cotton balls.** *These will be used for cleaning the ears, which should be done every week or so. Coconut oil has great natural anti-viral, anti-bacterial and anti-fungal properties, and will actually help prevent ear infections.*

- **A good 7 or 8 inch straight hairdresser's shears or a good pair of chunkers.** *If your Dood is curly, this is the scissors you want. Pro-line makes a good pair for around a hundred dollars, and if you don't use them for anything else or trim a sand-covered dog with them, they'll keep a good edge for a long time. For straighter and wavy coats, the chunker will allow you to achieve the "natural" look Dood owners like, and is by definition very forgiving of errors as you perfect your scissoring skills. The Pro-line 7-inch chunker is a good choice. Its $139 dollar price tag might seem steep, but not when you consider you'll spend at least that amount in three grooming appointments. Don't even TRY to trim your dog with a cheap pair of scissors – a good pair will last for decades and you simply won't be able to do a good job if you try to save money here. You'll end up with a ragged-looking dog and a bad case of carpal tunnel syndrome.*

- **A 5 or 6 inch straight shears with ball tips.** *Breaking the rule here, this one doesn't really have to be all that good, because you're not cutting much with it, so if you need to save money, this is the place to do it. Don't go much under $15 or $20 though, or they'll get dull in a couple sessions and you'll be sorry. Even if you plan to have your Dood trimmed professionally, you'll need this one for hygienic trimming around the eyes, butt and feet between times.*

- **A bag of special "grooming treats", reserved for grooming only.** *What's most important* *is that it's a treat he only gets when he's completed a grooming session, so he'll make the association and actually look forward to being groomed. It works—dogs who always get a treat after nails trimming will cheerfully offer up their paws rather than fight you.*

And except for the grooming table, which folds up when not in use, all this stuff will fit in a basket that can sit on a shelf in the laundry room.

Notice that the "slicker brush" recommended on so many websites is NOT on this list.

This is not an oversight.

In fact, if you already own a slicker, *throw it out right now*. First off, it is REALLY painful....seriously, try brushing your *own* hair with one and I guarantee you that you'll feel guilty that you ever subjected your poor dog to it! No wonder so many of America's dogs "hate being brushed" and won't hold still for it—if that's all they've ever been brushed with, you can hardly blame them. You'd run and hide, too—in fact, did you ever wonder why if it's so great they don't make a brush like this for people?

Unless you want to cause serious skin abrasion, there is absolutely no way a slicker, with that stupid bend in its nasty wire bristles, can get all the way to the root of the hair, which is why so many dogs come into the groomer's brushed on the outside and literally felted at the skin. This requires that they be sheared down like a Suffolk, because that's the only way the groomer can get under the felt, and *nobody ends up happy.*

As if *that* isn't bad enough, the slicker roughs up the cuticle on the hair shaft, which damages the hair and actually *causes* mats. Next to the retractable leash, the ubiquitous slicker brush is the worst thing to ever happen to dog ownership. Allowing a brush that looks like it was designed for scrubbing a barbeque grill anywhere near a dog just makes no sense at all. *It's probably not a coincidence that internet grooming instructions that involve the use of a slicker are invariably written by people who also misspell the word "mat", which ought to tell you something...it's not a "matt", folks. Never was.*

The other item intentionally missing from the list is a mat-splitter.

Another perfectly awful invention inflicted on the unsuspecting pet-owner, it's far better to learn to untangle a mat using a detangler spray, your fingers and cornstarch. If a mat cannot be teased apart (and almost any mat can be), it's really better to just use a scissors

blade as explained further on. Like slickers, mat-splitters and so-called "mat rakes" are hard on the coat and painful for the dog, and will also cause him to hate being groomed.

Line Brushing

Ok, now that you have all the right equipment, it's time to learn to *line brush*. Before you can do it, though, you need to train your puppy (or adult Dood if you're starting late) to lie on his side on the grooming table while being brushed, because that will allow you to easily get to the parts that are most likely to mat. It's really the ONLY way to line brush, no matter what size the dog.

Table-Training 101

1. **Set up your table** with have your supplies close at hand.

2. **Lift your puppy onto the table** with his head to your left and his tail to your right.

3. **Now lie him on his side.** The way you do this is to wrap your left hand around his right foreleg about halfway up (this is the leg farthest from you!) and your right hand around his right hind leg and pull gently towards you while saying "Rufus, side" (unless of course his name isn't Rufus, in which case you'll want to use his own name so as not to confuse him) in a firm and cheery voice. Voila! In one fell swoop your dog will end up lying flat on his right side with his feet facing you. He'll also be pretty surprised if he's never done it before, so you'll want to praise him like mad for learning this new trick. If he's big enough, he'll soon be hopping up there and lying down on his own like a seasoned show dog as soon as you give him the command. (Puppies and Minidoodles need to be lifted up but should lie on their side on command.)

4. *Now, as soon as he's on his side and before he has a chance to scramble back up, take your left arm and lay it firmly across his body.* Put your elbow at his point of shoulder, your forearm across his ribcage and your palm flat on the point of hip.

5. *With the brush in your right hand, GENTLY brush over his feet, legs and body.* Pick up each leg and brush lightly between them. (The goal here is not to thoroughly brush him so much as to get him used to being brushed while he's lying on his side.) Be sure and tell him what a good boy he is while you're doing it, because you want the whole experience to be positive. If he starts to get up, a quick tug on both of the right legs will put him neatly back on his side without having to wrestle with him. Repeat the "side" command while you're pulling and praise him when he's back on his side.

6. *When you've gone over his left side with the brush, do the same with the other side.* The easiest way to do this is to allow him to stand, turn him all the way around so his head is facing in the other direction and repeat step 3, this time with your left hand around his left hind leg and your right hand around his right foreleg as you give the "side" command, remembering to praise him lavishly when he's on his side once more. (This time when you lay your arm across him your elbow will be on his hip and your palm will be on his shoulder.)

7. *Once the second side is done, stand the puppy up and slide his head into the grooming loop.* Tell him to "stand" and "stay". Quickly brush his head and ears and brush the body coat down. Pick up his feet one by one, examine them and put them back down. Finish off with his special grooming treat, praise him lavishly, tell him he's gorgeous, and lift him down.

The whole process shouldn't take more than a couple minutes, and even an 8 week old puppy can learn this in a couple lessons. Once he's big enough (and brushing isn't a painful experience for him!), he'll be hopping up there and lying down on his side on his own like a seasoned show dog as soon as you give him the command. (Puppies and small Minidoodles will need to be lifted up.)

In fact, the "side" command can be used any time you want your dog to lie on his side – in case this hasn't occurred to you, it's the first step if you want to teach a dog to roll over.

"Stand" is another fairly easy command- it basically means don't go anywhere and don't sit down. Even the most dim-witted show dog learns this one with very little effort, so it should be no problem for your genius Dood. In both cases, it's good to practice these commands in lots of different places both indoors and out, lest the dog think they are only required on a table.

It goes without saying that even if your dog has the "stay" command down pat, no dog should EVER be left unattended on a grooming table, especially if he is attached to the grooming post— groomers don't call that loop that slides over his head a grooming "noose" for nothing!

Once your puppy understands the "side" command and will stay there on his own, you can actually begin line brushing.

Line Brushing Step by-Step

1. ***With the dog on his side, begin by misting lightly all over.*** *Now brush all the hair in the opposite direction of its natural growth—in other words....up.*

2. ***Start with the hind foot.*** *Mist the whole leg lightly, then take your Poodle comb and comb a small section back down, being sure to comb all the way from the root to the end. As soon as that layer's combed through, part off another layer maybe two inches above the first one with the last tooth on your comb (or a knitting needle if the coat is full-length) and then comb that one down, adding it to the bottom layer. Keep adding layers until the rear leg is combed through all the way to the spine.*

3. *Lift the leg slightly and comb out the inside of the opposite leg.* Keep your left arm across his body with firm but gentle pressure, Any time he starts to right himself, a slight tug on the offside leg will neatly put him back on his side without a wrestling match. (This quick movement will become second nature in short order.) Comb through the tail while you're back there.

4. **Move next to the ribcage area.** Start by combing out the first layer on the tummy from elbow to the already-combed-out hindquarters, adding layers as you go until you've combed everything to the spine. (If your Dood is really big, you may want to do the upper part by rotating him end-for-end while he's lying on his side until his feet are on the other side of the table ;this can save a lot of wear and tear on your back .)

5. **Move on to the front foot.** Using the same technique, add layers until you've combed down everything from foot to the spine, including the whole shoulder area.

6. **Lift the leg you just brushed and comb through the inside of the opposite leg, and then comb through the chest area between the front legs.** Make sure you have carefully combed out the area inside the elbow— that's a prime area for mats to form because the coat there rubs against itself with every step the dog takes. That hair can actually be trimmed short if you want.

7. **Turn the puppy around so his head is facing in the other direction, lie him down on his left side, and repeat the whole process.**

8. **Put your puppy on a sit-stay and slide the grooming loop over his head.** Adjust the slide so he can't back out of it. Now comb through his ears, neck, head and muzzle. (This is also when you'll want to clean ears, brush teeth and trim nails, all of which should be done weekly.)

9. *Stand him up (giving him the "stand" command), mist the coat lightly all over and brush the entire coat down with the pin brush.*

10. *Praise lavishly.* Give him his grooming treat, and lift him off the table. Take him outside to relieve himself, and then spend at least the next 5 minutes doing fun stuff with him.

If you actually follow the directions above on a daily basis, you will never need the following instructions, because your Dood will go through life mat-free. But since life often gets in the way of our best intentions, here's what to do if your comb actually hits a snag—*detangle* it.

What we call "mats" are really nothing more than tangled-up hair, some of which is probably attached to the dog's skin and some of which is not. Here's how to untangle it:

Detangling a Mat Step-by-Step

1. *Don't pull. Stop combing immediately.* Spray the area lightly with detangler and let it dry while you brush somewhere else.

2. *Take your shaker and sprinkle a little cornstarch or baby powder on the tangled area and work it in well with your fingers.* This will help untangle the mat by smoothing the roughed-up hair cuticles or something. (Never mind why—it just works.)

3. *Using only the thumb and index fingers of each hand, tease the mat apart bit by bit, always pulling sideways, until it looks more like a dust bunny than a mat.* Rub in more cornstarch as needed. (For some reason, this sideways pulling is not painful for the dog at all.)

4. *Pinch the area firmly at the roots. Now take your comb and use only the very last tooth to split the mat into small sections if needed.* You can also saw through it, using the blade of your opened scissors, sawing gently out from the root to the end. Remember to keep the scissors open and saw rather than cut (don't use your chunkers here.)

195

5. *Comb through the area with short strokes in stages, starting with the ends and working your way toward the root.* *Finish by brushing through it with the pin brush if needed.*

NOTE: This method will painlessly remove most "garden variety" mats—you can untangle a mat the size of your fist using this method if you have the time and inclination without causing pain or losing any hair that's still attached to the dog.

However, it WILL NOT work when the dog is matted in a "fleece" all over about a half-inch from the skin, so don't even try. That condition is almost always caused by improper brushing (usually from using a slicker brush) and the only painless cure for it is an electric clipper and a ten blade. If it happens, it's not the end of the world…your Dood will just look like a big shaved rat with long legs for a few weeks, and you'll know enough so that it won't ever happen again.

Bathing Your Goldendoodle

Many websites state that Goldendoodles "don't need frequent bathing". *I guess that depends on what you want your dog to smell like.*

Besides the doggy odor, dirty dogs mat faster than clean ones, and will carry more of the *Can f* proteins that cause allergic reactions, so if you got the dog for his hypoallergenic qualities, failing to bathe him frequently will be entirely counterproductive. Most Doods need to be bathed twice a month, although once a month may suffice. This can be done in the bathtub or shower with a handheld spray attachment or outside with the hose if it's hot enough. (Although most Doods like cold water well enough to swim in it, an outside hot/cold faucet will be appreciated at bath time.

Besides a source of water and a drain, here's what you're gonna need to do the job right:

- **Shampoo and cream rinse.** *If one of the reasons you got a Goldendoodle in the first place was because of allergies in the family, it's pretty dumb to cover him in shampoo and conditioner that's loaded with chemicals and artificial scents that provoke allergies. There are now lots of brands to choose from if allergies are a problem. Pawganics makes a line of non-toxic hypoallergenic unscented dog shampoos and conditioners* that are available on Amazon. If you want to turn it into a non-toxic flea shampoo, simply add two tablespoons of cedar oil to the shampoo and shake well. If allergies are not an issue, the Chris Christensen line of products are hard to beat, and beloved by show people everywhere. You can buy them online from their website, chrissystems.com. (Along with their shampoos and conditioners, their Ice on Ice Detangler is a total winner.)

- **An Absorber synthetic drying chamois or two and/or a couple of old bath towels.** Once you've used an Absorber to dry your dog, you'll never go back to regular towels. Way better than chamois cloths, they are more like big (like 27 x 17 inch) extraordinarily thin sponges and are the best idea to come out of Japan since the compact car. Actually made for drying cars, they will take a ton of water off a dog and can be squeezed out and used over and over until the dog is nearly dry. If you buy two, you'll think of lots of cool things to do with the second one. You may not even need the bath towels, although you can use one to finish him off if it makes you feel better. The Absorber can be purchased on –where else?–Amazon for under twelve bucks.

- **A Hair dryer on a stand** Unless you live somewhere very hot and dry, air-drying your dog year-round is probably not practical, and waiting "until the weather warms up" to give him a bath isn't a great idea if you happen to live somewhere like Duluth, when that could be awhile.   What everybody eventually figures out is that it takes three hands to dry even a well-trained dog, so you need a dryer on a stand.   A table-top stand dryer is useless for the average Goldendoodle, because there's not enough room on the table for both the dryer and the dog, and it'll only dry his feet and halfway up his legs in its little stand, so you have to pick it up to get the high parts, which sort of defeats the purpose. You need a FLOOR-stand dryer. The Rolls Royce here is the Oster Hi-Velocity Stand Dryer. Rock-solid, it will last forever and adjusts to every

position needed to dry every conceivable part of a dog of any size with little effort. It's
as good as a dryer can get. It also retails for around six hundred dollars. If that's more
than you want to pay for a doggy hair dryer, all is not lost. For $12.95 you can buy a
Jobar Hair Dryer Stand from Amazon to which you can attach your very own hand-
held hair dryer made for people. You'll save mucho dinero and still have both hands free.

Bathing Your Dood the Right Way

Now that you have everything you need to bathe your dog close at hand and you have him completely brushed out, it's time to actually get him wet and soapy. Although it seems like it should be pretty straightforward, the truth is 99% of people actually bathe their dog *wrong,* and in doing so cause the coat to mat. This is why even when the dog has been completely brushed out beforehand, you'll often encounter snarls when blow-drying that seemingly appeared out of nowhere. But they really didn't… you created them your veryownself by incorrectly bathing! Here's how to do it right, start to finish, in Eight Easy Steps:

Doodle bathing 101

1. **Wet the dog thoroughly and pour the shampoo down the spine from head to tail.** *Respray the shampooed part lightly to water down the shampoo a little and literally comb the shampoo through the dripping coat with your fingers only in the direction that the hair grows. Do NOT mash the hair around every which way to spread the shampoo – that's what causes matting, because the cuticles of each hair are softened and open at this point and will snag on each other when you do all that mashing around.*

2. **Add more shampoo to the legs,** *applying some at the top of each leg and combing it down the leg with your fingers from top to bottom, again without smooshing the hair up and down like you're scrubbing socks on a washboard.*

3. **Do basically the same thing on the head, ears and neck**, finger-combing the shampoo through in the direction the hair naturally falls, and then shampoo the tail, adding the shampoo along the top and finger-combing it down through the feathering.

4. **Rinse thoroughly and apply the conditioner** using the exact same technique.

5. **Squeegee off the excess water with your hands and then use your Absorber to remove as much water as possible**, again wiping firmly in the direction the coat grows rather than "against the grain" or around in circles. As soon as the absorber is pretty wet, wring it out and go over the dog again as many times as needed. Run it down each leg from top to bottom several times, wringing it out as needed. You can do this while he's still in the tub or shower, which will keep everything (including you) a lot drier.

6. **Once you have him at least halfway dry, cover him with the dry towel and blot, don't rub.** If you're going to let him air-dry, run the Poodle comb through and set him free. Otherwise go to Step 7.

7. **Spread the other towel on the grooming table and lift your Dood onto it, sliding the grooming loop over his head.** Turn on the dryer to low (always check with your hand to make sure it's not too hot) and use your pin brush to fluff the coat as you dry it in sections, rather than all over. A lot of it can be done while he's sitting, or even lying down. (Some dogs like to be dried in the "side" position, which works well, especially on longer coats, which you'll want to blow dry in line-brushing layers.) Give him the "stand" command to finish the underside.

8. **Reward with his special "grooming treat" and take him outside to play for a couple of minutes.** Be sure and tell him how gorgeous he is!

Trimming the Goldendoodle

One of the main advantages of trimming your Dood yourself is that you can scissor the coat to whatever length you want as often as you want, instead of the dog spending a third of his life much *shorter* than you like and another third much *longer* than you like! You can take an inch or so off whenever needed in an hour or less, which will keep him pretty much looking the same all the time.

These instructions are for scissoring only. It's best to learn to scissor first, and then, once you're comfortable, reasonably proficient and committed to grooming your dog yourself, invest in a good clipper IF you decide you need to do a faster job, or want to keep your Dood in a really short sporting clip. (The reason professional pet groomers mostly use an electric clipper is because it's faster, and for a pro groomer, time is money. It's *not* because it does a better job than a scissors, which is what the perfection-oriented show groomers use.)

On a dog like a Goldendoodle, a fifty-dollar "home pet clipper set" is just not going to do it—you'll be lucky to get through halfway down the back before it heats up and bogs down. You'll need a decent professional-quality 2-speed clipper like the Oster Golden A-5 or the Andis AGC, and then you'll need a couple of extra blades (like a 4 F and a 7F) and maybe a set of steel combs because the 10-blade that comes with them will only leave 1/16 of an inch of hair, so by the time you're done you'll have well over $200 in the project.

Contrary to popular belief, unless to plan to keep him in a buzz cut, learning to use a clipper is actually *harder* than learning to scissor, because you can make really big holes in the coat in a heartbeat if the dog moves at the wrong time, and clipper burns (the mark of the inept) are downright painful for the dog. Besides, scissoring is quieter and way more fun!

Now, until pretty recently, unless he was pretty curly, scissoring a Dood took a fair amount of skill and practice if you didn't want him to look like it had been trimmed by a first-grader. That changed with the scissors known as a "chunker". By definition, this scissors will leave a feathered edge that looks natural (unlike the "plush" look an electric clipper produces) and it's very forgiving of mistakes. It is the PERFECT scissors for the slightly wavy coat. (Curly dogs really do not need a chunker, although it works fine on them too.)

Before you start cutting on your dog, it's best to take a minute to practice with your scissors because nine out of ten people hold a scissors wrong, and odds are good you're one of 'em.

Here's how to use a scissors correctly, assuming you're going to cut with your right hand:

1, *Slide your right thumb in the hole that does NOT have a finger rest attached to it.*

2. *Put your RING finger through the other one, resting your pinkie on the finger rest.*

3. *Now move your thumb (and only your thumb!) to open and close the blade all the way.*

Holding the scissors correctly will keep you from dipping into the coat and making choppy little cuts with the last two inches of the blade (which is what happens when you use your thumb and index finger) instead of making long smooth cuts with the whole blade. Practice doing this until the motion becomes both comfortable and second nature.

If you're using a chunker on a wavy coat, there's actually a video by grooming maven Barbara Bird demonstrating the use of a chunker on a dog that's well-worth watching before you start— just go to YouTube, type in "GroomClassroom" and scroll down until you get to the video titled "Cool Tools for Pet Grooming". A picture is truly worth a thousand words here. (Barbara's grooming blog also has lots of wonderful information and photos on it, including stuff on grooming Goldendoodles.)

Until you and your dog are more experienced, it's good to have an extra person (a spouse or a large child works well) to help hold him, otherwise you'll just have to use your grooming post and the "stand" command, which you WILL have practiced beforehand if you're smart.

Note: If you're left-handed, follow these instructions as written, replacing "right" with "left" and "left" with "right", which you're probably used to by now. Don't even bother to look for left-handed chunkers.

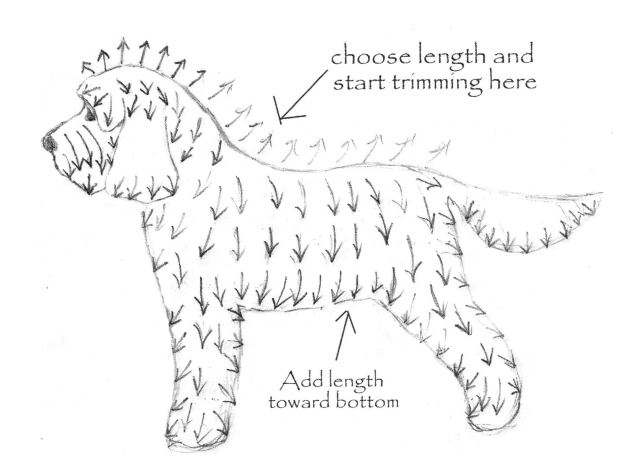

choose length and
start trimming here

Add length
toward bottom

Scissoring a Goldendoodle, Step-by-Step

1. With the dog standing on the table with his head to your left, lift the hair along the spine just behind the shoulders with your Poodle comb, which you should be holding in your left hand. Decide how long you want the hair to be, and with the scissors in your right hand, start cutting from the shoulders toward the tail at that length, keeping the scissors parallel to the spine and remembering to use the whole blade. (Instead of the single cut you'll make with a plain shears, you will need to make two or three rapid cuts with the chunker, moving the scissors very slightly each time to create a natural feathered finish to the hair.) Lift each area with the comb before you start cutting. Trim until you've got a swath about four to six inches wide cut down the back all the way to the base of the tail that's the length you want. Now "fluff and comb" through the whole area in the direction the coat grows to remove any cut hair that didn't fall off and touch up where needed.

2. With the scissors pointing down, start moving down the side of the rump closest to you, remembering to fluff the hair with the comb before each cut. Trim this hair to approximately the same length as the back. Make sure the tips of your scissors are not dipping in to the coat, and that you are cutting with the entire length of the blade.

3. Still working with the scissors vertically, move down the leg, trimming all the way around and making a straight column to the foot, leaving this hair slightly longer than the "jacket". Blend the coat at the elbow to get a smooth transition between the jacket and the leg. (This is easier than it sounds.)

4. Brush the hair around the foot straight down and pick up the foot, wrapping your hand around it. With your straight scissors, trim off all the hair that sticks out below the foot, and trim any excess hair between the pads. (You can use your little ball-tipped scissors to do the

pads if you're afraid of slicing a pad.) When you put the foot back down, you should have a nice round circle with maybe a tuft or two sticking out. Starting with the blade of your straight shears nearly flat on the table, tip it up about 45 degrees and trim neatly around the foot. The resulting angle will make the dog appear "well up on his toes".

5. **Next move to the ribcage, and work your way down that area (again keeping your scissors pointed down), fluffing as you go.** *To maintain the Goldendoodle outline, you want to leave it a little longer starting about halfway down the ribcage. Now working with your scissors parallel to the table, trim the underside, blending it into the sides and leaving enough length behind the ribcage to avoid a "poodley" or "greyhound" look. (In other words, you don't want to carve a lot of tuck-up under the loin.)*

6. **Move to the shoulder and trim the front leg** *pretty much as described in section 3. Lift the front foot and trim the same way as you did the back one.*

7. **Working from the head down, trim the neck, throat and chest, taking the throat and neck area down to the length of the back and leaving the hair slightly longer as you move to the chest.** *(Remember, you can always shorten an area afterwards, but you can't put hair back on!) Lift the ear and trim the entire area under it, blending into the neck- keeping the hair under the ear short will allow for airflow and will reduce the incidence of ear infections.*

Now stand back and check out what you've done so far. Make sure the line of the back is level, and neaten up the outline. Turn the dog around, and repeat the process on the other side. Check your work from the front and the rear, to make sure both sides match, trimming as needed down the shoulders, hips and sides of the legs to get there.

Trimming the tail

Once the body is done, brush through the tail and hold it out straight. Comb the feathering down and trim it into an elongated triangle from base to tip at whatever length you prefer. Use your ball-tipped scissors to trim around the anal and genital areas for hygienic purposes, including the first inch or so under the tail. (This ideally needs to be done every couple of weeks even if you are having your dog professionally trimmed.)

Trimming the head

First decide what length you want here, and keep a photo handy- tape one to the wall (a photo taken from the angle of the one below is most helpful) so you can look at it as you work. You'll get better results if trim the whole head at once rather than one side at a time, so you want the dog facing you dead-on for this part. He can be sitting down for this.

1.   Lift the hair on the top skull with your comb and trim it to the desired length, starting at the center of the head between the eyes and working front to back, trimming in an arch that follows the line of the skull rather than straight across. Now lift the hair between the trimmed area and the ear to your left with your comb. Turning your scissors so the tip is pointing to the ear, blend this hair into the top of the ear, again working in a curve rather than straight across.

2.   Next, brush the hair on the muzzle and beard, brushing toward the nose. Using your chunkers so that you get a natural finish, trim it to the desired length, trimming in a half-circle on each side rather than chopping it straight across. Some owners prefer to shorten the hair more around the jaw behind the muzzle, while others prefer a fuller face—there's no rule here, so go with your personal preference...you can always start fuller and remove more later if you like.

3.   Now, using your ball-tipped scissors with the tip up rather than down, trim the hair between the eyes into an inverted V shape. (It helps to cover the dog's eye with your left hand as you're doing this on each side, as it will keep him from jerking back.)

4.   Trim the bangs to the desired length, always working in a half-circle shorter in the center and longer toward the ears to avoid the Mamie Eisenhower look.

5.   Trim the ears to the desired length with the chunkers, making a rounded curve rather than a straight-across cut.

OK, you're done! Remember to give your Dood his special grooming treat, praise him lavishly for being such a great dog, compliment him on his good looks and take him out to play fetch for a couple of minutes.

It's also good to remember that, depending on your own temperament and the patience of your four-footed buddy, this trimming does not have to be done in one marathon session (although it really shouldn't take more than an hour tops once you've done it a couple times) but can be broken up into several sessions.

As with regular grooming, the important thing is to keep it from becoming a drag for the dog. And the best way to accomplish this is to *talk* to him while you're snipping way or combing…unlike everyone else in your life, *here's a friend who never tires of the sound of your voice*. He thinks you're brilliant, witty and the smartest person on the planet and your voice is music to his ears. Tell him about your job, or your love life, or practice chatting to him in a foreign language—at least he won't laugh at your accent! If you can carry a tune, you can sing the entire score of The Sound of Music while you're grooming. Come to think about it, you can do that even if you *can't* carry a tune…odds are good he's never heard Julie Andrews anyway, so he'll have nothing to compare it to.

Grooming Involves More Than Hair

In addition to an attractive tangle-free coat, a well-groomed dog also has clean ears, clean teeth and short nails. These are all things that you can and should tend to between regular haircuts, to avoid problems down the road.

Dental Care for Doods

A mere decade or two ago, anyone who suggested actually *brushing a dog's teeth* would have been widely considered certifiable. Today it's an integral part of responsible 21st century dog ownership.

Vets now suggest periodic professional cleanings at least once or twice a year (at $250-$500 a pop, depending on where you live), and there are now a wealth of doggy toothbrushes, special doggy toothpastes and doggy mouthwashes on the market, all of which you are supposed to use daily to prevent *periodontal disease*, which vets claim are associated with a host of other life-threatening diseases in dogs.

Is this just a new way for vets to make more money, or is it truly necessary for a dog's health and well-being? After all, dogs went for thousands of years without dental care and survived just fine. Unlike people, dogs don't even get *cavities*. And as older dog owners know well, not too long ago most dogs died of old age with all their teeth intact; simply gnawing on bones kept those teeth shiny and white. *Not so much any more.*

Veterinary data reveals that periodontal disease is now the most common disease found in dogs, and affects an astonishing 80% of dogs over the age of three.

OK, it appears this dental thing is pretty clearly not hype. So what's going on?

A wealth of new evidence now suggests that periodontal disease

in both man and beast is an *autoimmune disorder.*

Basically, what happens is the same old bacteria that have always adhered to the teeth and formed plaque are now causing an inappropriate response by the immune system (sound eerily familiar?), which then overproduces cytokines like TNF-alpha and interleukin 1beta, probably not coincidentally the same pair also involved in allergies. Ordinarily important for healing, in excess these cytokines produce inflammation and ultimately destroy the *periodontium*, the tissues that support the teeth. It's that same inability of the immune system to distinguish between self and non-self that is the hallmark of all autoimmune diseases.

This also explains the association between periodontal disease and heart and other organ problems that have been noted. It's not so much that periodontal disease causes heart and liver problems, but that all of them are caused by the same underlying inflammatory processes.

Armed with this new knowledge, it should be pretty obvious that the BEST way to avoid periodontal disease is *to protect your Dood's immune system in the first place* through careful choices in food, vaccination and anti-parasitic regimens, rather than trying to use band-aid solutions to treat the symptoms of an autoimmune disease after the immune system is overstressed by environmental factors

That said, brushing your dog's teeth is not a bad idea, and if you want to do it, by all means have a go— just make sure and use toothpaste made especially for dogs, because fluoride is toxic and dogs can't spit. The main problem with doggy tooth brushing is that most dogs hate it and most owners don't really *do* it— they mostly just buy the toothpaste and toothbrush from the vet and then feel *guilty* about it. A little casual research reveals that truth be told, the doggy toothbrush is right up there with the AbBlaster in the "Least Likely to be Used After Purchase" department.

If that describes you, all is not lost...luckily there are several products out there that will pretty effectively remove plaque and tartar that you can just spray in your dog's mouth a couple times a week.

One that a fair number of vets (who probably know damn well that their clients are not really going to brush their dogs' teeth every day no matter what they say) carry in their office is made by *Petzlife*; it comes in both a gel you can rub on the dog's teeth and a spray, which is hands-down the easiest. If your vet doesn't carry it, Amazon does. Actually buying this and using it a few times a week may well preclude the need for professional cleaning under general anesthesia, which both your dog and your pocketbook will appreciate, even if your vet does not!

Maintaining Healthy Ears

Your Dood's ears should be ideally be cleaned whenever he gets a bath. This is easily done with a cotton ball or two dipped in coconut oil. Coconut oil (which you can buy almost anywhere) is great stuff, and should be part of any holistic dog owner's dog kit. It's non-irritating and yet has strong anti-fungal, anti-bacterial and anti-viral properties.

The inside of a dog's ear is a little like the gut— there needs to be a balance of flora in there for optimum ear health. When that balance is upset (most often by strong antibacterial products) yeast overgrowth occurs, and you can end up with a secondary yeast infection. If he's shaking his head and scratching at his ears a lot, or if you detect a "yeasty" odor in his ears, he'll probably have to be treated for an ear infection. (If the vet puts him on a course of oral antibiotics, be sure and give him probiotics or Greek yogurt for a week or two after treatment to rebalance intestinal flora.)

Because of their Poodle ancestry, some Goldendoodles carry a lot of hair in the ear canal, which blocks airflow and consequently provides an ideal environment for infections. Groomers routinely pull this excess hair from the ears using a hemostat, which some vets agree with and others think is a really bad idea because it can cause inflammation.

his is one of those places where you probably need to ask for your own vet's opinion, because he is, after all, your dog's primary health provider. (However, do not be surprised if the various vets in a single practice hold differing opinions. here) It's good to keep in mind that like so much else, susceptibility to ear infections are a reflection of a dog's immune function at any particular point in time, and stressors like vaccination will often trigger them.

Trimming Nails

For some reason, this is one aspect of dog ownership that causes more anxiety on the owner's part than it needs to. Dog's being the intuitive creatures they are, this owner anxiety is transferred directly to the dog, and nail-trimming then becomes a Major Event, when it really should be no more traumatic for the dog to have his nails trimmed than it is for the owner, who rarely screams and carries on like she's being murdered during a manicure.

Because of this, most pet dogs are forced to endure nails that are too long. *Here's the rule of nail trimming: if you can hear the nails click when the dog walks across the floor, they are too long.* When this happens, your dog is going to have to adjust his entire skeleton to compensate, because he needs to put his weight on the *pads* of his feet, not the nails, and it will eventually cause him to break down at the pasterns.

Keeping your dog's nails off the floor is easy to do if you take a little bit off once a week, and if you cut them at the correct angle, which 99% of people do not do. In fact, most diagrams you'll find on the internet are incorrect! Cutting correctly will actually cause the quick to recede.

The diagram on the opposite page shows the *correct* angle to cut a dog's nails. If you hold the nail trimmer in the correct position and cut the nails vertically as shown, you can get them back where they should be in a couple of weeks without cutting into the quick. On the other hand, if you cut at a 45 degree angle, as most people do, your chances of bleeding the nails go way up, and you still won't be able to get his nails off the floor. (If you do cut into the quick, a dab of Qwik Stop will stop any minimal bleeding that results in short order, and odds are your dogs won't even notice.)

So here's the technique:

1. *With your dog's head in the grooming loop, lift each foot in turn without much ado and quickly snip off the end of each nail at the angle shown.*

2. *Follow with a couple of quick swipes of the file to smooth out the rough edges and you're done.*

3. *Reward him with one of his special "grooming treats".*

If you start trimming nails regularly when he's little and approach it with an air of cheerful confidence, it just won't be a big deal for the dog. Or you.

As you've probably figured out, keeping your Goldendoodle well-groomed is not rocket science, and is well within the average owner's capabilities. But it DOES require a commitment to investing a fair amount of time and effort on at least a weekly basis, even if you plan to use a professional groomer for the "haircut" part. If you are frankly unable or unwilling to make that commitment, this is probably not the right breed for you.

CHAPTER NINE:

Beyond the Basics

(or...cool stuff to do with Doods)

Everybody knows that Goldendoodles make great family dogs—in fact, it's that very trait which accounts for a large percentage of their popularity. But because they are intelligent dogs who actually *enjoy* training, there are lots of other things you can do with your Dood once he has mastered basic obedience. (In fact, the list is almost endless, and guaranteed to include more than a few spectacular jobs that you didn't even know existed.)

But more to the point, dogs were developed over thousands of years to work and thrive on it – because of their hard-wiring, dogs without a job are more prone to anxiety and health and behavioral issues than dogs with one. In other words, chronic unemployment is no healthier for a dog than it is for a person. This is especially true for breeds descended from working dogs, of which the Goldendoodle is one. So get your Dood off the dole and put him to work!

The Entertainment Industry.... AKA Stupid Dog Tricks

Everybody loves dog tricks...including dogs! Dogs are natural performers, and learning tricks is a huge confidence-builder for them, especially if you start when they're puppies. Any dog who has mastered the sit/stay and a decent indoor recall can learn a plethora of tricks.

Although people have been teaching dogs tricks on their own for eons, a good place to start if you want help is with the book *Dog Tricks*, by Captain Haggerty and Carol Lea Benjamin.

Any dog who works his way through these eighty-eight tricks, some very useful and some just silly, can go on to do *anything* in the world of dogs, since all these tricks involve a lot of the basics used in "real" work. Plus every trick your dog successfully masters will make the next one easier, because of a phenomenon known to behavioralists as *chaining*.

It's probably worth noting that Chapter Two in this book (which was written back in 1978) involves teaching the "retrieve" command using a collar twist, which is controversial in today's "positive-only" world of pet dog training, although many serious professionals still use it for working dogs.

Since Goldendoodles are good natural retrievers, you can easily teach him the "take it" command, which is necessary, without using a collar at all by simply tossing the desired object a very short distance and working your way *back* to dropping and then placing it directly in front of him instead of the other way around. (Forced retrieving is really only necessary for working dogs who don't naturally put things in their mouths, and odds are pretty good you don't have one of those anyway.)

Teaching him "out" to release an item on command is also critical, and the instructions given for doing that are pretty time-honored. But for heaven's sake don't try to teach "take it" or "out" with food treats, especially on a breed descended from some of the world's best natural retrievers....it's about as stupid as rewarding yourself for eating chocolate.

Agility, Obedience and Rally

Once entirely the province of purebreds, the AKC opened competition in their three Companion events to mixed-breeds under their new Canine Partners Program in 2010, much to everyone's surprise.

This decision effectively allowed Goldendoodles to enter and compete for titles as long as their breed is listed as "All-American" rather than "Goldendoodle". (Hey, it's a start...and as we all know, once Lady Sybil married the Irish chauffeur, things were never quite the same at Downton Abbey.)

In addition to the Companion events, dogs listed with the Canine Partners program are eligible for

AKC's new Therapy Dog title.

Undoubtedly one of the better financial decisions they've made in several lifetimes, over 20,000 entries by mixed breeds were recorded around the country in the first year alone, so you don't have to worry about feeling like the Lone Ranger if you decide to enter this longtime Bastion of Purebredness.

UKC is also accepting mixed breeds in Companion Events under their LP program, and also allows them to compete in dock-diving and weight-pulling events.

And not surprisingly for such an agile, intelligent and intelligent breed, there are a lot of Doods out there doing really well in Agility, Rally and Obedience, earning lots of titles, and between the two organizations there are trials in nearly every part of the country on any given weekend. Virtually every city in the US has Agility and Obedience training clubs where you can learn the basics even if you don't want to compete for titles. (AKC-affiliated clubs are listed on their website. Go to their homepage at www.akc.org , click on Clubs and Delegates, then click on Club Search.) Most Obedience and Agility Clubs, even if AKC-affiliated, have long accepted non-AKC registered dogs in training classes as long as you pay the fees.

OK, so my dog is maybe cut out for this stuff... but what about ME?

Unlike AKC's Conformation shows, which operate on the competitive principle that "the last dog standing" is the winner (much like beauty pageants for any species), all of these sports are non-competitive. Each dog "qualifies" by achieving the required score rather than by beating the other dogs, and a predetermined number of qualifying scores need to be accrued at each title level. You can enter as many trials as you need to in order to get your green (qualifying) ribbons.

In general, **Rally** trials are the easiest and least formal, and it's a good place for beginners, kids... and people with bad backs and dickey knees. Your dog should know how to heel and sit while on a leash. Basically, you and your dog follow whatever directions you find on the signs set around in a seemingly random and ever-changing pattern in a fenced-in course.

Obedience trials are more formal and precision-oriented (with half-point infractions for things like crooked sits) in their set routines, and the sport appeals to some human and canine temperaments far more than others. Speed is not of the essence here, except maybe for the dog's recall, so you don't have to be particularly athletic to compete, although you'll occasionally need to bend over and/or run a bit.

Agility trials are about speed as well as agility, as runs are timed. This sport does require both the handler and dog to be in pretty good shape, as the handler runs sort of beside the dog, although not through the tunnels and weave poles and over the jumps. Basic obedience is required for this one, because the dogs are by necessity working off leash.

More information on all of these programs for mixed breeds can be found at both AKC's website at www.akc.org and UKC's at www.ukcdogs.com , including dates and locations for trials near you.. Be sure and tell 'em I sentcha!

Dock Jumping

If your Dood likes water and retrieving out of it, this may be the PERFECT sport for him! One of the newest and fastest-growing dog sports, dock jumping as a competitive sport "officially" began in 1997 when Purina added it to their Incredible Dog Challenge Program, and most people have seen dock diving on TV.

Several organizations quickly emerged in the last few years to sponsor events and competitions, the best-known of which are probably Ultimate Air Dogs, which is affiliated with Purina and the UKC, and Dock Dogs, which is independent. Both groups have maps on their websites showing event locations.

Both organizations welcome newcomers to the sport and allow practice time for novice dogs in the pool between competitions. The whole sport is fun and casual and all breeds are welcome...the only requirement is that your dog be a strong swimmer, although life jackets are allowed.

Canine Freestyle

If Dock Diving is a sport that generally appeals to men (and a majority of its participants are males between the ages of 24 and 54) Canine Freestyle is a sport almost entirely dominated by women. More specifically, *women who like to dance.*

Canine Freestyle, often called "dancing with your dog", began in the 1990s and spread rapidly, with many local Obedience Clubs now offering classes. With choreographed routines performed in often flashy costumes to music, it probably resembles pairs figure skating more than anything else on the planet, except that it's done on the floor rather than ice and one of the pair is a dog.

Although any dog can learn freestyle, an agile dog with a love of performing will be easiest to work with, and the Goldendoodle is genetically well-suited for it—along with the almost ubiquitous Border collie, both his parent breeds are popular freestyle dogs.

You can find a class near you by simply googling "canine freestyle" along with the name of your nearest midsize city or your state. The Canine Freestyle Federation also maintains a list of classes available around the country on its website, which can be accessed at www.canine-freestyle.org.

If, on the other hand, this is something you maybe want to fool around with first in the privacy of your own home, the absolute best place to start is Sandra Davis's website at www.caninefreestyle.com. Sandra Davis quite literally wrote the book on canine freestyle, which is available for purchase here, as are several instructional DVDs. If you'd like to see how good Freestyle can get (and you've somehow missed them on TV) you can go to YouTube and search for one of Sandra and the amazing Pepper's many videotaped performances.

(As a side note, Ms Davis, who was one of the early pioneers of Agility in the 1980s before introducing a huge chunk of the dog world to Freestyle, is now pioneering a fascinating new sport she's calling **K-9 Dressage**. If you have a background in dressage and your interest is piqued, you can find out more about that also on her website.)

It's probably not surprising that in addition to their dancing skills, Canine Freestylers are often certified as Therapy Dog teams, and enjoy "taking their show on the road" to nursing homes and other health care facilities. And of course Therapy is another activity where Goldendoodles shine, so let's move to that one n

Animal-Assisted Therapy

Therapy dogs do not perform specific tasks for people with disabilities, but rather visit facilities like hospitals, special needs centers, schools and nursing homes with their owners. Goldendoodles, being social to a fault, excel here, and their low-shedding hypoallergenic coats make them especially welcome. Although they certainly don't need to be able to dance, therapy dogs DO need to have exemplary temperaments and good social skills as well as basic obedience.

And after a few visits with their Therapy vests on, Therapy Dogs quickly grasp the importance of the job they've been asked to do, and clearly look forward to it. An amazing number even know when it's "Therapy day" as soon as they wake up that morning—is it because dogs have an internal calendar, or are they reading the handler's mind? No one knows, and it really doesn't matter, but it's certainly cool.

Therapy work is one of the most singularly rewarding things you can do with your Dood, and there is a shortage of certified Therapy Dogs in many areas, as health care facilities have begun to realize their immense therapeutic value. Beyond merely brightening the days of those confined to a medical facility, the regularly scheduled presence of a Therapy Dog can initiate very real healing, for reasons we simply do not yet understand.

There are three large national organizations that partner with local groups to train, test and register dog/handler teams across the US. You can visit their respective websites to learn exactly what's required to prepare for therapy work and to find a group near you.

- **Therapy Dogs Inc:** Founded in 1990, they boast 12,000 handler/dog teams in the US and Canada. They can be found on the web at www.therapydogs.com

- **Therapy Dogs International:** The oldest and largest, TDI was founded in 1976 and has 24,000 handler dog teams registered. Their web address is www.tdi-dog.org.

- **Pet Partners:** Founded back in 1977 and long known as Delta Society, their name was changed in 2012 to better reflect the work done by their 10,000 registered dog/handler teams across the country. They can still be found at their www.deltasociety.org web address, however.

Service Dogs

When most people think of service dogs, the first thing that comes to mind is the classic Guide Dog working in harness to guide his blind partner through a maze of city streets, or perhaps the Assistance Dog performing a variety of complex tasks like opening refrigerator doors and pushing elevator buttons for the wheelchair-bound. And this breed is certainly capable—the first Goldendoodle to graduate from Guide Dog school was back in 2005 and an untold number work as Assistance Dogs around the country.

These dogs are traditionally donated by breeders to training facilities as puppies. They are raised by volunteers until they are ready for formal training and then placed with selected disabled owners as adults once their training is completed. This whole process takes the better part of two years, and is obviously not something we can (or even wish to) do with the family Dood.

But the world of Service Dogs has expanded greatly in recent years, and dogs now perform a variety of tasks for people with a wide range of physical and mental disabilities that can greatly enhance their ability to lead normal lives. Some of these "newer" service dog jobs now being performed by Goldendoodles across the country *right now* include:

- PTSD Assistance Dogs

- Diabetic Alert Dogs

- Seizure Response/Alert Dogs

- Autism Assistance Dogs

- Balance and Mobility Assistance Dogs

- Allergen Alert Dogs (also called "peanut dogs")

- Psychological Service Dogs (also called "psych dogs")

- Hearing Dogs

Obviously, there are some very cool jobs here! And although many are unaware of it, all of these dogs are granted the same public access rights as the better-known Guide and Assistant Dogs under the Americans with Disabilities Act of 1990, whether trained professionally *or owner-trained*. If you are interested in learning more about any of these newer kinds of Service Dogs just Google their name – there's lots of information on the internet

There is also a lot of *misinformation* floating around about Service Dogs and the law, so let's address that here first, just so you don't end up confused by conflicting information you may encounter from the usual internet "experts" The following information is from the US Dept of Justice and is current at the time of writing.

- *The definition of "disability" for purposes of public accommodation under the ADA is broader than that of agencies like SSA. It essentially covers anyone with "a physical or mental impairment that limits one or more major life activities". (Since "breathing" is actually on that list of activities, potentially life-threatening food allergies are covered,* just in case you were wondering about Allergen Alert Dogs.)

- **By Federal law, Service Dogs do NOT require any "certification" by any organization, nor do they need to pass any tests.** In order to be protected under the ADA along with their owners, they just need to be "individually trained to do work or perform tasks for the benefit of an individual with a physical, sensory, psychiatric, intellectual or other mental disability", at least according to the US Dept of Justice, which has the last word, bearing in mind that "the work or tasks performed by the service animal must be directly related to the handler's disability."

- **Service Dogs are not pets.** Because Service Dogs are not considered pets by the DOJ, municipal, county and state "no pets allowed" laws do not apply to them.

- **"Psychological Support dogs or Emotional Support Dogs are NOT considered Service Dogs and are not covered by the ADA.** Providing comfort or emotional support, while certainly useful, is insufficient—the dog has to be trained to perform specific tasks.

- **Contrary to popular belief, do you need "a letter from your doctor" in order to have a Service Dog.** In fact, the ADA prohibits anyone from requesting one.

- **Service dogs are not required to wear identifying vests or ID in order to be allowed public access.** However, since most people are not mind readers, it's a very good idea and will usually make access automatic.

- **Service Dogs in Training are not automatically guaranteed access under the ADA, although many state statutes grant them the same rights as trained Service Dogs.** In states that do allow access (California and Florida are two states that do) the dog must *be accompanied by his trainer*

It is, however, illegal to *pretend* your dog is a Service Dog, or to identify him as one with a vest or a tag, just to get him on a bus or allow him to ride in the cabin of the plane for free, even if you have a letter from your doctor claiming the dog provides needed emotional support. *Doing so is against the law in most states, and will result in heavy fines and possible jail time, so don't even THINK about it.*

The most up-to-date and accurate information on federal laws concerning Service Dogs is available at: www.ada.gov/service_animals_2010.

If you use a Service dog, it's worth printing it out and carrying it with you for reference if needed.

So, all that said…if you or your child have diabetes, or if you have a child with a severe peanut allergy (or *any* life-threatening food allergy for that matter) or autism or any other disability and you enjoy training, there are lots of resources available to help you train your own dog to be a Service dog, which will probably please him no end, since dogs *like* to have a job.

And if the truth be told, with the exception of seizure alerting, which some dogs just seem to be born with, it's really not all that difficult to train dogs for a variety of service tasks…for example, the average dog can be trained to do reliable scent detection with passive or active signaling in 8-12 weeks, maybe working with him an hour a day, by anyone with fair-to-middling training skills and a minimum of equipment. There are at least as many ways of training an alert dog as there are trainers, and no real evidence that one works better than the other, so just find a method you and your dog are comfortable with.

OK, so…if much of this training within the province of the average owner, why are so many people out there scrimping and fund-raising to afford the exorbitant price of trained Service dogs for their children? Are they being scammed?

Usually not. Although there are a few horror stories out there from people who paid thousands of dollars for trained Service Dogs from fly-by-nighters that turned out to be totally *un*trained, common sense dictates one should definitely do serious homework prior to shelling out big bucks on anything.

But the *real* reason trained Service Dogs are worth anywhere from $10,000 to $25,000 is not because trainers are carpet-bagging, or because the dogs are somehow special—in fact, Hearing Dogs have traditionally come from shelters.

It's simply because the costs of *raising the dog from puppyhood* – including early socialization, food, grooming, routine vet costs, health screening, and the basic obedience required before he begins task-specific training—are all factored into the cost, and many of the people doing that have to pay the mortgage, even if they have not-for-profit tax status.

If the trainer doesn't fund-raise to offset the costs (which legitimate charities like the Guide Dog organizations have traditionally done over the years) that cost will have to be borne by the new owner. Some Service Dog organizations do use the Guide Dog model, of course—*Tender Loving Canines* in San Diego is an exemplary example of a group that solicits donations and uses volunteer labor to provide PTSD and Autism Service dogs at no cost-- but others do not.

But you already *have* the dog, and you've already invested all that time and money and done the basic obedience work yourself, so you can move right to the fun stuff...and finding things is truly one of the great joys in a dog's life. To him, it's just another Stupid Dog Trick. Think about it—dogs unerringly detect drugs, bombs, peanut or dairy products or low blood sugar levels not because they intrinsically understand that these are "bad" things, but because they think it's FUN and he wants to please you.

If training your dog for a service job for yourself or another family member sounds like something you would like to try, a good place to start is of course the internet. There are wonderful YouTube videos put together by pros showing the basics of scent detection training and lots of other tasks... just go to You Tube and search for "detection dog training". There's a website at www.owner-trained-service-dogs.com that's a good place to start. Or you can work with a local search and rescue group, or an experienced trainer of detection dogs, because the basics are the same.

Bear in mind while researching that there are at least as many methods of training a Service dog as there are trainers, and no real empirical evidence that one works better than the other (although law enforcement dogs are never food-trained for a wealth of reasons), so just find a method you and your dog are comfortable with. Do beware of trainers who claim their method is the only one that will produce a reliable dog, though, because odds are they haven't been at it very long.

And a lot of this work can actually be started when they're still puppies. Learning the basics of searching is well within the capabilities of puppies 3- 4 months old, and once they've grasped the concept, they can be trained to search and signal for anything. *Including people.* And that, of course, is what search and rescue is all about.

Search and Rescue

Everybody loves a hero, and the highest-profile heroes in the canine world are inarguably Search and Rescue Dogs. From the events of 9/11 to Hurricane Katrina to the horrific earthquakes in Haiti and Japan, these dogs and their handlers have saved innumerable lives, as well as providing closure for the families of those for whom rescue was impossible. These dogs have been certified by FEMA as Disaster Search Dogs, and there are over 250 such teams in the US today. Trained to be *non-scent discriminatory*, they will alert on any scent of a given type (such as human scent) rather than an individual, and they are also certified as HRD (cadavar) dogs.

Maintaining a much lower profile but no less incredible, hundreds more teams are out in the field on any given day rescuing children and adults lost in wilderness areas, as well as recovering autistic children and mentally disabled adults in suburban and urban neighborhoods. These dogs must demonstrate proficiency in *scent discrimination,* which means they search for a particular missing person based on a scent article, usually using a combination of air scenting and tracking/trailing, based upon the situation and/or terrain.

Together, these owner/handler teams comprise one of the most elite

and highly specialized forces to be found

anywhere in the world,

and an astonishing number of them are unpaid civilian volunteers.

In a world where it often seems that there's a woeful shortage of heroes, these dedicated Search and Rescue teams give lie to the myth, because they are ALL heroes.

Of all the jobs that dogs can do, this one certainly requires the highest level of fitness, talent and training on the part of dog as well as the highest level of fitness, training and commitment on the part of the handler.

Training of an SAR team typically takes several years, because in addition to the dog's training, the human half of the team needs to be proficient in orienteering and wilderness survival and certified to the required level of emergency medical training. Most of this training and the travel required to achieve it, is at the owner's expense. Once certified, these teams provide search and rescue support for local, county and state law enforcement, and are on call 24 hours a day, 7 days a week, 365 days a year, so the human half of the team needs a flexible work schedule. And when they're not actually working, or doing public awareness and education on wilderness safety for schools and civic groups, these teams *practice,* because keeping skill levels sharp is critical to performance in emergency situations, and it is generally accepted that in order to be performance-ready a team must work at least once a week, usually for 4-8 hours. (SAR work requires an uncommonly high level of endurance, in case you haven't figured that out.) Needless to say, this sort of heroism isn't for everybody.

If it *does* appeal to you, however, there is certainly opportunity to get involved. Remember, the largest proportion of Search and Rescue Dogs teams are unpaid volunteers roughly organized into fairly small units around the country. This combination means they tend to be by definition inclusive rather than exclusive, and there's no gender bias as long as you're fit and tough and have a dog that can cut the mustard. Because there is no national directory, the best way to find a local SAR unit is to simply Google "search and rescue dogs" along with the name of your state or county, which should turn up a website or two. These units are all non-profit groups comprised of civilian volunteers who do not charge for their services to the state, county and municipal law enforcement agencies that they work with.

One such website is at www.americansearchdogs.org, which is the internet home of American Search Dogs, a volunteer group operating out of Utah, and pretty typical of what is out there.

Of course, given that you're reading this book, the first thing you'll probably notice on their homepage is that one of the dogs pictured is an extremely large and handsome Goldendoodle in glorious full coat. That would be Murphy, who's been a certified Search and Rescue Dog since 2006. He is also a certified Cadaver Dog and is certified in Water Rescue and Recovery. As a Therapy Dog registered with PetPartners, he visits nursing homes in his spare time, and enjoys long walks on the beach and finding socks in his backyard.

Murphy would especially like everyone to know that any donations made by Doodle fans to American Search Dogs to help defray the costs incurred in finding lost persons and saving lives will be greatly appreciated. Oh yeah, and that's him in the inflatable at the beginning of this chapter.

And that's pretty much everything

you need to know about Goldendoodles.

Now, I ask you....is this a GREAT BREED or what???

THE END

INDEX

A

agility trials, 217

Airline safety records, 95

Allergen alert dogs, 219

American Search Dogs, 224

Atopy, 140

Autoimmune disease, 142

B

Bathing, 198

Beds, 72

Books, 89

Bones, 79

Brushes, 190

C

Cancer, 143

Canine freestyle, 216

Check cords, 88

Chunkers, 184, 189

Coat genetics, 33

Combs, 76, 190

Crates, 71

D

Dental care, 207

Diabetes alert dogs, 219

Diets, home-prepared, 90

Distemper, 152

DLA genes, 134

Dock diving, 216

E-F

Ear care, 209

Essential oils, 175

Exercise needs, 17

Flea repellant, natural, 175

G-H

GMO ingredients., 113

Grooming tables, 75

Grooming tools , 188

Heartworm, 167

Hepatitis, 153

Housetraining, 100

I-K

Immune system, 139

Ivermectin, long-term safety, 167

Jumping, 92

Kong, 79

Kygen Hide-a-Squirrel, 84

L

Leashes, 87

Leptospirosis, 164

Line brushing, 193

Lyme Disease, 161

M-N

Mats, untangling., 196

Mini Doodles, 46

Nail trimming, 210

O

Obedience trials, 216

Octopomine, 173

Organic dog food, 112, 118

P-Q

Parasites, 168

Parvo, 153

Puppy shots, 147, 151

R

Rabies, 155

Raw feeding, 123

Retractable leads, 88

S

Search and Rescue , 223

Scissors, 189

Shedding, genetics of, 29

Slicker brushes, 190

T

T-brush , 187

Tapeworms, 169

Titers, 148

Toys, 83

U-Z

Vaccination, 145

Warranties, 83

Wheaten trim, 58

Made in the USA
Lexington, KY
03 January 2013